Understanding

Youth
Work
Law

SAGE has been part of the global academic community since 1965, supporting high quality research and learning that transforms society and our understanding of individuals, groups and cultures. SAGE is the independent, innovative, natural home for authors, editors and societies who share our commitment and passion for the social sciences.

Find out more at: **www.sagepublications.com**

Understanding

Youth
Work
Law

Brian P. McGinley

Los Angeles | London | New Delhi
Singapore | Washington DC

Los Angeles | London | New Delhi
Singapore | Washington DC

SAGE Publications Ltd
1 Oliver's Yard
55 City Road
London EC1Y 1SP

SAGE Publications Inc.
2455 Teller Road
Thousand Oaks, California 91320

SAGE Publications India Pvt Ltd
B 1/I 1 Mohan Cooperative Industrial Area
Mathura Road
New Delhi 110 044

SAGE Publications Asia-Pacific Pte Ltd
3 Church Street
#10-04 Samsung Hub
Singapore 049483

Editor: Kate Wharton
Editorial assistant: Laura Walmsley
Production editor: Katie Forsythe
Copyeditor: Audrey Scriven
Proofreader: Clare Weaver
Indexer: Elske Janssen
Marketing manager: Tamara Navaratnam
Cover design: Lisa Harper
Typeset by: C&M Digitals (P) Ltd, Chennai, India
Printed in Great Britain by
CPI Group Ltd, Croydon, CR0 4YY

© Brian P. McGinley 2014

First published 2014

Library of Congress Control Number: 2013947838

British Library Cataloguing in Publication data

A catalogue record for this book is available from the British Library

ISBN 978-1-4462-0185-5
ISBN 978-1-4462-0186-2 (pbk)

CONTENTS

This book is dedicated to:
My early educators and mentors for instilling the self-belief and drawing
out the intellectual curiosity; my family for their continuous encouragement
and love; my colleagues for helping to create the space to write; my publishers
for their patience and guidance.

ABOUT THE AUTHOR

Brian McGinley is a lecturer in Community Education within the School of Social Sciences at the University of Strathclyde. Prior to taking up his full-time academic career in 2005, Brian was a senior officer in a Scottish Local Authority with responsibility for developing inter-organisational partnerships under the umbrella of Community Planning. Throughout his twenty-one years in practice, he built up substantial experience at operational, middle and senior management levels, directing inter-disciplinary teams and delivering multi-dimensional services. These experiences have enabled him to carve out an academic profile through regular research, teaching, learning and writing.

Brian is also a Director of the Scottish Centre for Youth Work Studies and Editor of the *International Journal of Youth Work*. He is also an elected politician in South Ayrshire and is chair of the council's Scrutiny and Governance Management Panel. He was a member of Strathclyde Police Authority (2102–13) which is a tripartite governance arrangement with Scottish Ministers and the Chief Constable to execute statutory functions. Brian is currently a substitute member of Strathclyde Passenger Transport, a member of the Ayrshire Educational Trust and a Fellow of Higher Education Academy (HEA).

Brian's main research interests include investigating and substantiating different forms of community-based practice, especially youth work, with an emphasis on the learning process in informal educational settings. A main thread of his research has concentrated on the importance of the ethical learning relationship within informal educational settings to uncover the learners' voice and identify the pedagogical features that are valued most. His research also identifies the use of practitioners' reflective, personal and public voice as a way of encouraging improvements in teaching practice.

Another key feature of his research is exploring the extent to which the political and educational policy context in the UK continues to demand constant change which increasingly requires youth workers to be legally and politically aware, up to date and critically reflective. He also researches the effectiveness of policy implementation in establishing appropriate spaces and structures for meaningful and critical participation to overcome exclusion and help people to make a useful contribution to society.

PART 1

THE PRINCIPLE OF LAW AND YOUTH WORK

1

LAW, YOUTH WORK AND ETHICS

Chapter Aims

- Introduce the notion of law, youth work practice and ethics
- Discuss the contested nature and different dimensions of youth work
- Demonstrate an understanding of the social and legal interpretation of childhood
- Outline the legal context and operational guidance for the enactment of police powers
- Identify the age restrictions placed on children and young people
- Detail the importance of personal and professional values to developing ethical practice

INTRODUCTION

In simple terms, laws are the rules devised by government and enforced by an administration of justice to keep public order, outline and protect individual freedoms, regulate relationships, detail acceptable standards, and arbitrate on legal disputes. Although there are international laws, which are applicable to all countries in the world, each nation state devises its own laws which are socially and culturally bound. In Europe, for example, citizens are guaranteed the right of liberty, freedom of movement and freedom from discrimination. In England and Wales, there are different classifications of laws: international and national; public (including constitutional, administrative and criminal); and private/civil (including contract, family law, company law and tort).

THE CONNECTION BETWEEN LAW AND YOUTH WORK

At first glance, it may be difficult to see the connection between law and youth work practice other than the need for this social practice to comply with the law of the land in which it operates. However, there is another connection in that both practices provide a distinct societal function which operates along the same continuum. The main aim of the law is to provide for human protection while youth work exists to advocate for human development. The former practice, given its protective task, provides a framework and view that require both case law and new legislation to reflect current and emerging social circumstances, whereas the latter operates best in a developmental creative space which necessarily grapples with the real-life everyday circumstances of the young people it serves. Both practices optimally serve society, in the service of justice and social justice, and work best together when the rules are enriched and integrated with a human developmental understanding.

However, for our purpose here, the law provides an operational context for professional practice with young people. Although youth work is a non-statutory service, it is regulated and directed by a range of legislation, government reports and policies. Work with young people is subject to international and UK national laws, European legislation and policy directives, and shaped by organisational policies and procedures. While all laws will be relevant in particular situations, the main legislative focus for work with young people includes the areas of human rights, social welfare, youth justice, organisational law, management systems, and operational practice. These laws aim to ensure that the right attitudes, protections and procedures are built into the operational planning and practice for safe and enjoyable learning. However, it is also worth noting that the increase in recent legislation around children and young people is, at least in part, due to western societies becoming more risk averse and further aware of people's rights that are inherent in their understanding of citizenship in a particular society. It is also the case that laws do not always provide sufficient guidance when the principles are translated into reality through youth work practice.

SOCIAL CONTEXT FOR YOUTH WORK AND LAW

It could be asserted that a main rationale for the existence of youth work is that it is a practice which is aimed at a group of people who do not yet have full citizen rights and who need time and space with a significant adult, other than their parents, in which to explore their circumstances and come to a fuller understanding of themselves within the society in which they live. It is also a period of life where young people experience difference and seek the company of peers (Savage, 2007). However, in legal terms, there is not a clear age at which childhood ends and adulthood begins. In fact the laws concerning the rights and responsibilities of children and young people 'present a complex array of definitions which have been developed by the different institutions of the state, for different purposes and at different moments in history' (Cole, 1995: 7).

RESTRICTIONS BY AGE

In spite of the law's increasing recognition of the rights of children over the past fifty years or more, all people under the age of 18 years are legally regarded as children and are restricted by age in the type of actions that they can take. However, discriminating against adults, post 18, on the basis of age restrictions is prohibited by law except in defined circumstances: 'a proportionate means of achieving a legitimate aim' (Employment Equality (Age) Regulations 2006). However, it is still deemed appropriate by the state to pay a young person, over 16, less money than the minimum wage for adults and to receive no or reduced levels of social security rates when unemployed.

INCREASED LEGISLATION

In addition, over the past thirty years there has been a significant increase in specific types of legislation aimed at children: for example; the Children Act 1989, 2004; the Protection of Children Act 1999; the Crime and Disorder Act 1998; and the Youth Justice & Criminal Evidence Act 1999. This means that there is increased protection for children's rights and stricter requirements on local and other authorities to ensure that they are working together and sharing information for the protection of everyone's rights. In terms of law enforcement, parliament also provides guidance on how members of the public should be treated when an investigation is taking place to determine if a law has been broken.

LANGUAGE USED

At this point, it may be useful to point out that the language we adopt to describe what youth workers do reveals a set of expectations and assumptions which sets the operational position and determines the extent to which we can understand another's view and practice. This social discourse also affects the ability to reach out and effectively enter into dialogue with the other person and people. This interactive practice is inevitably framed within a societal framework which shapes the values, intentions and judgements that construct a legal, ethical and purposeful practice. It is useful to realise that language is not neutral and that it can be used to maintain unequal power relationships which will be to the detriment or benefit of particular groups (Spender, 1980).

It is important at the outset to be clear that while we would seek practice simplicity and clarity, the operational reality is often more opaque, diverse and complex. It is only by recognising the importance of personal and social development through reading, thinking, acting, reflecting and believing that we may develop experience, further understanding and a useful interpretation of what is perceivably occurring in practice.

Reflective Challenge – Questions

- Do you think that the law is supportive of children and young people?
- With increased legislation, nationally and internationally, over the past fifty years, do you think that children and young people are better protected now than in the past?

Comment

It is clear to me that young people are not prioritised in terms of legislation. Much of the law that related directly to young people in particular is now outdated. Young people would especially benefit from a fresh look at legislation around their status and rights through the development of laws based on capacity rather than age. Obviously, for children, it is vital that they are protected from harm, but evidence suggests that these laws are usually retrospectively based on reviews of cases and that safeguarding policies and procedures are not as effective as they could be.

WHAT IS YOUTH WORK?

In this section the first question which we may usefully consider is this: what is youth work? The answer to this important question will allow us to identify to what we are referring and will provide a framework for our discussion throughout the book. Unfortunately or fortunately, depending on how you view it, there are many different definitions and explanations of what constitutes the practice of youth work. This could be regarded as unfortunate if you are looking for a simple operational definition that will provide a security blanket for practice. On the other hand, you may see this as fortunate if you are a youth worker who finds pre-determined definitions restrictive and is liberated by defining the practice through creative meaningful interactions with young people. However, in spite of your perspective and preference there is an operational context to working with young people which is influenced by the current, dominant views of adults in society as expressed through laws, policies, and acceptable ethical judgements.

DIFFERENT PERSPECTIVES

The nature, extent and purpose of youth work have long been debated and rightly so, because at its best it is a dynamic developmental practice which is both highly disciplined and flexible in the moment. It is a practice which is defined by historical traditions and through legal, social, ethical, economic and political demands (Jeffs and Smith, 2010: 1–3) that delineate the key elements which define youth work: voluntary participation; education and welfare; young people; association, relationship and community; and being friendly, accessible and responsive while acting with integrity. Spence (2006: 48) suggests that youth work has a 'particular set of difficulties for the status, visibility and naming of the reality of youth practice'. Martin

(2006) also holds that there is no generally accepted definition of what the term 'youth work' actually means, but advocates for the nature of the youth work relationship as its defining feature. Notably, Merton (2004: 29) identifies that youth work does not operate in a political vacuum, or a neutral social context, which means that 'its purposes and principal forms of practice will differ as that context changes' and this provides the flexibility to meet young peoples' needs. In addition, Banks (2010) helpfully recognises three senses of youth work: as activities with young people; as a specialist profession; and as an academic discipline.

TEN KEY ELEMENTS

Davies (2010a: 1–6), drawing on historical and current sources, identifies ten key elements of youth work which help to define it. These are: voluntary involvement; starting from where young people are at; developing trusting relationships; tipping the balance of power and control in favour of young people; working with diversity and responding equally; promoting equality of opportunity and diversity; working through friendship groups; youth work as process; reflective practice; and disciplined improvisation. However, while this recognition of various aspirations and actions is helpful in articulating that youth work is not a singular practice, it does not recognise the broader human developmental and jurisdictional aspects of the practice.

Davies (2010b) is writing mainly for a UK audience that would recognise youth work in terms of informal education, which explains why the practice identified elicits educative intent through its voluntary nature, personal attributes for personal development, and a flexible approach to meet learning needs. In other parts of the world, youth work has a different purpose and perspective. For example, within the European Union, youth practice is tied up with an understanding of social pedagogy, and in the USA, youth work is largely synonymous with youth development which can be more interventionist and programme-focused with a remedial orientation. What is common to all these practices, across the world, is that they are shaped within a context and operate within the parameters of statutory laws and the implementation of policies.

FLEXIBLE INTERPRETATIONS

Youth work approaches need to transcend such definitional limits: these attempt to define the boundaries of practice because the circumstances and needs change over time, and youth policy in particular has articulated a range of contradictory expectations and requirements over the past century. We need a description of youth work practice which analyses the different types of practises generated that not only explains different elements but also places the practice in a historical, socially and politically aligned setting tied to a defined purpose.

For example, Coburn and Wallace (2011) identify three different practice traditions that represent a type of youth work: *functional youth work*, which essentially performs a socialisation function by working with young people who need to be fixed in some way; *liberal youth work*, which is open and developmental with negotiated activities and longer-term relationships with the location and the youth workers; and *critical youth work*, which recognises and builds on the capacities of young people, recognising the inherent injustices in society and encouraging them to participate in that society as part of their democratic and human rights. These are useful distinctions because each type is closely aligned to a purpose and setting.

POSING QUESTIONS

However, regardless of which tradition youth work belongs to, might it *not* be youth work if it is unaware of and/or subservient to current adult-dominated thinking about the status and role of young people? Is it still youth work if it fails to help shape the debate, with children and young people integrally involved, when adults are articulating their views about children? Is it self-evident that youth work becomes something else if it is a profession that maintains the status quo? Instead, given the unequal youth category, should it not defend the rights of children and young people and promote the debate about which form of youth work young people want? Should youth work be voluntary or state sponsored? Should it be open to all or targeted at those who are regarded as the most vulnerable? Is it about maximising potential or compensating for perceived deficiencies? (See Davies, 1999: 171–191; Davies, 2010a: 7–19.)

HUMAN DEVELOPMENT

Regardless of the nature, extent and purpose of youth work, one of its constant aspects is that young people need to be integrally and dialogically involved in shaping the nature of their participation, the type of content developed, and the learning experienced. Such an approach helps to mark youth work as a practice which is concerned with not just the individual and their relationships with others but also with the notion of community and human development. It is within these contested and competing ideas that youth workers needs to create a meaningful and ethical practice.

Reflective Challenge – Key Questions

- What is your definition of youth work?
- Are you the type of person who likes to operate within set parameters or work 'outside the box'?
- Which of the ten key elements of youth work are meaningful in your experience or understanding?
- What is your motivation for getting involved in youth work and what do you hope to achieve?

THE LEGAL AND SOCIAL CONTEXT OF CHILDHOOD

We need to acknowledge that our notions of childhood and youth are socially constructed, which means that these are culturally dependent as they remain subject to a changing political and legal interpretation. As a result our ideas on what constitutes a youth or child vary worldwide. In the UK it could be argued that the current overriding discourse, which underpins the service response of social practices, is that children are in need of protection and that young people are problematic either by giving cause for concern or being the source of that concern. Yet in spite of various social discourses, these individuals have the same protection under international law.

UNCRC

Although built upon the United Nations Declaration of the Rights of the Child in 1959, which charged governments with ensuring the best protection and promotion of children's rights, the establishment of the Convention thirty years later provided both the bedrock and the impetus for the development of current child policies across the world. The year 1989 proved a significant turning point in terms of moving away from an emphasis on the needs of the child and the duties of the adult to protect them, and turning towards a fuller recognition of children's own legal and political rights that enabled their views and wishes to be considered in law. Although there is still a qualification on these rights in terms of the parental duties of guidance and directions according to their level of maturity, there is still recognition that the child can hold separate views and claim different interests from those in authority.

In essence, the United Nations Convention on the Rights of the Child (UNCRC), fundamentally changed the nature and extent of the legal standing of children and young people. Through Article 12 the child has the right to freedom of expression and thought and the freedom to be heard by any judicial and administrative proceedings by which they are affected. Further, as outlined in Articles 13–16, the child has the right to freedom of expression, thought, conscience and religion, as well as the right to privacy and peaceful assembly.

Within the UN Convention on the Rights of the Child 1989, the notion of 'child' extends to 18 years of age, and all youth workers need to be aware of and must comply with its three underpinning principles:

- All rights under the Convention must be available to all children without discrimination of any kind.
- The child's best interests must be the primary consideration in all actions concerning them.
- The child's views must be considered and taken into account in all matters affecting them.

APPLICATION OF THE PRINCIPLES

These principles ensuring the child's protective rights, as well as a right to access education, growth, health and wellbeing, were enshrined in law through the Children Act (1989) and updated via the establishment of the Children Act (2004).

While these laws provide the principles on which children's rights are protected, youth work is based on a developmental approach to human growth which is in keeping with Erik Erikson's (1950) insights on developmental psychology that identified all humans as being in a constant state of *becoming*. This is an important idea for many developmental psychologists (Jung, 1957; Bronfenbrenner, 1974, 1979), one which challenges the dominant social idea that it is only children and young people who are in developmental phases and that adulthood is the preferred, dominant and fixed status in society. Therefore youth work is a people-based practice which holds that children and young people need to be involved in a dynamic process of participation in order to grow and to become fully human (i.e., the best that they can be). Previous, historical notions of 'being seen and not heard' are unhelpful and detrimental, as well as acts of corporal punishment that were routinely sanctioned, not so long ago, by many state institutions, including schools. This notion of *becoming* is central to the perception of the human being at all stages of development, in that a child begins the process of growing old from conception and continues the potential for human growth throughout life. In addition, the way that we perceive and treat the individual affects the process and potential of all human development. Each person, in their various capacities as citizen or professional, has a part to play in developing a society which both protects and develops each generation for the overall benefit of humankind.

This ethical duty, together with compliance with these and other laws, are the responsibility of all public servants, including those who are charged with a responsibility to uphold the law. Since youth workers sometimes work out on the street with young people, and they are also often asked by young people about their rights, it will be helpful to outline the role and responsibilities that police officers have in the public arena.

POLICE POWERS (PACE)

Under the Police and Criminal Evidence Act 1984 (PACE) in England, parliament has granted the police powers to stop, search and arrest people. Section 1 of PACE provides the power for police officers to stop, search and arrest people and vehicles in a public place if they have reasonable grounds for suspecting that the person is in possession of, or the vehicle contains, stolen goods or prohibited articles. A public place is considered to be all public roads and open spaces including car parks and play parks.

Given that these are significant powers, the act itself and codes of practice detail a range of safeguards in order to control police actions and protect all people, including children, as well as aiming to prevent harassment and encourage fairness, responsibility and respect. The first of four main conditions is that the police officer must state their name, give details of the station that they operate from, and provide a reason for the search. Secondly, if the officer is in plain clothes then they must provide documentary evidence to prove their identity, although under this legislation plain clothes officers do not have the right to stop vehicles. Thirdly, if the search is conducted in public then the officer can only request the removal of a coat, jacket, or gloves. Finally, every stop and search event needs to be written up by the officer as soon as possible after the event.

It is crucial to note that under PACE the police need to provide an expressed reason for the stop and search and do not have the right to stop someone because of their age, ethnic origin, or previous criminal record. However, it is also worth noting that other legislation, such as the Misuse of Drugs Act 1971, also allows searches under certain circumstances. Again, more recent legislation (for example, the Crime and Disorder Act 1998 which introduced Anti Social Behaviour Orders, and was supplemented by the Anti Social Behaviour Act 2003) can enact very specific restrictions on the movements of individuals which the police will enforce. There are also restrictions on particular behaviour in identified zones and therefore youth workers should keep abreast of developments in their local area. Also, youth work organisations should be involved in partnership work to ensure that governance decisions are based on reliable information and commensurate with the nature of the identified problem.

THE NECESSITY TEST

Notwithstanding, all arrests must comply with what is known as the necessity test which asks if there are reasonable grounds of an offence about to be or being committed. Recently the Equality and Human Rights Commission produced a report entitled 'Stop and think again: Towards race equality in police PACE stop and search': this identified that as a black person, you are at least six times as likely to be stopped and searched by the police in England and Wales as a white person. Following a programme of work initiated by the Commission, five police forces that were involved have seen reductions of up to 50 per cent in overall usage and a fall for some disproportionate usage against ethnic minorities (www.equalityhumanrights. com/key-projects/race-in-britain/stop-and-think-again/).

The Protection of Freedoms Act 2012 introduced a new regime for police stops and searches under the Terrorism Act 2000, and reduced the maximum pre-charge detention period under that Act from 28 to 14 days.

Reflective Challenge – Case Study

Les and Bev are detached youth workers working in an inner city neighbourhood in England. They have been working for the local authority for six and two years respectively. They have also worked the same patch together over the past year and have a good working relationship, as well as a significant degree of professional respect and confidence in each other's judgement.

(Continued)

(Continued)

One evening, while out on the street, they see a young person, with whom they have worked over the past six months, being accosted by two young police officers who jump out of their patrol car, push the young person up against a wall, and carry out a stop and search.

- What do you think these two experienced detached youth workers should do?
- (a) Walk by as if nothing was happening and speak to the young person later?
- (b) Take up a good vantage point, and observe and record what is happening for later use?
- (c) Intervene on the young person's behalf at the scene, asking the officers if they are complying with PACE guidance?

Comment

I think that option (b) might be the most useful response in the majority of circumstances as it allows you to be a witness for the young person if this is required.

CHILDREN, YOUNG PEOPLE AND LEGAL AGE RESTRICTIONS

Detailed below are a number of actions that can be legally undertaken at a certain age. One of the main difficulties in classifying people by age and restricting their behaviour is that this treats them as a homogeneous group which they are not. Although age is a key factor in development there is a danger that other factors will not be taken into consideration, such as gender, intellect, schooling, ethnicity, and religious beliefs. In other words, age is synonymous with a particular philosophical and practical view of childhood which is pre-determined and generic and overlooks a person's level of capacity, life circumstances, and personal aspirations.

The information below was correct at the time of writing and is an indicative list. However, as legislation continues to change and circumstances influence judgements, it is important that as youth workers we obtain particular advice from a qualified legal practitioner when required.

5 YEARS OF AGE

- Are duty bound to receive education by attending school or home tuition.
- May open a bank or building society account in their own name.
- May consume alcohol as long as they do not purchase it, nor have anybody else purchase it for them, nor consume it in licensed premises.

7 YEARS OF AGE

- May withdraw money from Post Office or savings account.

8 YEARS OF AGE

- Is the age of criminal responsibility in Scotland.

10 YEARS OF AGE

- Is legally responsible for crimes committed.

12 YEARS OF AGE

- May purchase a pet.
- May watch a 12A certificate film at the cinema unaccompanied or buy/rent a 12 certificate film on video or DVD. (Note that people under 12 can view a 12A movie at the cinema if they are with an accompanying consenting adult.)

13 YEARS OF AGE

- May begin work on a limited number of hours (7am–7pm) – although this is largely ignored.

14 YEARS OF AGE

- May enter licensed premises within certain hours to buy food and soft drinks.
- Are responsible for wearing their own seatbelts when travelling in vehicles.
- Can take accompanied flying lessons (can fly solo at 16).
- Liable to pay the full fare on public transport, buses and trains.

15 YEARS OF AGE

- May watch a 15 certificate film at the cinema or buy/rent a video or DVD.

16 YEARS OF AGE

- May smoke – but cannot purchase cigarettes or tobacco or cigars until the age of 18.
- May get married with the consent or at least one parent – but must be 18 without consent.
- May leave home and leave school.
- May have consensual sex – both heterosexual or homosexual in private (there are some differences in Scotland and Northern Ireland regarding age and offences).
- May join the armed forces with parental consent – but cannot enter a war zone.
- May work full-time, claim social security benefits, and join a trade union.
- May obtain a licence to ride a moped, and if disabled, obtain a license to drive certain vehicles.
- May select their own doctor.
- May buy Premium Bonds and play the National Lottery – but may not place a bet until 18.
- May drink beer, cider, port or perry with a meal in a restaurant.

17 YEARS OF AGE

- May obtain a licence to drive certain vehicles – but not some heavier vehicles like HGVs.
- May have homosexual sex, in private, in Northern Ireland.
- Will be treated as an adult when in police custody but will still attend a youth court.
- Can be sent to adult prison – but normally will be sent to a Young Offenders' Institute until 21.
- May go into a war zone as a member of the armed forces and give blood.
- Can buy an air rifle, be a street trader, and obtain a private pilot's licence.

18 YEARS OF AGE

- May purchase and consume alcohol in licensed premises and buy tobacco, cigars, and cigarettes.
- May buy fireworks and lighter refills.
- May appear before an adult court – although in exceptional circumstances younger people can also be tried in an adult court.
- May make a will or act as an executor of a will.
- May be required to sit on a jury and vote in an election.
- May sue and be sued, purchase land or property, and hold a mortgage.
- May see an 18 certificate film at the cinema or buy/rent one on video/DVD and get a tattoo.

21 YEARS OF AGE

- May drive any vehicle with an appropriate licence.
- May stand as a candidate in an election and adopt a child.
- May hold a licence to sell alcohol.

The issue of age is a consideration which contributes to the debate over what constitutes youth work. Yet again there are no definite age categories which can be specifically aligned with a particular type of practice. However, it would be fair to state that work with individuals under 8 years old would generally be regarded as children's work, with some practitioners extending this term to working with under 12s. It could be argued, therefore, that most youth work takes place post 12 and under 18, after which age the person would be legally regarded as an adult (although the European definition of youth extends to 25 years old). What is important for us in this debate is that the youth provision is built on friendship groups which are usually based within a confined age range appropriate to the social circumstances.

However, in certain circumstances it may be regarded as inappropriate to routinely organise the same generic youth provision for 12–18 year olds because of their different needs and levels of maturity. It is important for youth workers, in spite of the legal definitions for child and adult, to come to an understanding that our notions of childhood and adulthood are socially constructed, power laden and hegemonic, which in practice gives rise to the need for the term 'young person'. To add to this debate, organisations such as the Society for the Study of Emerging Adulthood (SSEA) and the Society for the Study of Human Development (SSHD) would recognise developmental periods of adolescence (11–18 years) and emerging adulthood (18–25 years).

Nevertheless, these positions and articulations are based on a set of known or hidden philosophical assumptions about what is acceptable practice which are open to both scrutiny and debate. To help us understand the rudiments and nature of youth work practice, and its role in society, we need to examine the notion of ethics and ethical practice. However, before doing so you may wish to look at the reflective challenge below to help you clarify your own thinking and think through a realistic practice scenario.

Reflective Challenge – Work Out Your Answer

As a newly qualified professional worker, you are asked by a local voluntary organisation to set up a youth club for teenagers who attend the local secondary school (11–17 years). You have access to a foyer area and a multipurpose room in a local community centre. The centre is available for use three nights a week from 7 to 9 pm. You also have permission to use the school gym hall, music room and art room one evening per week.

Outline the structure of a potential programme for the operation of the clubs by defined age groups and describe the type of processes and activities that you would adopt to suit each of the different age ranges. Also make a note of any activities, circumstances or events which would appropriately involve more than one or all age groups. Again, at this point think of any legal considerations that you are aware of and identify any operational restrictions that will need to be overtaken.

(Continued)

(Continued)

Comment

I think that it is vital to prepare, plan and train in order to make sure that everyone involved is clear about their job role and the reporting mechanisms. In addition, it will prove beneficial to build practice over time and not use rooms just because these are available: start small and build from this, making sure the necessary paperwork and registrations are in place.

ETHICAL PRACTICE

Ethics, or moral philosophy as it is sometimes known, is a concept that is not easy to definitively capture, and its interpretation will differ among people depending on their philosophical understanding and personal orientations. In such circumstances it may be helpful to dispel some myths by stating what ethics is not before delineating what it actually is.

ETHICS EXPLAINED

First, ethics is not a personal code based on individual feelings which dictate how a person feels about a particular situation. Secondly, ethics is not synonymous with religious practice as its use and interpretation applies to the behaviour of all people in a particular society. Thirdly, it not the same as following the law because although the law often incorporates ethical standards there is no in-built guarantee that it represents all ethical viewpoints. Finally, being ethical is not the same as doing whatever society currently accepts because society can become ethically distorted, and in any event it is very difficult to claim – with any degree of confidence – an overwhelming degree of social consensus in any given society.

Primarily, ethics is a set of moral principles which substantiate the consistent standards of right and wrong that determine the ways in which human beings act. Ethical standards are often expressed in terms of rights, for example the right to life, to privacy and to impose reasonable obligations on people to refrain from harming others. Again, it can also include a set of virtues such as honesty and compassion.

In addition, ethics is used as a concept to explain the study and development of ethical standards – to constantly examine those standards to ensure that they are reasonable and well-founded. Therefore, ethics also means a consistent attempt to study moral beliefs and conduct in order to ensure that people and institutions adhere to reasonable and dependable standards.

PHILOSOPHICAL ROOTS

In terms of classical philosophy, and for simplification, it is generally accepted that there are three broad traditional approaches to ethics: consequentialist, deontological, and virtue based. Proponents of consequentialism will directly relate the appropriateness of an action to the consequences that occur as a result. Deontologists, on the other hand, will maintain that moral judgements are inherent within the act itself, related to natural law and human rights. Supporters of a virtue-based approach will focus on the ways in which the act affects the person's potential to *become*. This is an aspirational view which supports the notion of human development, with creative growth based on sound values and choices.

APPLICATION IN PRACTICE

While it could be argued that elements of all three perspectives are present in both law formulation and practice with young people, it could be equally held that the first two theoretical positions are predominantly integrated and used to frame laws and social policy. Of course, consequentialist ethics will be attractive to those youth workers who operate by the rules. However, for the creative practitioner who works with the complexities of practice and is committed to the development of the whole person and humanity, the articulation of virtue ethics will resonate as a way of supporting a dialogically-based youth work practice. In relation to approaches to professional ethics, Banks (2010) expresses principle-based ethics in keeping with Kantian and Utilitarian stances and character/relationship-based ethics in keeping with virtue (Aristotelian) and the Ethics of Care. (For a fuller cogent and useful insight into ethics in youth work see Banks, 2010; Sercombe, 2010.)

ETHICAL PRACTICE AND WORKING VALUES

In this quest for ethical practice, values and meaning making are crucial, and these come from tradition, professional acculturation and training as well as a person's own preferred political, religious, or other beliefs. These beliefs, values and attitudes will determine what is regarded as suitable behaviour. This positioning indicates that values emanate from experience which helps to ascribe meaning to particular actions and events.

In addition, Young (1981) proposes that our working values and norms are a combination of four key elements: facts (cogitative understandings); feelings and values (affective understandings); our position in, and relation to, the world (cathectic understanding); and our motivation to act (directive understanding). Therefore, we can see from this that values and meanings are central to the way we operate, and these are shaped both by understanding and experience which help to develop good practice.

Reflective Challenge – Ask Yourself

- Why is it important to be ethical both in person and practice?
- What are my values and how have these been formed?
- How important are values related to practice?
- Which ethical theory do I find most useful when thinking about my experience of youth work practice?

CONCLUSION

Both the law and youth work serve different but related functions in society: the law protects people and youth work develops people. The law primarily provides for the protection of people based on consequential and deontological notions of what is ethical. Youth workers, in contrast, focus on developing with people, which fits with a virtues notion of ethics and encourages them to be the best they can be and to give of their best for their profession. All professionals and public servants work within a societal context which adheres to the current laws and contributes to the debate on the continued appropriateness of the law as it is interpreted and developed within a framework of continuous political and social discourse. However, youth workers have a special role in engaging and communicating with young people and developing an ethical relationship which is based on a good understanding of both their own and others' personal values, a sound commitment to an ethical practice based on dialogue, respect, and a determination to combat the deficit portrayal by adult power brokers. In this context, it is important that youth workers do not view the law as a technical act to be complied with, but rather as a means whereby the views, rights and treatment of children and young people can be enhanced and respectfully embraced. Finally, if the law is administered by a system which upholds and protects the law in the name of justice, then the task of youth workers is to advocate for social justice that will enable the free development of young people in their process of *becoming*.

Case Study 1

Jan, an experienced youth worker, is the newly appointed manager of a local inner city youth centre. The management committee had appointed her because of her experience and demonstrable knowledge of, and commitment to, young people. At the first formal meeting the committee, made up largely of local people and local authority representatives, told Jan of the local perception that the centre was never open, and asked her to open the centre seven nights a week in order to establish 'a traditional youth club for all the young people in the area and to get them off the streets'. They also thought that bringing in the community policeman would help to manage difficult behaviour and set the right tone for the club. Jan advised that she would want the centre to develop in a manner that was in keeping with youth work values, which would encourage the young people to decide how the centre was run and who supported them. She also suggested that representatives from other organisations would need to demonstrate similar values of ensuring that the young people's interests were at the heart of any decisions for any partnership to work successfully to their advantage.

Jan advised that, while understanding the good intentions of the committee, any plan should involve developing a balanced programme which would be both generic and targeted. She explained that their service should be based on aspirations that were clearly thought out and more robustly defensible. Jan also advised that it would be questionable to base a service on combating what was a legitimate right by young people to be on the street exercising their legal rights: trying to get all young people off the street would not only be impossible, it would also be counterproductive to their development and would negatively impact on the development of the community of which the young people were a vital part.

As a result of Jan sharing her experience and challenging the views of the committee in a helpful manner, the members recognised that she was advocating on behalf of the young people as well as applying a wider concept to perceived local problems which ultimately would enhance their own thinking and planning and offer a better service.

Following this honest and open communication, it was agreed that Jan should set out a range of principles on which the centre's programme should be based and developed. She thus went away to research and reflect and to identify a way forward.

Jan engaged in dialogue with local young people, centre users, youth work mentors, funders, committee members, and colleagues. She then devised and presented a 10-point plan to the management committee based on the work of a number of psychologists, educationalists and youth work writers (including Erikson, 1950; Jung, 1957; Freire, 1972; Davies, 2010; Sercombe, 2010; Jeffs and Smith, 2010).

The operating plan would be based on the following intentions that the centre would:

- provide a safe and protective learning environment;
- operate processes and procedures to comply with relevant legislation;
- develop activities based on the needs and desires of young people;
- work out a relevant interaction in, and between, different friendship groups;
- agree on an open and inclusive programme;
- complement, and be relevant to, local provision in the local environment;
- promote secure, empowering relationships;
- be inclusive by meeting the needs of particular disadvantaged groups;
- set up a youth committee, initially as a shadow group, to assess the decisions of the adult committee and develop their own proposals;
- advocate on young people's behalf with other adults when appropriate.

The management committee all agreed with the above operating principles but were surprised when Jan also explained to them that she wanted, within a period of five years, for the centre to be run by this group of young people and that the manager's job should be taken over by a qualified local young person within the same period.

(Continued)

(Continued)

The adult committee protested that the young people were too young to take on such responsibilities and that these new fancy ideas would contravene the current legislation. Jan advised that the law existed for the protection of all people and youth work existed for the human development of young people. She also advised that if the protective law allowed young people to marry, buy a rifle, fight in wars and fly a plane solo then surely the developmental role of running a youth centre should not be beyond the young people's grasp or the law's assistance. As manager her next task was to research and reflect and develop a plan to turn this aspiration into a reality.

Summary of Key Points

- The law provides an important framework for the ordered functioning of society.
- Youth work is needed because young people are regarded as a transitional group which needs opportunities to participate in society.
- Children and young people have basic human rights which need to be respected.
- The police need to follow set procedures (PACE) when dealing with members of the public.
- Blanket age restrictions are placed on children and young people, preventing some actions which are based on a fixed notion of childhood.
- Values are a key part of developing ethical practice with people in order to achieve their human potential.
- Both law and youth work can work together for the protection and development of children and young people in a common search for social justice.

REFERENCES

Banks, S. (ed.) (2010) *Ethical Issues in Youth Work* (2nd edn). Oxon: Routledge.

Bronfenbrenner, U. (1974) Developmental research, public policy, and the ecology of childhood, *Child Development*, 45: 1–5.

Bronfenbrenner, U. (1979) *The Ecology of Human Development*. Cambridge, MA: Harvard University Press.

Coburn, A. and Wallace, D. (2011) *Youth Work in Communities and Schools*. Edinburgh: Dunedin.

Cole, B. (1995) *Youth and Social Policy*. London: UCL Press.

Crime and Disorder Act 1998. Available at www.lbac.org.uk/Legal%20Notes/Crime%20 and%20Disorder%20Act%201998.pdf (last accessed 18.04.11).

Davies, B. (1999) *From Voluntarism to Welfare State: A History oOf the Youth Service in England, Volume 1: 1939–1979*. Leicester: National Youth Agency.

Davies, B. (2010a) What do we mean by youth work? In J. Batsleer and B.

Davies (eds), *What is Youth Work?* Exeter: Learning Matters.

Davies, B. (2010b) Policy analysis: a first and vital skill of practice. In J. Batsleer and B. Davies (eds), *What is Youth Work?* Exeter: Learning Matters.

Department of Health (1989) *The Children Act 1989*. London: HMSO.

Department of Health (1999) *Protection of Children Act*. London: HSMO.

Department of Health (2004) *The Children Act 2004*. London: HMSO.

Equality and Human Rights Commission (2013) *Stop and Think Again: Towards Race Equality in Police PACE Stop and Search*. Manchester: Author.

Erickson, E. (1950) *Childhood and Society*. New York: Norton.

Freire, P. (1972) *Pedagogy of the Oppressed*. London: Penguin.

Jeffs, T. and Smith, M.K. (2010) *Youth Work Practice*. Hampshire: Palgrave Macmillan.

Jung, C.G., Read, H., Fordham, M. and Adler, G. (1957) *Psychiatric Studies*, Vol. 20. London: Routledge & Kegan Paul.

Martin, L. (2006) *Real Work: A Report from the National Research Project on the State of Youth Work in Aotearoa*. New Zealand: National Youth Workers' Network of New Zealand.

Merton, B. (2004) *An Evaluation of the Impact of Youth Work in England*. Leicester: De Montfort.

Police and Criminal Evidence Act 1984. Available at www.legislation.gov.uk/ukpga/1984/60/contents (last accessed 10.01.2012).

Protection of Freedoms Act 2012. Available at www.legislation.gov.uk/ukpga/2012/9/contents (last accessed 08.07.13).

Savage, J. (2007) *Teenage: The Creation of Youth Culture*. London: Viking.

Sercombe, H. (2010) *Youth Work Ethics*. London: Sage.

Spence, J. (2006) *Youth Work: Voices of Practice*. Leicester: The National Youth Agency.

Spender, D. (1980) *Man Made Language*. London: Routledge & Kegan Paul.

Young, K. (1981) Discretion as an implementation problem. In M. Adler and S. Asquith (eds), *Discretion and Welfare*. London: Heinemann.

Youth Justice & Criminal Evidence Act 1999. Available at www.legislation.gov.uk/uksi/1999/3427/contents/made (last accessed 02.07.13).

United Nations (1989) *United Nations Declaration on the Rights of the Child*. Geneva: UN.

RESOURCE INFORMATION AND CONTACTS

Children's Rights Office
City Road, London,
EC1 V1U.
Tel: 020 7278 8222
www. cro.org.uk

Children's Society,
Edward Rudolf House,
Margery Street,
London,
WC1X OJL.
www.the-children's-society.org.uk

2

INTERNATIONAL CONVENTIONS

Chapter Aims

- Explain the societal context and functions of the law
- Outline the law's global perspectives in relation to international law and the litigious society
- Explore the relevance of the UDHR UN Convention articles for children and young people
- Provide details of the European legislative context for the UK
- Investigate the development of European youth policy and identify its key principles

INTRODUCTION

SOCIETAL FUNCTIONS OF THE LAW

The law, in western democracies, has a number of societal functions. The first is that it provides a legislative framework, set by the representative parliament, to shape citizens' rights and behaviours. To achieve this, parliament identifies and defines which actions and behaviours constitute an offence, which means that any action which is not forbidden could be regarded as an acceptable way to behave. It is also a process whereby the interpretation and enactment of these rules are carried out through a judicial system that includes prosecution lawyers, defence lawyers, judges, the police, and citizens. Other functions include providing adjudication in legal disputes and interpreting complex data to set meaningful and workable legal parameters. We can therefore glean from these roles that society puts much faith in the law to ensure that people's welfare and rights are at the heart of these processes. This has a resonance with youth work practice because it has young people's dignity, growth and development at its core and provides a very special service to society. In fact both professions, lawyers and youth workers, would recognise that in order to work effectively with other professionals a range of knowledge across subject disciplines will be drawn upon to support their main functions. Such knowledge, which determines the ways in which the person is perceived and represented, draws upon philosophical, historical, sociological, biological, political, psychological and cultural meanings. It also depends on custom and practice that shapes an agreeable understanding of the ways in which this knowledge is interpreted and translated into acceptable practice.

The law may be viewed as a network within the social system, along with the other social systems such as education, religion, economics, and politics which, through their own interpretation of the world, creates particular knowledge and determines truth within its own authoritative boundaries (King and Piper, 1995). This social systems view of society draws on theoretical work by Luhmann (2004) and Tuebner (1993) who identified the law as being self-referential, i.e., not that it ignores the external environment but that it needs to ensure that pronouncements and adjudications are in keeping with 'truths' previously established via the legal system. As a result the law operates within a closed system of communication that constructs 'legal semantic artefacts' to deal with particular issues and circumstances rather than attempting to reflect accurately the 'whole life of real people'.

Law is given a special place in social systems analysis, to the extent that it is accepted by other systems that in its role of neutralising contentious problems for the state (King and Piper, 1995: 29) it has the role of reinterpreting the truth to deal with emerging issues, such as those that have arisen in the recent legislative developments in child welfare (Monk, 2005) to protect children and vulnerable adults.

THE LAW AND POLITICS

Thus we can see that law making is a representative political process, as laws are devised by parliaments which are made up of political representatives from all parts of the country and many different walks of life. This also means that new laws will reflect the current issues in a given society that are influenced by political ideology, which in turn affects social understanding. An example of this will be given in Chapter 3 with details of New Labour's interpretation of the Crime and Disorder Act 1998. Such an example will help to demonstrate that laws are not value free and that these instruments are subject to change through political and social discourse. Also, it is worth noting that down through the ages individuals and groups of people have been treated differently and unfairly by legal structures and social processes. This has often been based on historical prejudice which limits the understandings and views held by both the vast majority of people as well as those who hold political and legal power.

As times become more enlightened such prejudicial treatment can be rectified as the absurdity of such inequity comes to light, often through a particular circumstance or situation which is drawn to the attention of the court. Such matters are dealt with by case law, which is the result of a verdict given by a judge in a specific case that is then used to sharpen the interpretation of the existing legislation as well as highlight the need for the development of new laws to remedy gaps or inconsistencies in the current legislation. In more recent times, for example, there has been a need to lessen the acceptance of intolerance and bigotry by devising anti-discriminatory legislation through the establishment of an Equality and Human Rights Commission under the Equality Act 2006: this has been used to help promote fairness in society through the promotion of guidance and good practice advice on equality issues (for more information see www.equalityhumanrights.com/).

AGE DISCRIMINATION OF YOUNG PEOPLE

Sometimes young people will be discriminated against just because of their age. Therefore the involvement of young people in society, through social and political participation, is a legitimate function and role of youth work, as the concept of a young person can be either constrained or enhanced by the exercise of societal control and a use of power. It is only by entering into the social and political discourse that young people can positively influence the ways in which they are viewed by society. In recent times, local and national politicians together with adults across society and in local communities (who are the power brokers in society) have given the police more powers to control public spaces using curfews and control zones. Whether this has made people safer is debatable, and it is unlikely that dealing with young people in this arbitrary way will have the desired long-term effect. In fact, there are other risks associated with increasingly driving young people underground and hidden from sight, including creating a potentially vulnerable situation for these young people which society claims it wants to prevent. Clearly, it is very short-sighted of the authorities to seek quick fixes by concentrating on dealing with, or masking, presenting behaviour rather than investing in and tackling the root causes of difficulties and problems (see Waiton, 2008).

SOCIAL PROTOCOLS

In enacting the second societal function identified above, the judicial system is operated by due process in an attempt to ensure impartiality, equity and fairness for all citizens. Thus it is helpful for youth workers to be aware of the operational mechanisms employed by the legal system which will help young people to understand the expectations and demands inherent within this and other powerful social systems.

However, it is also vitally important that youth workers recognise that they have no statutory role in this process and a limitation exists on their officially recognised involvement. This would be restricted to acting on behalf of the parents when the young person is a minor, with parental/guardian permission (*in loco parentis*), and acting as a responsible citizen in a given situation. As a result it is imperative that a youth worker ensures that where young people are involved in a legal process that they receive appropriate advice from a qualified legal practitioner who will represent their interests and advise them on how to navigate the judicial system. At the very least this is a common courtesy between professionals, and in the best interests of the client, but it is also a common concern to ensure that everyone has a right to speak (Freire, 1990: 76) to effectively ensure that their voice is heard and that they have access to effective representation. When we adhere to these principles and uphold individual rights, especially in difficult circumstances, we contribute positively to human development and make a small contribution that will build collective efficacy across the world.

Key Questions – Make a Choice

An 18-year-old young person comes to you and advises that he spent the previous night in the cells for being drunk and disorderly. What advice would you give this person?

- Tell the person to go to the police station to find out if he was charged.
- Advise the person to speak to his parents.
- Suggest that the person makes an appointment with a legally qualified practitioner.

GLOBAL PERSPECTIVES: INTERNATIONAL LAW AND THE LITIGIOUS SOCIETY

In today's world, no singular society can successfully operate on its own. While each country across the world has its own way of conducting its affairs, youth workers in the UK need to be aware that countries operate in a global environment, and that domestic politicians for example operate differently from elected representatives working in Europe and other parts of the world. Understanding the role and operational frameworks of elected representatives is important for youth workers because there are strong political elements in the practice. Such aspects may include the youth worker explaining and negotiating social systems, developing opportunities for social and civic participation which will involve the promotion of a meaningful dialogue with power brokers, and working to ensure that involvement brings about political change (Tisdall and Bell, 2006) and democratic renewal.

At a very basic level of co-existence, countries need to recognise the territory of countries on its borders and cooperate over the movement of people across those borders. Also, on a more complex level, economic and social systems are becoming both more intertwined and interdependent as the recent global financial crisis (2007–2009) has highlighted. Interestingly, this crisis was caused by individual and collective greed as well as a lack of transparency. However, and crucial to our discussion here, it was also due to failed regulation and poor credit rating systems which were subject to laws that were weak and poorly enforced. This global crisis occurred in spite of international cooperation becoming increasingly important in the twenty-first century, not just on global financial issues but also and particularly in terms of international peace and security.

TYPES OF INTERNATIONAL ORGANISATIONS AND COOPERATION

There are a number of international organisations which support the management and development of international cooperation, as well as a number of organisational types that form part of a process and movement known as globalisation (Bauman, 1998). The first type is *international nongovernmental organisations* (INGOs) or non-governmental organisations (NGOs) that operate internationally. Examples of these include the International Olympic Committee and the International Committee of the Red Cross. Also included in this group are multinational business corporations operating across world markets, including those operating in the food and drinks, car and oil industries.

The second form of international organisations are those that are deemed to be intergovernmental organisations and as such are often referred to as *international governmental organisations* (IGOs). Such organisations are mainly made up of sovereign or member states. Principal examples of these include the United Nations (UN), The Council of Europe (CoE), the European Union (EU), and the World Trade Organisation (WTO).

The third type of organisations is known as *global public policy networks* (GPPNs). These are made up of intergovernmental organisations, states and state agencies, and a range of public private partnerships. In essence, there are global institutions such as the Organisation for Economic Cooperation and Development (OECD); world trade organisations like the World Customs Organisation (WCO); international financial institutions such as the International Monetary Fund (IMF), and those that are concerned with food security (the World Food Programme), human rights (e.g., Amnesty International) and the environment (e.g., the World Wildlife Fund (WWF)).

One of the by-products of this increasing realm of international cooperation, organisational interface and enhanced relationships is that culture and behaviours are being influenced, changed, and mimicked. For example, it could be argued that while there are fundamental differences in the way that lawsuits are handled by the courts in Britain and the USA (Baye et al., 2005), close international interactions with the USA over a significant period of time have influenced Britain into becoming a more litigious society, one that is symbolised by the 'no win – no fee' culture. Through this globalised way of thinking and acting both individuals and organisations become more susceptible to claims against them when things go wrong. In this context it is important to be aware of, and comply with, the operating legal requirements as well as learning to manage risk effectively.

POLICIES AND PROCEDURES

As professional youth workers, there are a number of precautionary actions that we will need to undertake as the litigious society is the increasing operating situation for all professionals. One of the main tasks is to ensure that our employing agency has a written policy and procedures manual that adhere to relevant legal requirements. In addition, it is our responsibility to read and understand the written instructions and advice. If we are unsure about the meaning or implications of any information then we should raise this with our line manager, and if necessary other more senior managers, until we are satisfied that we understand and feel able to comply with the written statements. We should also speak officially to our manager if we feel that, for any reason, the advice is either not relevant, not substantial enough, or is in any sense unworkable in our practice situation.

It is also necessary to make sure that we, and the staff and volunteers that we work with, are trained regularly and feel comfortable with the legal obligations when acting on behalf of the employing agency. While compliance is an essential feature in all aspects of law, in youth work it is particularly important to be fully conversant with the limits and process associated with confidentiality, child protection and duty of care, all of which will be explained in more detail in subsequent chapters.

To increase our confidence about demonstrating compliance with the law we will need to be highly organised and methodically rigorous in developing both planning and recording processes. For example, we may find it appropriate to keep a current written record of important information in our files (such as contact details for young people and any notable instances such as complaints made). Also, any recording will need be in keeping with the laws on data protection and other relevant legislation, such as the Reporting of Injuries Diseases and Dangerous Occurrences Regulations 1995 (Riddor) and when we need to report accidents (see: www.hse.gov.uk/contact/faqs/riddor.htm). However, it is vital that we do not solely rely on peer or management advice, that we keep ourselves up to date and informed through official sources and, where necessary, that we seek particular legal advice about a specific situation from a qualified legal practitioner.

Reflective Challenge

As professional youth workers we are duty bound to comply with the law and adhere to the policies, principles and procedures of the employing agency and as such this is fine as a principled position. However in practice this is not always quite as straightforward or clear cut. As workers we can encounter tensions and dilemmas as we attempt to make ethical judgements about meeting the needs of young people in situations that require a perceived contravention of the rules. For example, if as a youth worker you are working with a young person using drugs

(Continued)

(Continued)

and are aware that this person is in possession of a controlled substance, what would be the advantages and disadvantages of reporting this situation to the police? In this situation, can you foresee any possibility of criminal intent or a potential litigation based on the decision you make?

Comment

This situation raises issues about who is the primary concern in this relationship and what is best course of action to suit their needs and circumstances. It also demands, in order to protect human rights, that any other agenda the youth worker has (alongside the context and limitations of confidentiality) should be made explicit in advance with the young person.

THE RELEVANCE OF THE UN CONVENTION ARTICLES

The UN Convention articles have been put in place to protect individual and communal rights and bring peace and stability to the world. The United Nations, as a global institution, was founded in 1945 at the end of the Second World War by 51 countries committed to maintaining international peace and security. This international organisation has its headquarters in New York that, while based within US territory, has its own jurisdiction, and America holds no special power or control over it. Currently, there are 192 member sovereign states that are committed to establishing and protecting basic rights and freedoms as well as adjudicating on worldwide disputes. Three years after its establishment the General Assembly of the United Nations made a Universal Declaration on Human Rights (UDHR) that provided for human rights and freedoms based on the values of human dignity, mutual respect and equality, as well as limiting state power.

The UDHR aims to protect citizens, in democracies across the world, by setting out the context and principles that govern the making and enactment of public decisions. The initial declaration contained thirty articles that have since been extended through a range of mechanisms, including the establishment of international treaties, specific human rights instruments, and the adoption of the human rights principles in national constitutions and laws. In Europe this was drafted into the 1950 European Convention on Human Rights (ECHR) by the recently established Council of Europe.

In the UK this was latterly translated into the Human Rights Act 1998 as a UK Act of Parliament, that while it received royal assent in November 1998 mainly came into force in October 2000. One of the main reasons for establishing this act was that it gave UK courts a way of dealing with convention breaches without having to refer such matters to the European Court of Human Rights in Strasbourg. However, as a last resort, there is still the facility for a British citizen to take their case to the European courts.

The existence of such an act helps to ensure that people are treated in a humane and dignified manner. This act recognised the right to privacy and a family life, to choose associations freely, and to have the freedom to express beliefs. However, as youth workers will recognise, there is a balance to be struck between individual rights and the rights of others in society. This act is based on five principles of fairness, respect, equality, dignity and autonomy which underpin our relationships with others. These rights are important for all but are particularly necessary for the vulnerable and less powerful in our society, such as people in care, young children and young people, as well as those with learning difficulties. These are often the types of groups that youth workers will engage with in community settings.

Human rights are expressed via a range of articles detailed in the legislation. These are:

SCHEDULE 1 - THE ARTICLES

PART I: THE CONVENTION RIGHTS AND FREEDOMS

ARTICLE 2 - RIGHT TO LIFE
ARTICLE 3 - PROHIBITION OF TORTURE
ARTICLE 4 - PROHIBITION OF SLAVERY AND FORCED LABOUR
ARTICLE 5 - RIGHT TO LIBERTY AND SECURITY
ARTICLE 6 - RIGHT TO A FAIR TRIAL
ARTICLE 7 - NO PUNISHMENT WITHOUT LAW
ARTICLE 8 - RIGHT TO RESPECT FOR PRIVATE AND FAMILY LIFE
ARTICLE 9 - FREEDOM OF THOUGHT, CONSCIENCE AND RELIGION
ARTICLE 10 - FREEDOM OF EXPRESSION
ARTICLE 11 - FREEDOM OF ASSEMBLY AND ASSOCIATION
ARTICLE 12 - RIGHT TO MARRY
ARTICLE 14 - PROHIBITION OF DISCRIMINATION
ARTICLE 16 - RESTRICTIONS ON POLITICAL ACTIVITY OF ALIENS
ARTICLE 17 - PROHIBITION OF ABUSE OF RIGHTS
ARTICLE 18 - LIMITATION ON USE OF RESTRICTIONS ON RIGHTS

Other parts of this legislation deal with the right to protection of property, and to education and free elections, as well as abolishing the death penalty (further information and details on the focus of these articles can be found at www.legislation. gov.uk/ukpga/1998/42/schedule/1).

Research and Writing Task

Download the Human Rights Articles above and write a summary of the main points contained in each article. From these identify the extent to which these rights, freedoms, restrictions and prohibitions affect the way that youth workers engage with young people.

THE EUROPEAN LEGISLATIVE CONTEXT FOR THE UK

As briefly mentioned above, in 1950 (a year after it was established, and two years after the United Nations Universal Declaration) the Council of Europe adopted the European Convention on Human Rights. It is worth noting that the Council of Europe is a larger separate international structure from the European Union which cannot make binding laws. The European Economic Community was first established in 1957 by six members under the Treaty of Rome which enabled it to make laws for those member states. Subsequently, the extended European Union (EU) was established in 1993 by the Maastricht Treaty with 27 member countries, including the United Kingdom. These two treaties were amended by the Lisbon Treaty which was signed by all member states in December 2007 and came into force on 1 December 2009.

There are four decision-making institutions in the EU: the Council of Ministers; the European Commission; the European Parliament; and the European Court of Justice. The Council of Ministers is made up of ministers from the EU member states that are there to represent the interests of their national governments supported by Brussels-based permanent staff. This body is presided over by whichever country currently holds the presidency (these are rotated every six months in alphabetical order) and usually makes the final legal decisions on proposals made by the European Commission. However, in more recent years, the European Parliament has also had a role in the lawmaking process since the establishment of the Maastricht Treaty.

THE EUROPEAN COMMISSION

The European Commission, based in Brussels, is the institution responsible for ensuring that the measures in the various treaties are carried out. Members of the European Commission (commissioners) are nominated for a five-year term of office by each member state. The UK traditionally appoints one commissioner from the government and another from the opposition. The president of the European Commission is appointed by the governments of member states.

COMMISSIONERS

Commissioners may act only in the interests of the EU and are solely answerable to the European Parliament. Their principal duties include administering EU funds and investigating breaches of EU law that are brought to their attention by member states. It is therefore important that they act impartially and do not take directions from any national government or other body including the Council of Ministers. Commissioners are supported by staff organised under Directorates-General (DGs). Each DG covers a particular subject area (which is similar to a UK government department).

EUROPEAN PARLIAMENT

The European Parliament is made up of elected Members of the European Parliament (MEPs) from each member state who are elected for a five-year term. The European Parliament is co-located since it is based in Strasbourg and committee meetings take place in Brussels. It has the power to both recommend and decide on legislation in certain subject areas. The members coalesce around political groupings rather than a party organisation and it is up to the MEPs to choose which group they will align with.

EUROPEAN COURT OF JUSTICE

The European Court of Justice (ECJ) is based in Luxembourg and is comprised of judges and advocates-general who are appointed by the governments of member states. Some of the main functions of the European Court of Justice involve:

- assessing the validity of actions proposed or taken by EU institutions;
- providing clarification on EU law at the request of national courts by issuing preliminary rulings;
- giving legally binding opinions on proposed agreements with other international bodies;
- taking action against member states which have failed to comply with EU law.

Access to the ECJ is not open to individual citizens: if people wish to challenge EU legislation or force a member state to implement EU legislation, then they must initiate a case through the domestic legal system of the member state concerned. It will then be the relevant domestic court that will subsequently, if it is deemed appropriate, refer the case on to the ECJ for further consideration.

REGULATIONS AND PROTOCOLS

Under UK law Acts of Parliament cannot be challenged unless these conflict with European law which is developed through treaties, regulations and directives. Treaties are made up of a range of conventions, protocols and agreements that overarch the European Union.

Although European regulations will take precedence over any member state's domestic law if these are inconsistent with it, member states are not required to make additional domestic laws to implement regulations. However, individuals can rely on regulations in any court cases in their own country. An example of a regulation is Regulation 1408/71 which deals with EU nationals' entitlement to social security benefits when in other member states. Directives, on the other hand, set a goal which must be reached by a certain date. Member states are responsible for making their own laws in order to reach this goal. For example, the European Parliament and

Council Directive 2004/38/EC of 29 April 2004 gave citizens of the Union and their family members the right to move and reside freely within the territory of the member states, thereby amending Regulation (EEC) No 1612/68 and repealing previous directives. Another example would be the updated Toy Safety Directive 2009/48/EC which extended safety provisions and replaced the previous Toy Directive 88/378/EEC: this also brought in improvements to make enforcement across the Union more effective.

Investigation

Find out who is the Member of the European Parliament for your area. Consider contacting this person to ask what they have done that is helping young people in your area. Research their voting history in the European Parliament and identify any European Directives that are directly aimed at or indirectly affect young people.

THE DEVELOPMENT AND KEY PRINCIPLES OF EUROPEAN YOUTH POLICY

The current aim of EU youth policies is to meet the changing expectations of young people while encouraging them to make a contribution to society. These policy aspirations are supported by a dedicated funded programme for young people called Youth in Action. In the European Union Council the youth issue is dealt with by the Education, Youth and Culture Council (EYC) where ministers meet on a quarterly basis.

Although the Council of Europe identified a need for research on youth problems across Europe in 1967, the recognition of 'youth' as a concept in European policy is a relatively recent phenomenon. Prior to the Treaty of Maastricht in 1993 there was very little specific recognition of the needs and aspirations of young people across the European Union. Prior to 2001, activities by European institutions in the youth field mainly focused on considering and implementing specific programmes, for example the 1988 'Youth for Europe' initiative. However, as time progressed a consensus developed that the programmes would be a solid launch pad to get young people more involved and to seek more genuine cooperation between member states.

WHITE PAPER

This momentum resulted in the production of the White Paper on Youth which was adopted by the European Union in November 2001. This was a refreshed policy approach identified in the European Commission paper *New Impetus for European Youth (*Commission of the European Communities, 2001).This contained a proposal for the EU's member states to increase cooperation across four main areas: participation; information; voluntary activities; and a greater understanding and knowledge of youth. It set out clear objectives for member states to achieve and the countries making up the UK all have systems and processes in place to meet these aims. The main requirements are based around meaningful participation, listening to young people, and providing a forum for local initiatives. In addition there was a focus on meaningful volunteering opportunities and getting involved in local communities.

The White Paper also proposed to take the youth dimension more into account when making other relevant policies, such as education and training, employment and social inclusion, health and anti-discrimination. This policy, with its integrative dimension, was deemed to be a response to young people's unhappiness with available forms of social participation, and it also recognised young Europeans' right to become active citizens. Each government and local authority across the UK should have strategies in place to address these demands, while youth workers need to know about these in order to inform their practice.

STRATEGY

In 2009 the European Commission produced a new strategy entitled 'Youth – Investing and Empowering'. For the first time this document acknowledged that young people were one of the most vulnerable groups in society as well as a very precious commodity, not least because of the aging population. Its strategy focuses on youth education, employment, creativity and entrepreneurship, social inclusion, health and sport, civic participation, and volunteering. It also recognises and privileges the important role of youth work and makes a clear commitment to ensure that youth policies at EU level are implemented more consistently and fairly. This strategy is based on extensive consultation with a significant number of stakeholders during 2008 and aims to create more opportunities, improve access, and foster solidarity between youth and society. The Commission stated its commitment to a new way of working and articulated this as a continuous process of dialogue between the EU and its youth.

YOUTH POLICY

It would be fair to assert that youth policy is firmly fixed on the public policy agenda within the European Union and across the 48 countries in the Council of Europe. However, this does not mean that all is positive and progressive in terms of youth policy. At national levels there are a range of criticisms, ranging from an over-reliance on developing strategy without adequate follow-through resources, to an over-emphasis on short-term fixes (Green et al., 2001) and a lack of sustained engagement, and poor monitoring mechanisms for the effectiveness of participation over a significant period of time (McGinley and Grieve, 2010).

These criticisms infer that we should not rely on policy alone and makes youth research all the more important to ensure that the youth work approach is based on strong evidence on what benefits young people's real lives the most. In the Council of Europe a resolution was put forward and adopted which led to the Declaration of the Future of the Council of Europe Youth Policy – Agenda 2020, and youth workers and young people should monitor and be involved in this to make sure it happens.

One of the main problems with policy in general, and youth policy in particular, is that it is based on an understanding of the 'tripartition' (Kohli, 1987) of the human development life course, which is standardised and emphasises difference rather than intergenerational reciprocity. Trinitarian notions of childhood (not youth), adult-hood and old age are outmoded and have dislocated people's lives from policy struc-tures. This simplistic approach makes policy easier to ascribe but it also makes it less relevant to people's lives and more obtrusive than helpful. A refreshed policy frame-work is required that will emphasise the intergenerational relationships of depend-ence and interdependence in terms of the truths that encourage community living, fairly define and enact agreed understandings on crime and disorder, recognise the contribution of all citizens, promote the just payment of taxes, and ensure security in old age.

However, at least at the European level, there is increasing recognition that policies can have unintended consequences. In the EU's 2009 Youth Report ('Youth – Investing and Empowering', section 5.2.) the recommendations to youth workers included a mandate to, inter alia:

> ensure that they are aware of any unintended outcomes of policies to promote the inclusion of young people in society. There can be a danger that some such policies may have the effect of excluding significant numbers of young people because of a lack of education and/or training.

Perhaps this type of honesty in recognising that policy can have an adverse affect and including a commitment to monitor the affects of policy could provide the basis for a refreshed policy framework which both invests and empowers.

Reflective Questions

- How much did you know about Europe before you read this chapter?
- Is Europe a subject that is routinely discussed between you and your friends?
- Is your Member of the European Parliament a visible politician?
- How is Europe portrayed in the newspapers you read?
- In what ways is Europe useful to the youth work profession?
- What can youth workers and young people do to improve youth policy?

CONCLUSION

The law has an important function in society and increasingly laws are being made outwith local jurisdictions. This has some benefits in that the making and interpretation of laws takes place within a wider social, organisational and political context and good ideas and practice from a range of states can be commonly adopted. It can also cause some problems, for example by a loss of cultural uniqueness in the search for standardisation and common conventions.

Increasingly, the European Union is setting the legal and policy frameworks although it is the member states that translate these into practice. However, the level of commitment and resources can vary which gives rise to varying degrees of success as these decisions are rightly tempered by the local political ideology and prevailing social discourses in those countries. The development of devolution and the role of local authorities across Britain with particular reference to social and welfare policy will be the topic of the next chapter.

Some would hold that in recent years European policy has become more youth friendly and has declared itself open to a continuous dialogue with young people. Yet the challenge remains of finding meaningful ways for young people and youth workers to engage effectively in this dialogue with politicians and other adults. Since youth work is about promoting dialogue and participation youth workers must try to encourage young people to contribute to this debate with politicians, policy and law makers. Youth workers and young people should not stand back from this opportunity because youth work is essentially concerned with social democratic renewal in a globalised world. Both the law and youth work are concerned with protecting the rights and freedoms of individuals to enable them to contribute to a society that recognises our shared humanity and provide the foundations for continuous growth and human development.

Kit is a youth worker in a local youth club in an inner city housing estate. Kit relates this case as an example of the way in which an ordinary incident in a youth club can be turned into a series of positive outcomes based on reliable information, sound procedural knowledge, and reflective practice.

Jan was a young person whom Kit had known for six years since coming to the club at the age of 12. Jan stated that she wished to make a complaint about one of the club leaders.

Jan came into Kit's office and told a story that a group of boys and girls were arrested the previous night for drinking in the local park and that Jan had been part of the group. She did not know if they were charged as none of the group understood what the police sergeant said to them before they left the police station.

Jan explained that earlier in the evening Lesley, the club volunteer, had been asked for advice about how to handle the situation and sort it out. Lesley advised that the parents should be informed and that if they did not do it themselves then the club would make sure that they knew about it. Lesley asked Jan for the names of the other people so that parents could be advised and that they would be required to attend a drug awareness programme that would be put on in the club.

Case Study 2

(Continued)

(Continued)

Jan was not happy about this because, in her opinion, 'Lesley is trying to go behind my back and has no right to ask for the names of the other people involved, club members or not'. She was adamant that parents should not be told because it would only upset them.

Kit reassured Jan that as the club leader any action to be taken by the club would need to be approved and be subjected to an agreed procedure in which Jan would be fully involved and informed. Kit also reminded Jan that all 18 year olds were treated as adults under the law which meant that they could make decisions on their own and be responsible for their own actions. Both of these statements helped to calm Jan and give her the reassurance that no action would be taken without her knowledge.

Kit then informed Jan that because this was a complaint against a leader that there would be a record of the way the complaint was investigated, a note on the findings, and a record of the actions taken to prevent any reoccurrence if appropriate. Jan acknowledged the need for this and agreed to cooperate fully.

After hearing the fully story Kit was able to chat through the options open to Jan to remedy her situation. She judged that involving Jan's parent would not be productive because of Jan's experience of poor parenting and changes in the family set up. Kit cautioned against Jan going back to the station to speak to the sergeant on her own as she had first suggested and advised that it was important that Jan make use of the facilities available to protect a person's interests. Kit, with Jan's full agreement, was able to make a referral to a local legal advice centre to speak to a qualified legal representative. This person was able to advocate on Jan's behalf and discovered that a police warning had been issued. They were also able to describe in detail what this meant in terms of Jan's future behaviour. She subsequently responded positively to this and kept out of further trouble.

Kit then had a meeting with Lesley and recorded this side of the story. It transpired that, although well intentioned, Lesley had made comments and decisions outwith the lines of the volunteering responsibility. This also reminded Kit of the organisation's responsibility to train Lesley appropriately in what the role involved and how it should be preformed, as would be the case with any employee.

As a result of this incident Kit put an action plan in place after consulting with her line manager. She realised that the young people did not differentiate between the different roles and responsibility levels of leaders within the club so badges were made with each worker's name and job role. Kit also put in place a regular supervision and training programme for all staff and volunteers. Lesley was trained up to deliver the anti-drug programme after which she took a special interest in confidentiality issues. Appropriate records were also kept up to date on personnel, incidents, complaints and achievements.

Finally, Kit arranged a meeting with the local police commander and they agreed an action plan to recruit detached youth workers who would work with the young people drinking in the local park.

Summary of Key Points

- The law has societal functions that can be viewed from a social systems' perspective.
- Laws are not value free and are subject to current political ideas and social circumstances.
- Young people have a legitimate right to have their voice heard and to influence the debate, and youth workers have a role in encouraging this.
- Most societies across the world are influenced by the process of globalisation.

- There are an increasing number of international organisations that are gaining increasing influence and exerting wider powers.
- People are becoming more aware of societal process and there is an increase in litigation which places a greater emphasis on rules, operating procedures and the recording of evidence.
- The Universal Declaration of Human Rights (UDHR) was established by the United Nations General Assembly to protect individual rights and support communal development.
- The European Union (EU) was established in 1993 under the Maastricht Treaty and is made up of 27 member countries, including the United Kingdom.
- The most recent treaty was the Lisbon Treaty in 2007 and there are four decision-making institutions in the EU: the Council of Ministers; the European Commission; the European Parliament; and the European Court of Justice.
- Traditionally Europe has been slow to recognise the concept of youth, but in recent years it has started to value young people and now not only desires a constant dialogue with them but also recognises the value of youth workers.
- Youth workers and young people need to be fully involved in the development and monitoring of policy so that it works both for them and everyone else in society.

REFERENCES

Bauman, Z. (1998) *Globalization: The Human Consequences.* New York: Columbia University Press.

Baye, M., Kovenock, D. and de Vries, C. (2005) Comparative analysis of litigation systems: an auction-theoretic approach, *Economic Journal*, 115 (505): 583–601.

Commission of the European Communities (2001) European Commission White paper: *New Impetus for European Youth* ((COM) 2001; 681). Brussels: European Commission. Available at http://eur-lex.europa.eu/LexUriServ/site/en/com/2001/com2001_0681en01.pdf (last accessed 06.12.2013).

Equality and Human Rights Commission. Available at www.equalityhumanrights.com/ (last accessed 04.06.11).

EU Youth Report 2009 *Youth: Investing and Empowering.* Brussels: Commission of the European Communities.

Freire, P. (1990) *Pedagogy of the Oppressed.* New York: Continuum.

Green, A. ,McGuire, M. and Canny, A. (2001) *Keeping Track: Mapping and Tracking Vulnerable Young People.* Bristol: The Policy Press and the Joseph Rowntree Foundation.

King, M. and Piper, C. (1995) *How the Law Thinks About Children* (2nd edn). London: Arena.

Kohli, A. (1987) *The State and Poverty in India: The Politics of Reform.* Cambridge: Cambridge University Press.

Luhmann, N. (2004) *Law as a Social System.* Oxford: Oxford University Press.

McGinley, B. and Grieve, A. (2010) Maintaining the status quo? Appraising the effectiveness of youth councils in Scotland. In B. Percy Smith and N. Thomas (eds), *Children's' Participation Handbook.* London: Routledge.

Monk, D. (2005) (Re)constructing the head teacher: legal narratives and the politics of school exclusions, *Journal of Law and Society*, 32 (3): 399–423.

Tisdall, E. and Bell, R. (2006) Included in governance? Children's participation in 'public' decision making. In E.K.M. Tisdall, J. Davis, M. Hill and A. Prout (eds), *Children, Young People and Social Inclusion: Participation for What?* Bristol: The Policy Press.

Treaty of Maastricht 1993. Available at http://eurplex.europa.eu/en/treaties/dat/11992M/htm/1992M.html (lat accessed 22.01.2014).

Tuebner, G. (1993) *Law as an Autopoietic System.* Oxford: Oxford University Press.

Waiton, S. (2008) *The Politics of Antisocial Behaviour.* London: Routledge.

White, N.D. (1997) *Keeping the Peace: the United Nations and the Maintenance of International Peace and Security.* Manchester, UK: Manchester University Press.

RESOURCE INFORMATION AND CONTACTS

Office of the European Commission (Brussels)
Commission of the European Community,
200 Rue de la Loi,
B-1049 Brussels,
Belgium.
Tel: 0032 2 235 1111

European Parliament Information Office (UK)
2 Queen Anne's Gate,
London,
SW1H 9AA.
Tel: 020 7227 4300

Office of the European Commission (UK)
England
Jean Monnet House,
8 Storeys Gate,
London,
SW1P 3AT.
Tel: 020 7973 1992

Scotland
The Tun,
4 Jackson's Entry,
Holyrood Road,
Edinburgh,
EH8 8PJ.
Tel: 0131 557 7866

Wales
2 Caspian Point,
Caspian Way,
Cardiff,
CF10 4QQ.
Tel: 029 2089 5020

Northern Ireland
Windsor House,
9/15 Bedford Street,
Belfast,
BT2 7EG.
Tel: 028 9024 0708

The European Ombudsman
The European Ombudsman can investigate maladministration in the activities of the European community institutions and bodies, including administrative issues, refusal of information, discrimination and abuse of power.
1 Avenue du President Robert Schuman
B.P.403
F-67001 Strasbourg Cedex
France
Tel: 00 33 388 172313
Fax: 00 33 388 179062
www.ombudsman.europa.eu/home/en/default.htm
E-mail: euro-ombudsman@europarl.eu.int

Europe Direct
This service provides information and advice about citizens' rights in the European Union, for example, to work live or study in another country of the EU, and is staffed by a team of multilingual lawyers in Brussels.
Free phone hotline: 00800 6789 1011
Website: ec.europa.eu/eurodirect

Euro Info Centres (UK)
There are 26 Euro Info Centres in the UK. They are sometimes called European Business Information Centres. They are usually based in existing organisations which have links with the business community. Their function is to provide EU information that is likely to be of value to small and medium-sized businesses. For the address of the nearest Euro Info Centre, people should contact their local Chamber of Commerce, or check the website of the National Euro Info Centre Network.

European Consumer Centres
There are European Consumer Centres (ECCs) throughout most of the EU member states. They can provide information and advice on EU consumer issues and help if goods or services have been purchased from another EU member state. To contact the UK's ECC, visit www.ukecc.net, or call 08456 040503.

3

NATIONAL AND LOCAL GOVERNMENTS

Chapter Aims

- Provide a historical account of acts that established local government
- Explore the development of the local/national relationship in terms of central and local government
- Locate youth work practice in relation to policy development and law creation
- Consider the ways in which devolution has changed governmental relationships across the UK
- Outline the relevance of recent local government acts
- Draw out the relevance of certain aspects of social welfare policy to youth work practice
- Outline the notion of new public management within the political and professional discourse
- State the importance of an informal learning pedagogy to enable youth workers to work effectively in an ever-changing unequal society

INTRODUCTION

Since Anglo Saxon times the relations between national and local governments across Britain have been a constant source of tension, with both sides attempting to secure power and exert influence over local people. However, over the last seventy years or so the central/local divide has been the subject of continuous research and public debates (see Chester, 1951; HMSO, 1977; HM Gov., 1996; Cabinet Office, 1999) as the different forms of representative government endeavour to claim their democratic territory. Traditionally, there has been a drive by national governments to make sure that their parliamentary acts and policies are implemented across the country in spite of the political allegiances and mandates of the locally elected local government councillors.

Over the past thirty years and more there has been the persistent accusation of government becoming increasingly aloof from the people, with a subsequent legislative and organisational drive by government to demonstrate a connection to the electorate it represents. This has resulted in significant and continuous change at both central and local levels, involving structural changes like parliamentary devolution and the adoption of different voting systems in some parts (for example, proportional representation to elect local councils in Scotland).

TENSION BETWEEN NATIONAL AND LOCAL GOVERNMENTS

It is important for community-based services, such as youth work, to recognise the existence of this tension and the potential implications for practice in terms of satisfying national and local authority funding requirements allied to meeting local young people's needs and demands. Youth workers will recognise that traditionally central government, and more recently the European legislature, set the broad legal parameters within which local government operates. Consequently, local authorities interpret the requirements of these acts and develop local policies to meet those same requirements. Normally, in such an enabling or parent act, parliament outlines the broad legal framework giving other individuals and organisations the power to make more detailed laws through delegation. Three main examples of this would be: the Queen and the Privy Council who can make laws under the Emergency Powers Act 1920; ministers and government departments that make rules and regulations through the use of statutory instruments; local authorities who make bylaws pertaining to their local areas to manage issues like parking and public drinking. Youth workers need to be aware of these powers and the ways in which these are enacted locally, in addition to having a working knowledge and understanding of the legal requirements inherent in the operation of practice.

LEGISLATIVE BASIS AND RESOURCING ARRANGEMENTS

Although youth work as a social practice does not currently have a singular dedicated mandatory basis for its operation it is used as a mechanism, principally by local authorities, to demonstrate compliance with legislative requirements laid down in various acts; Education, Social Welfare, Anti Social Behaviour, Equity and Human Rights. Therefore, local authorities will generally provide the operating context for locally funding community-based youth work directly or indirectly, as from time to time central government will fund national initiatives at a local level, usually on a short-term basis. Youth work provides a useful function in terms of empowering local young people to participate and find a voice by which to express their needs and tackling inequalities in keeping with equality legislation (Equality Act 2010) and youth work history, process and practice (Freire, 1972; Jeffs and Smith, 2005; Ord, 2007; Packham, 2008; Banks, 2010).

In essence, the policy framework under which youth work and other organisational practices operate is determined via a number of routes, namely Acts of Parliament, codes of practice, statutory guidance, regulations (also known as statutory instruments), good practice and professional guidance and case law.

POLITICAL AND PROFESSIONAL DISCOURSE

In addition to the legislative and youth work practice framework, another context that needs to be taken into account is the political and professional discourse about the best way to organise and manage local government. Since the 1980s, local government has been significantly and continuously affected by a set of strategic principles and operational assumptions which has come to be classified under the terminology of 'new public management'. This approach has promoted business ideals, largely uncritically, to be incorporated into public service delivery, and has served to highlight the influence that central government has had over the ways that local government, across different political persuasions, has viewed and organised itself to deliver its functions and remit for local people. For youth workers, however, there is a need to ensure that their professional awareness includes an understanding of the ways in which society is organised and to work with young people in an informative, progressive, and empowering manner.

THE ROOTS OF LOCAL GOVERNMENT IN ENGLAND

The roots of local government have a long history and distinctive traditions across the UK. In England the basis for local government as an organisational unit can be traced back to the time of the Anglo Saxon kingdoms that established the 'shire' as an area of about 100 houses until this became 'county' after the Norman Conquest. This was the origin of establishing local administrative units that would give the ruling classes a way of centralising control in order to help ensure consistency and conformity. These original organisations were mainly self-elected and operated by the Anglican and liberal elites. It should be noted from the outset that the status and powers of local government do not emanate from a single local government law, but remain a government mechanism that implements a whole raft of legislation passed by the Westminster parliament. Thus local government exists at the behest of central government: it has no constitutional basis as an entity, and is subservient to the extent that its functions could potentially be diminished or demolished by an Act of Parliament at Westminster.

In fact local government in England is not uniform and comprises a rather complex network of institutions. There are currently four principal types of district-level sub-division: 326 districts made up of 36 metropolitan boroughs; 32 London boroughs; 201 non-metropolitan districts; and 55 unitary authorities (as well as the City of London and the Isles of Scilly which are also districts but possess distinctive features).

ESTABLISHMENT OF LOCAL GOVERNMENT IN ENGLAND

Although the Municipal Corporations Act (1835) was the first recognisable act to establish a local government in England, it did not introduce elected councils across the whole of the country. Those areas that had previously been incorporated by royal charter, and were governed by locally appointed leaders, were to have an elected council. However, those cities and towns which had not been incorporated could potentially be established via a right to petition parliament to enact the conditions set out in the act. Parliament was the body responsible for determining if the petitioning territory would have an elected municipal council based on the merits of each case. Each of the incorporated municipality consisted of a mayor, councillors, and aldermen. Subsequently, the borough councils became elected entities through the Local Government (England and Wales) 1988 Act which democratised the county councils and set up 40 administrative counties, 61 county borough councils, and the elected body for London. These seismic changes occurred as a result of the demands of the Liberal Unionist Party as a condition for supporting the minority-led Conservative administration. The county councils took over the functions of the magistrates courts, devised urban and rural districts based on the sanitary districts, and were made up of a mixture of elected and nominated councillors.

The Local Government Act 1894 created urban and rural districts as sub-divisions of administrative counties. A further reform in 1900 established 28 metropolitan boroughs as sub-divisions of the County of London. However, the two-tier principle in English local government, the separation of town and country, had already been introduced by the Local Government Act of 1888, with county borough status all-purpose councils being granted to large urban populations of 50,000 and over. The size of population was increased to 100,000 in the Local Government Act 1958, before being abolished altogether by the London Government Act 1963 and the Local Government Act 1972 in favour of unitary councils.

CURRENT COMPOSITION AND FORMATION FOR LOCAL AUTHORITIES IN ENGLAND

The current composition and formation for local authorities in England began in the 1960s with the creation of Greater London Council and its 32 London boroughs, although this platform has been subject to continual change ever since that time. In the mid 1970s the 'shire' counties, also termed 'metropolitan counties and non-metropolitan counties', were established throughout England only to be changed again in 1986. During the 1990s the unitary authority was brought into being, combining the functions and status of county and district. Subsequent reforms and reorganisations of local government have continued to come about following the passing of Acts of Parliament, with the exception of unitary councils that were created after the Local Government Act 1992. Under the provisions made in the 1992 Act unitary councils can be formed through ministerial initiative, via statutory instrument, which means that doing so does not require specifically initiated Parliamentary legislation.

This 1992 Act also gave rise to the Local Government Commission for England which replaced the Local Government Boundary Commission for England and set about reviewing the structure of local government in England for the subsequent ten years. The commission carried out structural reviews at the request of the Secretary of State, and although some unitary authorities were created the work of the commission was subject to continuous legal challenge and political debate. As a result of this central/local tension the organisation was replaced by the Boundary Committee for England in 2002 which largely ended this cycle of reviews.

LOCAL GOVERNMENT IN SCOTLAND, NORTHERN IRELAND AND WALES

The Local Government (Scotland) Act 1994 replaced the two-tier Scottish local authority system, regions and districts that had been in place since 1975 with 29 new unitary authorities that came into being on 1 April 1996, while the three island councils remained in place. There were no structural changes to Northern Ireland's local authorities as this time, but the Local Government (Wales) Act 1994 replaced the system of counties and county boroughs with a new unitary system.

UK DEVELOPMENTS

In more recent years the thinking around the role and responsibilities of local authorities across the UK has changed and these have been granted 'empowering powers'. Until recently local authority powers were curtailed by specific Acts of Parliament, which meant that they were authorised to carry out only those specific functions specified within acts, for example under the Local Government Act 1972 in England. If councils were deemed to be operating outwith their powers (i.e., *ultra vires*), they would be subjected to a judicial review.

However, the Department of Communities and Local Government (DCLG) issued information on the 'Power to promote well-being of the area: Statutory guidance for local councils' in England. This document recognised that:

> as the first tier of local government, local councils have a vital role to play in improving local services and invigorating local democracy. These reforms provide the statutory underpinning to help increase the capacity of local councils to deliver better public services and represent their communities' interests. Local people via local councils will have more say and ownership over how their communities are run and managed. (DCLG, 2009: 3)

This was however still subject to some safeguards, for example the Prescribed Conditions Order. There were similar developments in other parts of the UK.

Notwithstanding, the principle has been set that rather than being able to act only when the law states that they can, the new Localism Act 2011 has given local authorities the freedom to do anything as long as they do not break any other laws in doing so. Essentially, this takes the question of local authority powers beyond the reach of a judicial review and limits, to some extent, the role of the courts in democratic decision making. But it must be pointed out that under S.5 (1) of the act the power lies with the Secretary of State who can still repeal any part of another parliamentary act that is deemed to prevent a local authority from doing what it wants. This is a significant change in the balance of power, moving away from parliamentary and judicial scrutiny towards increased personal power invested in a single political office.

CENTRAL/LOCAL RELATIONS

There are four main points that are worthy of note when considering the establishment, organisation, and democratisation of local authorities. Firstly, that it has been traditionally viewed principally as a welfare service provider in preference to its role in representing people in a locally elected political institution. Secondly, that it is heavily reliant on central government for its remit and finances which causes tensions, particularly when there is a clash in local/central political mandates. Thirdly, that local government is being continually centralised, amalgamated and reduced in number by its having to cover larger areas. Fourthly, that the funding from central government is released with conditions attached and government ministers are seeking to take more control over what is allowed to happen locally. These circumstances, and the relationship between central and local government in England, are germane to the situation experienced by local government in the devolved nations where issues of control, influence and local democracy are very much at the forefront of public debate.

Key Challenge – Researching, Thinking and Writing

Write two paragraphs which sum up the relationship between central and local government and describe the ways in which this could affect youth work practice.

Comment

Central and local governments perform different functions but there are complications in their relationship because of levels of funding, issues of control and centralisation, and various shades of politics.

Youth workers should be aware of these tensions and operate within and between these situations to achieve the best possible outcomes for the young people they serve.

HOME COUNTRIES CONTEXT (DEVOLVED AND RESERVED POWERS)

The rationale for devolution, introduced by the Labour Government in 1997, was three-fold: to improve the policy-making process; to strengthen the Union; and to restore public confidence in both politics and politicians (Paterson, 1998). The main driver for this initiative was that it formed part of a constitutional reform programme that aimed to decentralise power, reform politics, and bring people closer to the decision-making processes. This development took place following a positive vote in a referendum, as well as giving cognisance to the new rights that citizens were set to enjoy under the European Convention of Human Rights and the opening up of government that would happen through the freedom of information acts that came into force in 2005. At the time it was seen politically as a settlement that would prove beneficial not just for the devolved nations but also the UK as a whole.

Yet it would be wrong to suggest that this was entirely a modern-day political initiative. For example, in the Scottish context power had been continuously, (albeit slowly) devolved to Edinburgh over the years, with the post of Secretary for Scotland established in 1885 and the functions of the Scottish Office being transferred from London in 1939. In fact there had been a proposal to establish a Scottish Assembly in the late 1970s following the publication of a report by the Kilbrandon Commission (1975) which recommended devolution for both Scotland and Wales but interestingly not for England. This recommendation subsequently led to a national referendum in Scotland in March 1979 which achieved a positive majority result. However, the legislation was not enacted because, although a majority of 77,000 plus (33.9 per cent) voted in favour of it, it fell short of the 40 per cent majority required. Notably, as broader support for this latest devolution initiative there had been a cross-party campaign in existence since 1988 which, as well as senior political figures, also involved unions, business leaders, and church and civic groups.

WELSH DEVOLUTION

As with Scotland, Welsh devolution is not a very recent phenomenon and aspects of administrative devolution for Wales can be traced back to the early twentieth century. In 1952 a government initiative devised the formation of separate Welsh departments within the ministries for Education, Agriculture, Insurance and Health, initially managed by a Minister for Welsh Affairs (a post that was upgraded to Minister of State in 1964 as other functions were increasingly transferred).

In relation to the Welsh Devolution Settlement, after a successful vote in 1997 a National Assembly was established in 1999 following the passing of the Government of Wales Act 1998. This initial settlement was virtually a transference of the Secretary of State's existing powers, with a limitation on the ability to legislate on all matters contained within the original settlement. The Welsh people had to wait until the Government of Wales Act 2006 to be granted increased legislative powers, referenda capabilities for further powers, and extended structural changes to improve the devolved governance mechanism. The full enactment of the prime settlement was realised in May 2011 subsequent to a positive referendum result in March 2011. The Assembly's increased legislative responsibilities were set out under 20 broad headings covering similar territory to those listed within the Scottish and Northern Irish devolution frameworks.

NORTHERN IRELAND

Northern Ireland, in devolution terms, has differences and similarities with both Scotland and Wales given its particular history and political allegiances. Devolution in Northern Ireland is distinctive in at least three principal ways: its rationale and integrity are integrally linked to the peace process based on the Belfast or 'Good Friday' Agreement (April 1998); the assembly is not based on a traditional nation state and it was therefore established within a broader geographical context; and its powers have been suspended from time to time since its establishment in December 1999. However, since October 2002 it has operated continuously, denoting an extended period of political commitment that has secured increased social stability through cooperation.

The Northern Ireland Assembly is similar to those in the other devolved nations in that it was established on the basis of a referendum and Act of Parliament in 1998. Also, it has similar devolved powers in terms of transferred, excepted and reserved matters as defined in the act. Again, as with its neighbours devolution is a process which is continuing to evolve, with Northern Ireland ministers playing an equal part in establishing more formal administrative and other agreements with central government and the other devolved governments.

THE UNITED KINGDOM

As a result of the devolution settlements across different parts of the United Kingdom, the UK government remains responsible for the areas of policy that were deemed to be best run on a UK basis (e.g., the UK constitution, foreign policy, defence and national security, fiscal, economic and monetary system, common markets, employment legislation, social security and the main aspects of transport and safety regulation). There are some small variations but devolved matters across the three devolved powers are broadly the same, and include education and training, health, local government, social work and housing, economic development and transport, the law and home affairs, the environment, agriculture, fisheries and forestry, culture, sport and the arts, and research and statistics as these relate to the devolved nation.

THE RESULTS OF DEVOLUTION

The level to which the devolved parliaments have been successful in making the most of this opportunity is open to debate, but there are clearly some differences that have emerged that are worthy of note. Firstly, there is significantly more legislation with different policy preferences and direction in the devolved states. Secondly, there is more scope for coalition politics, and thirdly, there is an appetite for more wide ranging legislative powers but whether there is also an appetite for outright independence remains to be seen. However, what is clear is that devolution is a continuously changing process that has real implications for the shape, nature and extent of local services. Interestingly, as part of this constantly changing political and administrative context brought about by devolution, in June 2011 the Memorandum of Understanding was agreed involving the UK government and the devolved administrations in Wales, Scotland and Northern Ireland: this articulated the overarching principles on which formal relations between these administrations would be conducted, and included provision for a joint ministerial committee and the publishing of bilateral concordats.

Using Scotland as an example, research has found that citizens in the devolved countries found that Westminster was less relevant to them. They also felt that contact between local councillors and Westminster MPs had diminished, and that the capacity for local authorities to engage in policy development had been thwarted by local government reorganisation, reductions in management levels, and public spending cutbacks (Bennett et al., 2002).

These relatively recent changes in governmental structures have influenced the ways in which local governments are perceived and place a continuous focus on their governance role. The relation between local governments and devolved governments has brought the relationship closer and made it more directional and competitive. However, in this situation England is different in that it does not have a devolved legislature and its local authorities deal directly with the central Westminster government which is a UK parliament. This absence of separate decision-making powers for the representatives of voters in England is a growing concern for UK politics, along with the issue of increasing developed powers and the independence referendum for Scotland in 2014.

Investigative Task – Research

Research the ways in which youth work practice has changed in your country since the onset of devolution.

Comment

My thinking is that youth work traditionally and historically, across the UK, had its foundations built on an informal education, club-based approach. Since devolution there have been a number of developments which have impinged upon youth work's focus and remit. In Scotland it has been influenced by the Curriculum for Excellence policy which has brought it closer to schools and learning hubs. In Northern Ireland it has strengthened its community roots. In England, youth work has been strongly directed by the development of the training, employment and advice-based connexions service which is individual and problem-based. In Wales the most recent direction has been through partnership development and integrated services. One constant across all of the UK though, is that the funding for youth work is inadequate, unstable and controlling. Has your research led you to similar or different conclusions?

SOCIAL AND WELFARE ACTS AND POLICY

This section articulates three of the main integrated legislative areas (education, children and young people) that will be of interest to youth and community professionals, as these help to explain the roots and focus of professional practice as well as providing an example of the ways in which laws and policies change over time and influence that professional practice. Other relevant legislative areas of significance to youth work, such as anti oppressive legislation, human rights, child protection and emotional well-being, are discussed in more detail in other chapters of this book.

Education acts are important to youth work in the UK as these have, throughout their history, maintained a focus on both welfare and informal education, and post war have been aligned with the organisation of education through Local Education Authorities (LEAs). The epistemological basis of informal education in youth work has strong roots in the UK youth work discourse as well as a coherent set of principles, values and approaches which inform practice (see Dewey, 1916; Freire, 1972, 1992; Jeffs and Smith, 1999; Ord, 2007). Within the legislative and social policy context we have seen a significant movement in youth work from its original voluntary and philanthropic roots to state intervention seeking to control its practice and development. Alongside this, there has been a continuous strong tradition for local people to get involved in their local communities in the belief that they are best placed to come up with solutions to local problems.

SOCIAL POLICY

Across the social policy agenda moving into the twenty-first century, at least two broad themes can be identified which are relevant to youth work. The first is an increased recognition of the importance of the contribution of community members through, for example, volunteering and participation, which is useful for young people as it helps them contribute to society as citizens. The second is the drive to integrate services through multi-agency and partnership work which aims to hold the person at the centre of the service rather than organisational methods or professional boundaries. Both of these developments are in keeping with youth work values and approaches, in terms of valuing the relationship with the young person over any other concern and working with other professionals to help ensure that young people's needs and views are given appropriate and judicious consideration.

The first formal legislative recognition of youth work, in education terms, can be traced to the Education Act 1944 which established the youth service in England and Wales. It did so as a result of the Board of Education (1939) issuing a circular (number 1486) where the board took direct responsibility for youth welfare. This circular encouraged LEAs to set up youth committees to complement the National Youth Committee. Other documents (such as the White Paper on Educational Reconstruction (1943), the McNair report (1944) and the National Youth Council, 1943, 1945) all helped to ensure that the youth service became an integral, albeit junior, part of the education service.

As a funded local authority service, the Albemarle Report (1960), chaired by the Countess of Albemarle, provided youth work in England and Wales with a foundational rationale and operating framework along with a substantial investment in infrastructure and funding resources. The committee was set up by the Minster of Education in 1958 with the following terms of reference:

> To review the contribution which the Youth Service of England and Wales can make in assisting young people to play their part in the life of the community, in the light of changing social and industrial conditions and of current trends in other branches of the education service; and to advise according to what priorities best value can be obtained for the money spent.

INCREASED FOCUS ON EDUCATION

As part of this growth and development in education, we can begin to see that it is being increasingly viewed in policy as being more than the provision of schools and curriculum timetabling, with the steady growth in after-school clubs, youth work in schools, outdoor education, and special provision for those with special needs. However, while the development of the youth service was proposed as part of Circular 133, under 'schemes of FE Development', the sector was to lack the significant investment promised and thus set about building a 'structure without support' (Wylie, 2010). Much of what was achieved was as a result of pragmatic collaboration and partnership development and cocktail funding. Since the Education Act (1981) professionals from education, health and social services have been encouraged to work together to support children and families.

This trend has continued up until today where, for example, the Education Act 2002 required every local authority in England to develop extended schools which would provide integrated, wraparound services from 8 am until 6 pm. This was aimed at using the school as a community hub involving community groups, health initiatives and the co-location of multi-disciplinary teams.

Quite specifically, section 175 of the act places a legal duty on the school to safeguard and promote the welfare of children, requiring staff to:

- provide a safe environment for children and young people to learn in education settings;
- identify children and young people, who are suffering or likely to suffer significant harm, and take appropriate action to make sure that they are kept safe both at home and at school;
- contribute to effective partnership working between all those involved in providing services for children.

FOCUS ON CHILDREN'S SERVICES

From this we can see that children's services were refocused around extended schools as a result of the government policy inherent in *Every Child Matters* (Chief Secretary to the Treasury, 2003; House of Commons Education and Skills committee, 2004/2005) which saw the establishment of new safeguarding children's boards and new directors of children's services, with a duty of care for corporate parenting. Children's trusts have also been established, set up by local authorities, to integrate staff and services and ensure that children and young people are consulted about service development. Some critics have pointed out that using schools as a hub for social service interventions may be of limited value as those who are most in need have not experienced school in a positive way. Nevertheless, children's trusts were New Labour's way of amalgamating all the commissioning for children's services. This integration of service aspects includes LEAs, children's social services, health services, youth offending teams, connexions and police to provide integrated service provision, develop operating systems for protection and tracking, and offer advice, guidance and prevention strategies. However, in the past such concern about the welfare of children was not a priority for politicians, government, and other powerful adults.

CONSTRUCTION OF CHILDHOOD: DEBATE

In the academic literature about the construct of childhood there are two schools of thought. There are those authors who argue that in medieval times, the Middle Ages and the Victorian era the childhood state was not recognised, and that parents tended only to their children's biological needs and remained emotionally neutral about them (Aries, 1962; De Mause, 1974). On the other side, are those writers who hold that there were significant notions of childhood in earlier times, but that the extent of and attitude to child rearing depended on levels of education, class, gender, status, circumstances and location (Pollock, 1983; Shahar, 1990). However, what we can all agree on is that legislatively recognition of the child in law and their need for protection has increased over the years. This protective trend started with a series of factory acts, including the 1833 Act which improved working conditions for children in factories, prohibited the employment of children under 9 years of age, and limited the working day to nine hours for children aged 9 to 13 and to twelve hours for those aged between 13 and 18. It also required factory owners to educate children for two hours a day.

CHILDREN ACTS

Following the Victorian era, a series of children acts had been introduced, appearing in each decade from the 1933 Children Act until the two most recent in 1989 and in 2004. These acts developed the focus from being concerned with employment protection issues through to safeguarding and protecting children, and from there to getting professionals to work together and giving children rights and a voice. The Children Act (1989) and *Every Child Matters* (2003) both enhanced the need for integrated working. However, the Children Act (2004) made it a duty for professionals to cooperate, safeguard and promote the welfare of children, and brought in organisational interprofessional collaboration through the establishment of children's and young people's services to make sure that this happened on an operational basis. This legislative development has been further supported by such initiatives as the Children's Workforce Strategy (DfES, 2005), the Children and Young People's Workforce Strategy (DCSF, 2008), and the Children's Plan Two Years On (DCSF, 2009). More details on this will be provided in Chapter 10 which is specifically dedicated to child protection, but at this point we need to recognise that this current focus on protection is allied to a youth development discourse which views young people as troublesome.

ADOLESCENCE DISCOURSE: POLICY AND LAW

Although we noted in an earlier chapter that in terms of human rights law all people under 18 years old are classified as children, in practice the way that adolescence is viewed is through both sexualisation and criminalisation (Griffin, 1993). The underlying discourse about young people, which influences policy and law making, is that not only are young people 'at risk' but that they are also involved in risk taking and risky behaviour which lead to delinquency and criminal behaviour (Heaven, 1994: 208). However, any risky behaviour could be equally attributed to the fact that young people are largely marginalised, the opportunities for them to income generate are limited, and they are particularly vulnerable to exploitation by the economic system (White, 1989). In recent years, laws passed in the UK to tackle crime and disorder have been largely aimed at controlling young people's behaviour in public that is seen as threatening and out of control.

Although like many acts which appear to be a collection of diverse and miscellaneous measures, this type of discourse, that support the unruly teenager view, is evident within the Crime and Disorder Act 1998. This act introduced Anti Social Behaviour Orders (ASBOS), Sex Offender Orders, Parenting Orders, racially aggravated and religious offences, and abolished the 'rebuttable presumption' that a child is *doli incapax* which is the presumption that a young person between 10 and 14 years old is incapable of committing an offence. It also established the Crime and Disorder Reduction Partnerships across England, which are inter-agency forums made up of LAs, police, health, social landlords, the voluntary sector, local residents and businesses. This thinking and approach were further cemented, in England and Wales, by the Anti Social Behaviour Act 2003, which made ASBOs stricter, introduced fixed penalty notices, and banned the sale of spray paints to under 16s. It also addressed truancy, gang membership, fireworks, and public drunkenness. The focus of such acts on the prevention of potential behaviors and actions of young people, along with the organisation of adult-dominated forums, demonstrates that young people are not regarded as responsible and cannot be trusted to act safely. However, it is not only young people who cannot be trusted as those who hold the dominant central power seek to change and direct those who operate at a local level.

Activity

Make a note of any effective collaboration or partnership arrangement that you have been involved in with others. Reflect on and record those aspects that made this successful or unsuccessful, and show how this practice related to any responsibility you had under any of the social welfare acts.

Comment

Partnership work will only be successful if the partners have similar values and common aims. There are different types of partnerships: those that are community based which provides a recognisable structure for working with local people, and multi-agency partnerships which can bring interdisciplinarity across professions as well as assist with planning and the integration of services.

NEW PUBLIC MANAGEMENT

At this point we will now turn to the political and professional discourse which gives rise to a debate about the most appropriate and effective way to organise and manage local government. In recent decades this debate has been dominated by ideas around New Public Management (NPM), which is a term devised in the early 1980s that is used to describe a way of thinking and acting that has been adopted by national and local governments with the central aim of modernising the public sector. It is an encompassing and complex shorthand description, used to reflect the significant changes and reforms which have taken place both across Britain and throughout the western world. The main idea behind this management philosophy is that greater market orientation in the public sector and a fusion of best practice (see Clarke et al., 1994) will result in greater cost-efficiency for governments.

The impetus for NPM is driven by a combination of political, economic, social, and technological factors. However, an overriding motive for countries promoting the NPM course has been the experience of economic and fiscal crises as it triggered the desire for efficiency and provides an acceptable rationale and mechanism by which to cut the cost of delivering public services.

NPM: A MOVEMENT

NPM therefore is essentially a movement that aims to limit public spending and enhance opportunities for private firms to provide services that were formally provided by the public sector. In order to achieve this, demands are placed on the public sector to replicate private sector behaviours. For example, there is an emphasis on accountability and performance management, a focus on competition and contracts, and an insistence on flexibility in working conditions along with increased management control (Hood, 1995).

Compared to other public management philosophies NPM is more focused on outcomes and efficiency, which is held to be achieved through better management of the public purse and the creation of competition based on economic principles. NPM views the recipients of public services as customers and citizens as shareholders, which helps to shift the emphasis from traditional public administration to public management. An example of such a shift was the introduction of compulsory competitive tendering laid down in the Local Government Act 1988, which required LAs to tender for some of the services that it provided directly in house.

NPM: ALIVE OR DEAD?

Over and above this type of approach, NPM measures show themselves in a number of different ways: through ways of decentralising management within public services; creating autonomous agencies and devolving financial control; increasing use of markets and competition; contracting out and other market-type mechanisms; and increasing the emphasis on performance, outputs and customer orientation. Some commentators would argue that NPM has peaked and is now in decline, while other critics (e.g., Dunleavy et al.) now proclaim that NPM is 'dead' and the cutting edge of change has moved on to digital era governance that is focused on reintegrating concerns into government control, holistic (or joined-up) government, and digitalisation (exploiting the Web and digital storage and communication within government).

THIRD WAY THINKING

NPM has been challenged by a range of related critiques such as Third Way thinking (Giddens, 1998) and in particular by the rise in ideas associated with Public Value Theory. This position reasserts a focus on citizenship, networked governance and the role of public agencies in working with citizens to co-create public value and generate democratic authorisation, legitimacy and trust. It also emphasises the necessity of recognising the complex adaptive systems domains within which public managers are working, as with characteristics which are qualitatively different from simple market forms or private sector business principles.

Most significantly, while recognising the arguments about the search for efficiency and the differences in organisation, values and intention between the public and private organisation (Boston et al., 1996), youth work and community professionals must emphasise the importance of local accountability in service provision and promote the primacy of meeting local needs through the creation of local democratic opportunities.

Key Challenge – Question

What are the values and principles that inform your discourse and position on the rationale for, and the shape of, local services?

Comment

My ideas are that locality can be key part of understanding society and is the environment by which local participation can come alive. Locality is a feature of community and is the place where social systems interface with people. It is also the environment where meaning making takes place with opportunities for relationships to grow and networks to develop. It is the place where communal social action can take place and where the vulnerable can be protected. Therefore it is the right space for some services that if these were delivered centrally, for example, would be less efficient and effective.

CONCLUSION

It is important that youth work is not swallowed up by its uncritically accepting new public managed thinking which is latent, pervasive, and incremental. Youth work must obviously comply with and operate within the law, but it must also take the opportunity to articulate its raison d'être and clearly detail its democratic intention, contribution and pedigree. It must help to create the discourse that enables it to influence and shape future laws and develop an acceptable enhanced practice that values young people for who they are.

Although some of the language and emphasis changes, it has been recognised that the role of the informal educator is principally three-fold: to create space for association and conversation; to encourage self-directed learning and act upon this knowledge; and to utilise a critical perspective on society and circumstances which helps to focus the participation (Smith,1988; Banks, 1999; Ord, 2007; Packham, 2008). The relationship of democratic values to the process of informal education is identified in the academic literature (Jeffs and Smith, 1999: 25) where conversations and ontological orientations are 'central to democracy'. In policy terms it is often referred to as a process of engagement ([Scottish Executive, 2004). It is within this context that youth workers need to see beyond the current political discourses and take a higher-principled view when conducting 'democratic audits' (Smith and Jeffs, 2007) over the longer term. This approach may help to explain the tension that youth work has with some policy drivers which require compliance rather than discussion.

A youth worker, as an informal educator, needs to be self, socially and politically aware, and able to articulate either their own or others' ideological and critical perceptions. We should not assume that those youth workers who engage in a critique of bureaucratic modernity carry out this task either to criticise tradition or out of a more liberal sentiment. Instead this critical approach is necessary to help ensure that the structures and processes remain relevant, that individual student needs are satisfied along with those of the masses, and that students endeavour to participate in the meaningful and constructive path that they must make and own.

Youth workers, as with other social professionals, need to recognise that they are a product of their own time, and thus can only influence and work through that time's events and recognise the fundamental shape that any particular part of history will have on the way life is lived. In this context youth workers will recognise the importance of knowing the ways in which society works, and will also endeavour to make a study of these because they are the main way for judging and acting upon them.

We can draw from these educationalists that youth workers go about the job with a notion of liberation which is not temporally confined by structure, processes and rules. Instead, the engaging youth worker inspires and moves through a dialogue which has everything to do with knowledge, aspiration, conviction, commitment, and being fully alive.

Case Study 3

Advice from Central Government to Local Government

Annex A: Example of a statement of intent as to community engagement

This annex provides examples of the type of information that a council may wish to include in its statement of intent. The breadth and type of information that a council includes in its statement will, to a large extent, depend on the size of that council, and therefore some of the examples listed below may not be appropriate to all councils. However, it is recommended that, when preparing its statement, the council considers all of the suggestions carefully. The examples listed below are not exhaustive. Quality councils who have prepared community engagement strategies will be able to draw on these.

The types of information that could be included are listed below.

Aims and objectives

A statement setting out the council's aims and its objectives for seeking community engagement as well as the outcomes it hopes to achieve.

Defining the community

A statement describing the individuals, groups and organisations the council intends to proactively engage with (e.g., the elderly, the young, Third Sector partner organisations).

Provision of information to the community

A statement setting out the types of information the council will make available to the community and the methods it will utilise in order to make such information accessible (e.g., how and when the annual report will be published and what level of detail it will include on spending).

Opportunities for community involvement

A statement setting out the opportunities the council will make available to the community to facilitate and encourage their involvement (e.g., councillors' surgeries, surveys, open days, web discussion forums, the allocation of a 'public representation' session at council meetings).

Opportunities for formal representations to the council

A statement setting out the processes in place to facilitate formal representations from individuals/ groups/partner organisations (e.g., details of the timetable for receiving and responding to representations, the process for evaluating consultation).

Involvement in partnerships

A statement setting out the council's participation in partnerships/networks (e.g., council representation on the Chamber of Commerce).

Role of council members and officers

A statement setting out how council members and officers will engage with the community.

Specific areas for community involvement

A statement setting out specific issues that the council intends to consult the community on (e.g., the development of a community centre, the preparation of community-led plans).

Task

Evaluate the example above and attempt to discern any discourse that is identifiable in this suggested approach.

Summary of Key Points

- There is a significant history between central and local government which is continuously changing and full of tensions.
- The process of devolution has increased these tensions and in three of the countries it has added another layer of government between central and local.

(Continued)

(Continued)

- Youth work practice has differed across the UK as devolution governments have shaped its development.
- Youth workers must be conversant with their responsibilities under the various social welfare acts and look for opportunities to contribute to the development of policy.
- New Public Management is a political and professional discourse which is latent and open to challenge.
- Partnership work can be a main vehicle for delivering good effective youth work practice.
- Youth work is a practice filled with tension, but youth workers must be able to see behind the presenting situation in order to place young people's interests at the heart of the process.
- Informal education pedagogy is an important basis for the practice to ensure that youth work meets its obligations.
- Youth workers need to be well-informed, self-reflective, and socially aware.

REFERENCES

Albemarle Report (1960) *The Youth Service in England and Wales*. London: HMSO.

Aries, P. (1962) *Centuries of Childhood*. London: Penguin.

Banks, S. (1999) The Social professions and social policy: proactive or reactive, *European Journal of Social Work*, 2 (3): 327–339.

Banks, S. (ed.) (2010) *Ethical Issues in Youth Work* (2nd edn). Oxon: Routledge.

Bennett, M., Fairley, J. and McAteer, M. (2002) *Devolution in Scotland: The Impact on Local Government*. York: Joseph Rowntree Foundation.

Boston, J., Martin, J., Pallot, J. and Walsh, P. (1996) *Public Management: The New Zealand Model*. Auckland: Oxford University Press.

Cabinet Office (1999) *Role of Central Government at Regional and Local Level*. London: Author.

Chester, D.N. (1951) *Lessons of the British War Economy*. Westport: Greenwood Press.

Chief Secretary to the Treasury (2003) *Every Child Matters*. Norwich: HMSO.

Clarke, J., Cochrane, A., & McLaughlin, E. (1994) *Managing Social Policy*. London: Sage.

DCSF (2008) *The Children and Young People's Workforce Strategy: DCSF -01052 -2008*. Nottingham: DCSF Publications.

DCSF (2009) *The Children's Plan Two Years On: DCSF-01162-2009*. Nottingham DCSF Publications.

De Mause, L. (ed.) (1974) *History of Childhood*. London: Souvenir.

Department for Communities and Local Government (2009) *Town and Country Planning (Consultation) (England) Direction 2009*. London: DCLG.

Dewey, J. (1916) *Democracy and Education*. New York: MacMillan.

DfES (2005) *The Children's Workforce Strategy: A Strategy to Build a World-Class Workforce for Children and Young People*. Nottingham: DfES Publications.

Dunleavy, P. and Margetts, H. (2006) New public management is dead: long live digital era governance, *Journal of Public Administration Research and Theory* (July).

Equality Act (2010). London: Office of Public Sector Information.

Freire, P. (1972) *Pedagogy of the Oppressed*. London: Penguin.

Freire, P. (1992) *Pedagogy of Hope*. New York: Continuum.

Giddens, A. (1998)*The Third Way: The Renewal of Social Democracy*. Cambridge: Polity Press.

Griffin, C. (1993) *Representations of Youth*. Cambridge: Polity Press.

Heaven, P. (1994) *Contemporary Adolescence: A Social Psychological Approach*. Australia: Macmillan.

Her Majesty's Government (1996) *Government Response to the Report of the House of Lords Select Committee on Relations Between Central and Local Government 'Rebuilding trust'*. London: HMSO.

HMSO (1977) *Relations between Central Government and Local Authorities: Report*. London: Author.

Hood, C. (1995) Contemporary Public Management: a new global paradigm?, *Public Policy and Administration*, 10 (2): 104–117.

House of Commons Education and Skills Committee (2004/2005) *Every Child Matters*. London: The Stationery Office.

Jeffs, T. and Smith, M. (1999) *Informal Education: Conversation, Democracy, Learning*. Ticknall: Education Now.

Jeffs, T. and Smith, M. (2005) *Informal Education: Conversation, Democracy and Learning*. England: Educational Heretics.

Localism Act 2011 accessed at www.legislation.gov.uk/ukpga/2011/20/contents/enacted (last accessed 06.12.2013).

Ord, J. (2007) *Youth Work Process, Product and Practice*. Dorset: Russell House.

Packham, C. (2008) *Active Citizenship and Community Learning*. Exeter: Learning Matters.

Paterson, L. (1998) *Diverse Assembly: The Debate on a Scottish Parliament*. Edinburgh: Edinburgh University Press.

Pollock, L. (1983) *Forgotten Children: Parent–Child Relations in England from 1500 to 1900*. Cambridge: Cambridge University Press.

Scottish Executive (2004) *Working and Learning Together to Build Stronger Communities*. Edinburgh: Scottish Executive.

Shahar, S. (1990) *Childhood in the Middle Ages*. London: Routledge.

Smith, M. (1988) *Developing Youth* Work. Milton Keynes: Open University Press.

Smith, M. and Jeffs, T. (2007) *Fostering Democracy and Association*. Available at www.infed.org (last accessed 06.05.09).

White, R. (1989) Making ends meet: young people, work and the criminal economy, *Australian and New Zealand Journal of Criminology*, 22 (2): 136–150.

Wylie, T. (2010) HMI Inspectorate and youth work, 1944–2009. In R. Gilchrist, T. Hodgson, T. Jeffs, J. Spence, N. Stanton and J. Walker (eds), *Reflecting on the Past: Essays in the History of Youth and Community Work*. Dorset: Russell House.

4

OPERATIONAL LEGAL REQUIREMENTS AND MANAGEMENT SYSTEMS

Chapter Aims

- Outline the importance of having robust organisational and practice policies and procedures
- Emphasise the importance of record keeping and procedure compliance
- Stress the importance of training, regular employee communication and reliable information
- Introduce the main aspects of employment law and offer information on further sources of guidance
- Present some of the key ideas behind the introduction of recent equality legislation
- Highlight the centrality of Health and Safety legislation and establish the role of the HSE
- Underline the ways in which data should be handled and present the functions of the ICO
- Compare the role of data protection and freedom of information in terms of record access and keeping

INTRODUCTION

Youth work takes place in many different locations and situations which can make it difficult to anticipate some of the circumstances that may arise. Due to this fact, it is imperative that youth workers ensure that they have policies and procedures in place that will be helpful to analyse and act in a particular situation. In these fluid situations many potential problems can be averted by good planning and preparation which should engage all those involved. A key tenet of any advice would be to take personal responsibility by not leaving it to others, either a colleague, volunteer or young person, to conduct the preparation and planning. It would be advisable that you make sure yourself that the necessary levels of 'checks and balances' have been carried out appropriately in accordance with the stated policies and procedures. There are a range of different laws that need to be recognised when operating within a practice situation and the degree to which any particular legislation applies will be dependent on the particular situation.

However, in general terms, and regardless of the operating situation, a key point to remember for all stakeholders is that the individual practitioner should not be left to determine what is required in order to comply with legislative requirements. Therefore, it is both your right and responsibility as a professional worker to ensure that your employing agency has the relevant written policies and procedures, held in an accessible form (for example, a reference manual), that will outline guidance and advice which, if followed, will comply with the relevant legal requirements. From this, it will subsequently be your responsibility to read and understand the policy and procedures manual and then make sure that all those for whom you are managerially responsible perform in the same way. If you discover anything that needs clarification, or an issue has not been covered within the policy and procedures manual, then you should make a formal written request for management to develop a policy on this issue. Similarly, if you find that a policy is not workable then draw this to the attention of management immediately and ensure that policy is altered so that it becomes workable and appropriate. Monitor any changes to make sure that the situation is remedied to your satisfaction, and record any shortcomings in operation that remain. Request further improvements until you are satisfied that the systems and operations are compliant and workable. If you are still unhappy about the circumstances after this seek legal advice from a registered legal practitioner.

ADMINISTRATION

In addition to this, do make sure that your record keeping and administration are kept up to date so that you can demonstrate clear organisational processes, ensure informed consent, and record agreements including the details of all parties. Keep a written record of important information in your files such as contact details for the young people you are working with. Also record any complaints made, no matter how trivial these may first appear, and ensure that all injuries are appropriately documented in keeping with the organisational and legal requirement. When an incident does occur ask a team member to take notes as the incident develops and write up a full account, with everyone involved, during (if appropriate) and as soon afterwards as possible. In doing this, you will have the background notes to be able to comply with the requirements of the Data Protection Act, the reporting of injuries requirement, and child protection polices (which are all covered in more detail in subsequent chapters in this book). This position is adopted not only to promote the notion of 'floating responsibility' (Bauman, 1994) where employees are devoid of responsibility if they adhere to the rules, but also to help ensure that young people learn in a safe and enjoyable environment.

LEGAL COMPLIANCE

All staff and volunteers need to be regularly trained in their legal obligations, particularly in relation to privacy, confidentiality, and duty of care. You may wish to consider undertaking a NEBOSH (National Examination Board in Occupational Safety and Health) course which is provided by a recognised organisation that delivers vocational qualifications in health, safety, and environmental practice and management.

Young people should also be informed about their rights and responsibilities. Parents, guardians and young people need to be given appropriate and regular information, and so you must always seek particular legal advice, from a qualified legal practitioner, that is tailored to your specific circumstances and situation.

Making sure that your organisation and operation are legally compliant can be a complex task, and it is vital that those responsible for this organisation and practice receive the best advice for their own protection and the safety of those they employ. As this is a complex field, organisations should seek professional help which can be obtained from a range of free and paid sources. If possible, and especially if you have to pay for it, seek advice from a specialist in the area that you wish to address. There are also a range of strategic organisations in the voluntary sector who will offer free advice and support, as well as other services such as the Arbitration, Conciliation and Advisory Service (ACAS) which will also help with employment matters.

This chapter will offer information on five main areas of the law which, subject to the specific situation, could be relevant to the type of youth work practice you are likely to encounter.

EMPLOYMENT LAW

It is often said, but not always evidenced in action, that people are the most important resource and greatest asset to any organisation. People are a prime asset but they can also be the most difficult part of any manager's job, because dealing with people is complex, multi-dimensional, and very changeable over a short period of time. However, employment law is in place (and should be used) to help ensure that employees are treated fairly and equitably. Employment law is important and should be followed but it can be complex, mainly because it changes over time and inter-relates with aspects of other legislation. Good youth work managers should see these statutory instruments as being the minimum requirements and recognise the significance of a more holistic empowering approach to people management in keeping with their professional values and attributes. The legislative requirements set out the basic principles, rights and responsibilities, along with any arrangements to be followed and particularly when things go wrong. It is necessary to recognise here that laws do not, and indeed cannot, deal with other vital operational aspects such as motivation, happiness, and feelings of self worth (Argyris, 1960), which are equally vital to organisational stability and success.

There are also some other significant aspects of people management which are not detailed in law, such as the significance of induction processes, providing appropriate support, conducting effective supervision, developing teamwork, handling day-to-day conflict, and being a good leader. (For more guidance on these elements in youth work settings to develop effective youth work, see Adirondack 2006; Tyler et al., 2009.)

Employment law is both a generic and specific term. Its generic use is often used to distinguish it from other branches of practice, such as family law, immigration law, and criminal law. Employment law is sometimes used to cover all aspects of the law that relate to employment matters, and when it is applied more specifically, it refers to particular legislation that aims to prevent discrimination in certain identified areas such as gender and marital status. The Sex Discrimination Act 1975 (which as well as employment related to training, education, harassment, the provision of goods and services and the disposal of premises) also established the Equal Opportunities Commission. Under this 1975 Act, discrimination is identified in two forms: direct and indirect. The first is evident when a woman, for example, is treated less favourably than a man. An illustration of this, which is clearly unacceptable, is when two people, one a woman and the other a man, are both performing the same job but are paid different rates of pay. This act states that men and women should receive equal pay for work of equal value, but there have been many examples over the subsequent years when it has been shown that this inequity still exists and that, for example, there remains a 'glass ceiling' on women's pay in some sectors. Indirect discrimination can be hard to prove, but it could be for example a height restriction that prevents many women from applying for a certain job, and this is often only noticeable after statistical analysis over a period of time identifies an imbalance in the workforce. A number of equal pay claims, both individual and for work groups, have been settled over the past few years, with a significant number of claims still outstanding.

EMPLOYMENT RIGHTS

The Employment Rights Act 1996 introduced a whole host of significant requirements, including the protection of wages, Sunday working arrangements, safeguards for suffering detriments, time off working, and maternity, paternity, parental and adoption leave, as well as flexible working, termination rights, and minimum redundancy payments. In relation to employment particulars, the Employment Rights Act 1996 states that all employees, if employed for over one month, should be given, within the first two months, a written statement detailing the employment particulars. This information must detail the employer's and employee's names, the job title and job outline, the commencement date, the place and hours of work, and entitlements such as leave and holiday arrangements. In any event, a full contract should be written up which outlines all the employment conditions and benefit: this is normally signed by the employee and a copy kept, by both employee and employer, for future reference. The professional services of a person qualified in law and/or human resources management should be engaged for this purpose.

ASYLUM AND IMMIGRATION

Another act that youth workers should be aware of which affects potential employment is that according to the Asylum and Immigration Act 1996 (note that it is also unlawful for any person who is not entitled to work in the UK to do so, and procedures should be put in place to verify a person's eligibility to work in the country). Again, youth workers must note that part-time staff should not be treated any differently from full-time staff, and should also enjoy, pro rata, the same conditions of service under the Part Time Workers (Prevention of Less Favourable Treatment) Regulations and Amendment 2002. In terms of gender matters, this original 1970 Act has been amended by the Employment and Equality (Sex Discrimination) Regulations 2005, which makes it unlawful to discriminate on the grounds of pregnancy and maternity leave. This European directive also provides a definition of harassment and sexual harassment, and makes harassment by an employer unlawful.

GENDER RECOGNITION

Amendments were made to the seminal Sex Discrimination Act 1975 by the Gender Recognition Act 2004 and the Sex Discrimination Act 1975 (Amendment) Regulations 2008 in relation to transsexuals. Other amendments were introduced by the Sex Discrimination Act 1986, the Employment Act 1989, and the Equality Act 2006. The act was repealed in full by the Equality Act 2010 which is discussed in more detail below.

ARBITRATION AND CONCILIATION ADVISORY SERVICE

It is important that when a youth worker is working with others, both formally and informally, that this is always predicated on reaching a mutual understanding and agreement as well as applying the principles of equality and transparency. However, it must be recognised that this is a complex operating situation and that appropriate help should be sought through organisations such as the free Arbitration and Conciliation Advisory Service (ACAS).

Checking Understanding – Key Questions

What are the main purposes of employment law? Why is it important to have a contract of employment? To what extent does employment law relate to other laws? Why are specific aspects of employment law updated on a regular basis? Describe the role of the Arbitration and Conciliation Advisory Service (ACAS). In what ways are employment laws relevant for youth work practice?

Comment

The answers are contained within the section above. Employment law exists to help ensure that workers are treated fairly and equitably. There are some duties placed on public bodies to promote racial equality but not on private sector organisations. However, a recent report by the JRF (2011) found that SME's continue to show signs of poor equal opportunities practice, and that workplace discrimination and workplace cultures favour some groups over others and thereby add to work poverty.

EQUALITY LEGISLATION

The Equality Act 2010, which came into force on the 1 October of that year, was introduced in an attempt to streamline and combine previous disability and race relations legislation to make the requirements less complex. This act has the same goals as the four major EU Equal Treatment Directives, whose provisions it reflects and implements in requiring equal treatment in access to employment as well as private and public services. The act applies to all those who employ other people and/or provide goods or services to the public, and puts in place measures to help protect minority groups and prevent discrimination.

In brief, it is unlawful to discriminate against people at work due to the protected characteristics of:

- age;
- disability (including mental health and clinical obesity);
- gender reassignment;
- marriage and civil partnership;
- pregnancy and maternity;
- race;
- religion or belief;
- sex;
- sexual orientation.

TYPES OF DISCRIMINATION

The two types of discrimination mentioned above, identified in the Sex Discrimination Act 1975, have been added to and included in a list of seven major types of discrimination, which introduces the notion that these areas are referred to as protected characteristics:

1. *Direct discrimination* – this is unacceptable discrimination judged in terms of an identified protected characteristic.
2. *Associative discrimination* – this is direct discrimination but against someone because they are associated with another person with a protected characteristic. This would include carers of disabled people and/or elderly relatives, who may claim that they were treated unfairly because of the care duties they carried out at home. It also covers discrimination against a person who is treated less favourably because, for example, their partner is from another country or culture.
3. *Indirect discrimination* – this exists when a rule or policy, which applies to everyone, disadvantages an individual with a protected characteristic.
4. *Harassment* – this situation is recognised when behaviour is viewed to be offensive by the recipient. Please note that employees can claim that they find something personally offensive even when it's not directed at them. In these circumstances this has the purpose or effect of violating a person's dignity or creating an environment which is intimidating, degrading, humiliating or offensive to that individual.
5. *Harassment by a third party* – this situation may arise when employers are potentially liable for harassment of staff or customers carried out by people who they don't directly employ (for example, a contractor working on behalf of the organisation). This is sometimes referred to as the 'harassment by a third party' rule.
6. *Victimisation* – this is discrimination carried out against someone who experiences detriment because, for example, they made or supported a complaint under the Equality Act legislation.
7. *Discrimination by perception* – this is direct discrimination against a person because other people think they have a protected characteristic, even if they do not.

HEALTH

Another aspect that you should be aware of under this legislation is that generally employers can no longer question a prospective employee about their health before offering them work. This also means that an employer cannot ask at interview, or in an application form, how much time an employee has taken off work in previous jobs.

Two main exceptions to this are if the employer can prove that this is necessary in order to monitor diversity or determine if this is necessary to ascertain the person's suitability for an essential task like heavy lifting. You can screen for health, both physical and mental, after making a job offer, but you cannot withdraw the offer based on disability grounds. In essence, a person cannot be treated unfavourably because of something connected to a disability (for example, discriminating against a person with dyslexia because they would make spelling mistakes).

AGE

Interestingly, age is still the only protected characteristic by which you can justify direct discrimination, as long as the employer successfully argues that the person is being treated differently because of their age and is meeting a legitimate aim. At present an employer can still operate a default retirement age of 65 years, although this is likely to alter with the proposed retirement age legislation changes.

GENDER

In addition, under this legislation, mothers are free to breastfeed in public or on the premises, and cannot be asked to move to a more private location. Again, because gender reassignment is a protected characteristic, then workers who are changing their gender cannot be discriminated against and must also be given time off work to complete the process. Employers cannot put restrictions on staff discussing their levels of remuneration as individuals are now free to discuss their wages openly with each other, which may help ensure that employees are paid in relatively fairer terms. People making claims can also now bring a 'dual discrimination' claim which enables the tribunal to assess the impact of the two protected characteristics together to help uncover a fuller extent of the discrimination.

DISABILITY

In the case of disability, employers and service providers are under a duty to make reasonable adjustments to their workplaces to overcome the barriers experienced by disabled people. It is worthy of note that tribunal judges can recommend changes to the operational procedures of the organisation and not just to the way an individual is treated.

There is some evidence (ECU, 2011) that organisations, such as higher education institutions, are failing to meet their duties under the Equalities Act by not providing disability leave. There is also some evidence of continuing pay gap levels in the public sector and across the wider economy. In spite of some improvements in recent years, the gender pay gap for higher education teaching professionals identified by ASHE in 2011 was 14.4 per cent, with significant gaps recorded in other professional areas working with young people (secondary education 11.8 per cent, and primary and nursery Education 10.4 per cent).There are no statistics available for the situation within youth work, which is telling by their absence.

EQUALITY ACT (2010)

Essentially, the Equality Act (2010) demands that there is action to promote equality, to tackle and reduce inequalities through positive action and comply with the equality duty by ensuring that public bodies make sure that their work supports equality.

Self-reflection Exercise

- Think about and then write down your views on equality.
- Are you able to remember an incident when someone was being discriminated against? If so, what did you do at the time? What, if anything, would you do differently if a similar incident happened today?
- Do you think that people who are discriminated against are getting a better deal as a result of the Equality Act 2010? Can you provide any evidence for your stated assessment? In what ways can/does youth work promote equality?

Comment

Every social interaction is mediated via an interface with a range of equality issues, including gender, race, age, sexuality, class, religion, and power. A youth worker needs to be aware of their personal prejudices, cultural discrimination, and structural positions. Values and experience, both personal and professional, provide the bedrock for working with others, and these need to be articulated to ensure that we can work equitably with difference.

HEALTH AND SAFETY REQUIREMENTS

Health and Safety is a crucial aspect of strategic and operational management function in every organisation. Youth workers will find themselves in a variety of working situations and these will require adherence to various aspects of health and safety, from managing buildings to lone working arrangements, and from using new technology to operating machinery. Health and Safety is an important aspect of safe and professional practice, and each worker should ensure that they are familiar with the standards expected and only undertake an activity for which they are appropriately trained.

HEALTH AND SAFETY AT WORK ETC. ACT 1974

The foundational legislation in this area, in more recent years, has come via the Health and Safety at Work etc. Act 1974, which itself builds on other legislation such as the various historic railway and factory acts. This main act is also supported by the Management of Health and Safety at Work Regulations 1999. However, as with previous acts, this seminal legislation has been consistently added to as operational environments change, lessons are learned from incidents, and new knowledge is created. More specifically, additional acts reflect situations that require further guidance: for example, dealing with offences for non-compliance (Health and Safety Offences Act 2008), the wider protection of the environment

(Environment Protection Act 1990), and a more proactive approach to ensuring that responsible staff are given advice and guidance about carrying out risk assessments that are appropriate to their operating context (the Regulatory Reform (Fire Safety) Order 2005: see www.communities.gov.uk/publications/fire/regulatoryreformfire), as well as many others.

WHAT'S INVOLVED?

In organisational terms, this is an area that requires a dedicated resource and involves continuous updating and training for all staff. It will be your responsibility to ensure you are operating safely, and the organisation you work for should give you sufficient support to enable you to comply. This is a complex area and as such there are over 60 acts that relate to Health and Safety at work, as well as hundreds of regulations emanating from the UK and European parliaments. However, not every act and regulation will be relevant to your operating circumstances (but you will need to know the ones that are).

RANGE OF HEALTH AND SAFETY LEGISLATION

There is a whole range of legislation here covering a wide variety of topics, and taken together this is too vast to cover in detail in this section. In general terms however the legislation applies to issues such as controlling noise at work and ensuring the safe provision and use of work equipment.

You may be somewhat surprised by the number of areas covered where health and safety requirements are relevant, but you still need to become familiar with these requirements for practice. There is a range of areas, not a full list, related to youth work which could be relevant, including Safety Induction and Training Procedures; Health and Safety in Education and Training; Emergency Evacuation Procedures; Fire Fighting Equipment; Food Hygiene; Managing Violence at Work; Work at Height; Lone Working Risk Evaluation; Grounds Maintenance Safety; Personal Protective Equipment (PPE); Display Screen Equipment (DSE); Risk Assessments; Manual Handling; Control of Substances Hazardous to Health (COSHH); Accident Investigation and Recording; Stepladder Pre-Use; Manual Handling: Machinery Safety; Pregnant Employees; Asbestos Safety; and Temporary Workers.

THE IMPORTANCE OF TRAINING

In general terms, many of the regulations require an employer to complete staff training and keep training records, as well as make sure that operatives are competent under the Street Works (Qualifications of Supervisors and Operatives) (England)

Regulations 2009. In addition, there are a number of distinct actions that are required under certain pieces of legislation. For example, an organisation is required to appoint a competent adviser/competent person and complete risk assessments to satisfy, inter alia, the Management of Health and Safety at Work Regulations 1999, the Control of Substances Hazardous to Health Regulations 2002, the Control of Noise at Work Regulations 2005, the Regulatory Reform (Fire Safety) Order 2005, and the Dangerous Substances and Explosive Atmospheres Regulations 2002. Also, organisations are required to produce a company Health and Safety policy under the Health and Safety at Work etc Act 1974, appoint a first aider, record the training for all first aiders, and provide adequately stocked first-aid box with contents list in order to comply with the Health and Safety (First-Aid) Regulations 1981.

EMPLOYEE CONSULTATION

Under the Health and Safety (Consultation with Employees) Regulations 1996 and the Safety Representatives and Safety Committees Regulations 1977, organisations are required to keep evidence that the management team (including the director named on the health and safety policy and the health and safety manager) do consult with employees. If you are operating in an environment where pressure systems are in place and/or there is lifting equipment, then you should make sure that statutory inspections are undertaken in order to comply with the Pressure Systems Safety Regulations 2000 and the Lifting Operations and Lifting Equipment Regulations 1998. It is also necessary to ensure that any machinery is safe to operate under the Supply of Machinery (Safety) Regulations 2008. The organisation must also undertake statutory health surveillance, if appropriate, carry our specific surveys under the Control of Asbestos Regulations 2006, and not use certain substances under this and the Control of Substances Hazardous to Health Regulations 2002 and the Ionising Radiations Regulations 1999.

GENERAL WORKPLACE SAFETY

In addition to the above, there are other requirements which youth workers should know about: for example, the requirement for temperatures to be maintained in the workplace under the Workplace (Health, Safety and Welfare) Regulations 1992; the need to have insurance under the Employers' Liability (Compulsory Insurance) Regulations 1998; and need to provide protective equipment to comply with the Personal Protective Equipment at Work Regulations 1992, which could apply to circumstances attached to detached youth work for example. Finally, if you are involved in building installation or demolition work then you need to be aware of the requirements of the Construction (Design and Management) Regulations 2007. (For further detailed information and specific guidance please consult the Health and Safety Executive (www.hse.gov.uk/) and/or contact the appointed safety officer in your organisation.)

Key Challenge – Research Task

Access the HSE website given above and make a list of the range of legislation, instruments and guidance that relate to youth work. Also, identify the type of activities in a youth work situation that you have experience of, have read or know about that would require specific practice action to comply with Health and Safety legislation.

Comment

It is obviously vital that youth workers are aware of the legal parameters which inform their decisions and actions when working with young people. When doing so it is likely that youth workers may encounter issues of stealing, assault, offensive weapons and the use of illegal substances, and before they encounter these it would be worthwhile their knowing what the law says about such matters. It is also important that the employing organisation trains its youth workers appropriately in legal responsibilities and organisational procedures. However, every youth worker needs to keep up to date through continuous professional development in order make informed choices when ethical dilemmas occur in practice.

DATA PROTECTION

In this broad area of information management, there are four inter-related legislative areas: the Data Protection Act; the Freedom of Information Act; the Privacy and Electronic Communications Regulations (PECR); and the Environmental Information Regulations (EIR) and INSPIRE Regulations. We will deal with the first two acts in more detail in this chapter, but for quick reference the PECR deals with unsolicited marketing across the internet and give individuals the right to stop unsolicited direct marketing communications, the EIR gives rights to environmental information such as air quality and contamination in the food chain, and INSPIRE relates to access to spatial or geographical information based on EU Directive 2007/2/EC.

PRINCIPAL AIM

One of the principal aims of the Data Protection Act (1998) is to give individuals the right to know what information is held about them. This helps individuals to protect their interests and reputation by making sure that the information held about them is processed in a proper manner. It also gives individuals the right to ensure that the data held about them are correct and an opportunity to change that information if it is wrong. As well as this they have the right to seek compensation through the courts, for distress and financial loss for example, if an organisation is found to be in breach of the act.

FOI REQUEST

This is usually done through a subject access request but these do not have to be submitted in a particular format as long as it is a clear FOI request. A genuine request should be responded to within 40 calendar days of receiving the request. Each public organisation should appoint a data controller to oversee the operation.

FRAMEWORK

The act provides a framework to ensure that personal information is handled properly and in line with the eight principles of the Data Protection Act. The personal information held must be:

1. fairly and lawfully processed;
2. processed for specified purposes;
3. adequate, relevant, and not excessive;
4. accurate, and where necessary, kept up to date;
5. not kept for longer than is necessary;
6. processed in line with the rights of the individual;
7. kept secure;
8. not transferred to countries outside the European Economic Area unless there is adequate protection for the information.

The act is relevant to any organisation that collects, holds and uses data about people and organisations with which it works, and such data as it enables it to conduct its business. This may include members of the public, current, past and prospective employees, clients, customers, contractors, partners and suppliers. In addition, the public authorities may be required to collect and use personal data in order to comply with its statutory obligations.

PRINCIPLES

All public organisations must abide by the eight principles of the Data Protection Act.

Notification is a statutory requirement of the act and therefore a council must notify the Information Commissioner's Office (ICO) and give details about its processing of personal information. The ICO publishes certain details in the register of data controllers, which is available to the public for inspection. The council's entry in the Data Protection Public Register is published and available on the Web.

If, as a youth worker, you are asked to share information that you hold on record with a partner or agency, then this must be carried out in compliance with the Data Protection Act 1998. Such information sharing should be subject to organisational protocols where the decisions are clearly recorded about the level, type, and purpose of the information to be shared, (more detailed information and advice can be obtained from the Information Commissioners Office at www.ico.gov.uk/for_organisations/data_protection.aspx).

Key Challenge – Interpretation and Practical Processing

Think about the nature and type of data that would be collected in a particular youth setting. Use your knowledge, experience or research skills to identify the type and nature of actions that would need to be taken practically to ensure that such data were handled in keeping with the eight principles identified above.

Comment

A key point to remember is that data should only be collected for specified purposes and only held for as long as that purpose is still relevant. You also need to remember that any information held about someone can potentially be accessed by the person, so do make sure that any written comments are judicious, accurate, and defensible.

FREEDOM OF INFORMATION ACT

The Freedom of Information Act 2000 came into force in January 2005. The time lapse from approval to implementation gave public organisations time to review their procedures and put processes in place to enable an effective response to the requirements of the act. The difference between this act and the Data Protection Act (DPA) is that the latter deals with the processing and accessing of personal information whereas the Freedom of Information Act (FOI) deals with public information. In short, an individual is entitled to see all official information held by public authorities, including government departments, local authorities, hospitals, schools, colleges and universities, police forces, and prison authorities.

WHO CAN APPLY?

Anyone can make an FOI request irrespective of their age, nationality or geographical location. Any person can request any piece of information held by a relevant public body, and if this is refused then a reason has to be provided by the organisation. If you are unhappy with the reason for withholding the information then a complaint can be made to the Information Commissioner's

Office (ICO). There is guidance about how to make such a complaint on the ICO website.

PROCESS

In order to make a request, you will need to write or email the public body giving your name, contact details, and a description of the information you require. It will be helpful to the organisation if you make a specific request and curtail the extent of the search: this will then affect the time and cost of producing the information. A response should be provided within 20 days or an explanation given to you if it will take longer. It is noteworthy that while most requests are free you can be asked to make a small contribution towards photocopying or postage. You can also ask to have the information in a format that is suitable for you, and in addition, under sections 9 and 13 of the act, a request can be turned down if it costs more than £450, or £600 for central government (deemed to be an 'appropriate limit', which emphasises the need to be specific in your request).

FURTHER GUIDANCE

Further guidance is provided to public authorities, through codes of practice, and issued under sections 45 (updated 2004) and 46 (updated 2009) of the Freedom of Information Act. The section 45 code gives more detailed information on the practices to be adopted when dealing with requests, the provision of advice and help to applicants, the transference of requests to other authorities, the use of confidentiality clauses in contracts, and the provision of an internal complaints procedure. The code, issued under section 46 of the Freedom of Information Act, gives further information on good practice in relation to record keeping, and offers guidance on the review and transfer of public records for permanent archiving.

IMPLICATIONS FOR YOUTH WORKERS

For youth workers it is clear that the information systems adopted, when operating in practice, need to be organised in such a way that these comply with both the Data Protection Act (1998) and the Freedom of Information Act (2000). As a result youth workers will want both to comply with the law and ensure that records are necessary, factually based, and with balanced judgements when required, and be sure this will help young people to know about their access rights to information held about them. This also reaffirms the advice in the introduction to this chapter about the need to keep accurate, purposeful, and up-to-date records.

Key Challenge – True or False?

The Information Commissioner Office (ICO) is a UK-wide office which has a remit to oversee the application of the Data Protection Act 1998. The Information Commissioner aims to uphold the confidentiality of personal information and ensure that when confidential information is shared then this is justifiable under the terms of the act. The ICO also has a regional office in Edinburgh, although Scotland has the Scottish Information Commissioner who is responsible for increasing access to the information held by public authorities under the Freedom of Information Act 2002.

Comment

True.

CONCLUSION

It is important to note that legislation changes continually and professional youth work practitioners should find a way of keeping themselves up to date, which is sometimes achieved through a form of Continuing Professional Development (CPD). A good barometer and source of potential changes is to take note of the Queen's speech at the opening of parliament as she outlines the future legislative programme intended by her government. Each government determines its own priorities and the current coalition government (2011–15) has announced its intentions on a New Enterprise and Regulatory Reform (ERR) Bill, which aims to change the way employment tribunals work; a Children and Families Bill, which will give greater choice over when parental leave is taken; and a New Pensions Bill, which will bring forward the state pension age to 67 between 2026 and 2028, and make reforms to public sector pensions.

In addition, the current government is consulting on amendments to the Equality Act 2010. Aspects under consideration include reducing the consultation period for redundancy dismissals, introducing protected conversations which cannot be used in subsequent tribunal claims, simplifying TUPE regulations, modernising maternity and paternity leave, simplifying the national minimum wage, and introducing no fault dismissals.

As this chapter current has demonstrated the legal requirements around safe and legal operations are continually changing and it is vital to keep up to date. In addition to the advice given above there are also opportunities to take specific registered courses: as mentioned in the introduction, a Certificate in Health and Safety organised under the auspices of the National Examination Board in Occupational Safety and Health, or a Certificate of Competence in Environmental Noise Measurement, accredited by the Institute of Acoustics, are examples of this. Such courses will allow you to become a member of a professional body and access all the necessary support and updates which such membership brings.

Finally, it is important to note that, at the time of writing, there are a number of legislative areas under active consultation and consideration which will result in changes to existing laws. Part of the professional approach we adopt demands that we keep informed and up to date with changes for the protection and benefit of the young people we serve. It is also important as professionals that we adopt an informed holistic approach to operational management, taking cognisance of the legal framework, but also linking developments to promote health and wellbeing with wider reform strategies for social and economic policies and practices in the European Union (Walters, 2001).

Case Study 4

You have just been appointed as a youth worker for Grangehill under special initiative money: the area is deprived and statistically in the bottom 1 per cent of the government's Deprivation Index. The Crime and Disorder Partnership has built a community centre which is designed to be a meeting place for all community groups. The previous community centre, an old school built in 1910, was burned down and demolished two years ago.

Since that time the youth groups have been meeting in makeshift accommodation throughout and beyond the area. These groups are agitating to gain access to the centre which was completed two months ago but has yet to be occupied. There are also some signs of external vandalism, and on your first internal inspection of the building as part of the interview process you noticed that there were a number of small jobs that remained unfinished. You also noticed that there were no fire evacuation signs or fire extinguishers in place, and the entrances to rooms with plant equipment were not marked.

You have since been employed under the auspices of the local authority with officer conditions and now have access to other council support services. You have been successfully appointed because at interview you convinced the panel that you had a good understanding of the legal requirements that had to be adhered to in order to open and manage the building and demonstrated that you were a team player.

You have been asked to appoint a new group of five youth workers to the project to staff and operate this new youth centre. You have been told to develop a plan to be presented to local councillors and the community groups at a public meeting next week. You have also been advised that local parents have expressed concern about poor record keeping by a previous youth worker.

Your task is to develop this initial plan and produce a time-lined six month action plan using the information above as well as your own knowledge, research and experience. You should include in your plan details about employment, equality, information systems and health and safety, in addition to thinking about team building, work systems, quality assurance, and job design.

You could also specifically justify parts of your plans and actions by making reference to relevant organisational research and theory and stating the legal requirements which lie behind your plan.

Summary of Key Points

- A main way of demonstrating compliance with the laws relating to youth work practice is to ensure appropriate training, quality planning and preparation procedures, and robust practice operations.

- Employment law is in place to help ensure fair standards of practice by building in operational safeguards and support so that employees are treated accordingly.
- Specific pieces of legislation are continually brought in as society develops its thinking and recognises particular areas of operation which need further safeguards and protection.
- The Equality Act 2010 is the latest principal piece of legislation which aims to consolidate the previous anti-discriminatory legislation and place a duty on public bodies to ensure that their work supports equality.
- Health and Safety is a key organisational and professional management consideration.
- Youth workers need to be aware of and comply with health and safety legislation when carrying out their professional practice.
- The data collected by youth workers must be processed in keeping with the eight principles of the Data Protection Act 1998.
- Youth workers should keep records to enable compliance with the Freedom of Information Act 2000, and support the rights of young people to access such information held about them.
- Youth workers should engage in CPD and keep up to date with changing legislation.

REFERENCES

Adirondack, S. (2006) *Just about Managing? Effective Management for Voluntary Organisations and Community Groups*. London: London Voluntary Service Council.

Argyris, C. (1960) *Understanding Organisational Behaviour*. Chicago, IL: Dorsey.

Asylum and Immigration Act 1996. Available at www.legislation.gov.uk/ukpga/1996/49/contents (last accessed 10.01.2014).

Bauman, Z. (1994) *Alone Again: Ethics after Certainty*. London: Demos.

Construction (Design and Management) Regulations 2007. Available at www.legislation.gov.uk/uksi/2007/320/contents/made (last accessed 03.07.12).

Control of Noise at Work Regulations 2005. Available at www.legislation.gov.uk/uksi/2005/1643/contents/made (last accesed 24.06.12).

Control of Substances Hazardous to Health Regulations 2002. Available at www.legislation.gov.uk/uksi/2002/2677/contents/made (last accessed 24.06.12).

Dangerous Substances and Explosive Atmospheres Regulations 2002. Available at www.hse.gov.uk/fireandexplosion/dsear.htm (last accessed 24.01.2014).

Data Protection Act 1998. Available at www.legislation.gov.uk/ukpga/1998/29/contents (last accessed 13.04.12).

Employers' Liability (Compulsory Insurance) Regulations 1998. Available at www.legislation.gov.uk/uksi/1998/2573/contents/made (last accessed 24.06.12).

Employment Rights Act 1996. Available at www.legislation.gov.uk/ukpga/1996/18/contents (last accessed 05.05.12).

Equality Act 2010. Available at www.legislation.gov.uk/ukpga/2010/15/contents (last accessed 30.06.12).

Equality Act 2010 (Amendment) Order 2012. Available at www.legislation.gov.uk/uksi/2012/334/made (last accessed 30.06.12).

Equality Challenge Unit (2011) *Enabling Equality: Furthering Disability Equality for Staff in Higher Education*. London: UCU.

Freedom of Information Act 2000. Available at www.ico.gov.uk/for_organisations/freedom_ of_information.aspx (last accessed 10.05.12).

Health and Safety at Work etc. Act 1974. Available at www.legislation.gov.uk/ukpga/1974/37/ contents (last accessed 03.04.12).

Health and Safety Offences Act 2008. Available at www.legislation.gov.uk/ukpga/2008/20/ contents (last accessed 10.05.12).

HMSO (1990) *Environment Protection Act (1990)*. London: Author.

INSPIRE Regulations 2009. Available at www.legislation.gov.uk/uksi/2009/3157/contents/ made (last accessed 25.06.12).

Ionising Radiations Regulations 1999. Available at www.legislation.gov.uk/uksi/1999/3232/ contents/made (last accessed 28.06.12).

Lifting Operations and Lifting Equipment Regulations 1998. Available at www.legislation. gov.uk/uksi/1998/2307/contents/made (last accessed 28.06.12).

Management of Health and Safety at Work Regulations 1999. Available at www.legislation. gov.uk/uksi/1999/3242/contents/made (last accessed 26.06.12).

Personal Protective Equipment at Work Regulations 1992. Available at www.legislation.gov. uk/uksi/1992/2966/contents/made (last accessed 28.06.12).

Privacy and Electronic Communications Regulations. Available at www.legislation.gov.uk/ uksi/2011/1208/contents/made (last accessed 24.06.12).

Pressure Systems Safety Regulations 2000. Available at www.legislation.gov.uk/uksi/2000/128/ contents/made (last accessed 27.06.12).

Regulatory Reform (Fire Safety) Order 2005. Available at www.legislation.gov.uk/ uksi/2005/1541/contents/made (last accessed 30.06.12).

Sex Discrimination Act 1975. Available at www.legislation.gov.uk/ukpga/1975/65/contents (last accessed 16.01.2014).

Street Works (Qualifications of Supervisors and Operatives) (England) Regulations 2009. Available at www.legislation.gov.uk/uksi/2009/2257/contents/made (last accessed 28.06.12).

Tyler, M., Hoggarth, L. and Merton, B. (2009) *Managing Modern Youth Work*. Exeter: Learning Matters.

Walters, D. (2001) *Health and Safety in Small Enterprises: European Strategies for Managing Improvement*. Oxford: Peter Lang.

Workplace (Health, Safety and Welfare) Regulations 1992. Available at www.legislation.gov. uk/uksi/1992/3004/contents/made (last accessed 24.06.12).

PART 2

THE APPLICATION OF LAW IN YOUTH WORK

5

OUTDOOR EDUCATION

Chapter Aims

- Introduce the recent changes in political thinking about health and safety and proposed supervisory arrangements for managing health and safety at outdoor activity centres
- Explain the relevance and importance of outdoor activities to youth work programmes
- Give information on specific legal duties as well as practical organisational and emergency advice when organising trips
- Offer practical safety information when using transport on trips
- Provide information on the importance of training and certification in managing risk

INTRODUCTION

Outdoor education, recreation and development opportunities are a key part of many youth work programmes, and it is important that such activities are carried out safely and enjoyably. Traditionally, these have been successfully managed through a combination of statutory regulations, staff training, skills certification and equipment safety checks. The statutory framework has included the Health and Safety at Work etc. Act 1974, the Health and Safety Management Regulations 1999, and the Activity Centres (Young Persons' Safety) Act 1995 which laid out the requirements relating to safety at activity centres in the Adventure Activities Licensing Regulations 2004 (AALR). These licensing requirements related to the paid provision of four adventure activities (trekking, water sports, caving and climbing) for young people under 18 years old.

However, the current coalition government has announced a review of all existing health and safety law (Löfstedt, 2011) and introduced changes to Britain's health and safety system to support the government's growth agenda. The intention is to cut red tape by focusing regulation on high hazard sites, tackling rogue employers and consultants, and freeing Britain's businesses from unnecessary red tape. As part of this agenda, the Health and Safety Executive, in order to implement the recommendation in Lord Young's report 'Common Sense Common Safety', is seeking to abolish the licensing of these four adventure activities by the Adventure Activities Licensing Authority. The licensing system will be replaced by a code of practice which will oversee and monitor adventure activities. The main reasons given for this change are that it is expensive to administer (£750,000), costly for small businesses, and does not reflect the wide variety of adventure activities now on offer. The Health and Safety Executive (HSE) holds that there is enough enforcement power in the 1974 act, and the Management of Health and Safety at Work Regulations 1999 together with issued codes of practice and guidance are sufficient.

REASONS FOR CHANGE

Part of the rationale for the change by this government, as the Prime Minister David Cameron notes in the foreword of Lord Young's document, is a recognition that while:

> good health and safety is vitally important ... all too often good, straightforward legislation designed to protect people from major hazards has been extended inappropriately to cover every walk of life, no matter how low risk.

Again, he advises that the government aims:

> to put a stop to the senseless rules that get in the way of volunteering, stop adults from helping out with other people's children and ... Instead, we're going to focus regulations where they are most needed; with a new system that is proportionate, not bureaucratic; that treats adults like adults and reinstates some common sense and trust. (HM Government, 2010)

Although the rationale and approach here do appear reasonable, it is vital that youth workers receive guidance that will help them make sound judgements and be certain that young people are kept safe. It is also important that youth workers receive specific certified training from a qualified person to build their confidence, knowledge and competence. In addition, youth workers need to be aware that that there is still a need to ensure that specific pieces of legislation are complied with when working with young people: for example, there is a need to have trained first aiders in keeping with the Health and Safety (First Aid) Regulations 1981; a requirement to report and ensure compliance with the Reporting of Injuries, Diseases and Dangerous Occurrences Regulations 1995 (RIDDOR) when appropriate; to adhere to the requirement for portable appliance testing by the Electricity at Work Regulations 1989 when using a portable electrical device; and to be aware of the Work at Height Regulations 2005 if engaging in activities at a height.

THE IMPORTANCE AND RELEVANCE OF OUTDOOR EDUCATION FOR YOUTH WORK PROGRAMMES

There are many different types of educational experiences which can come under the banner of outdoor education, from taking classroom learning into the immediate environment, undertaking trips and visits as part of a social education programme (Davies and Gibson, 1967), taking part in a Duke of Edinburgh expedition, and undertaking a hill walk, to participating in a residential adventure activity centre or being involved in a wilderness camp experience. However, for youth workers the emphasis is not so much on the medium or the activity but on the purpose, educational intent and the growth and development that can occur in all participants (i.e., young people and youth workers alike).

Education in the outdoors is a key feature of many youth work programmes because it can provide numerous opportunities for developing experiential learning (Dewey, 1938/1997; Kolb and Fry, 1975). Learning without walls (Wilmington, 2011) is an important facet of informal learning which can be fun, offer personal growth and development, enable teamwork and leadership opportunities, and build significant relationships. The use of outdoor experiences in youth work programmes is often adopted because its approach is based on a common philosophy and values, is a conducive way of working, and facilitates the aims and objectives of holding the young person at the heart of the learning process.

Education outdoors is crucial for youth work because it is a natural operating environment which can help to build physical and personal confidence through exploring risk and enhancing self worth. Working in, and appreciating, the outdoor environment can help to instil a sense of community and belonging, as well as develop shared goals, experience the power of interdependence, and create positive relationships.

OUTDOOR EDUCATION: THE PROCESS AND BENEFITS

For some educationalists, outdoor learning experiences are regarded as more authentic (Cooper, 1983) than other forms of learning because these involve taking action in keeping with internal feelings and emphasise the collective mutual reliance on others. It is also argued that outdoor learning requires deep thinking, disturbs 'taken for granted' learning patterns, and requires decision making based on the unpredictability of the operating environment. This is learning which is emotional, significant and potentially deep, transformative and long-lasting.

On another notable level, outdoor activities are an excellent medium for advancing the important aims of traditional youth work to be inclusive and promote equality in practice (Sapin, 2009). Education in the outdoors can be a great location and situation for working with people with disabilities due to the flexible nature of the space, the opportunity for creative self-expression, and the ability to interpret and learn in the everyday natural environment (see for example Greenstein, 1993).

The educational process of outdoor education could be regarded as being based on an 'eclectic' theoretical framework in the sense that it draws on a range of other ideas, knowledges and practices, such as groupwork, experiential learning, cognitive dissonance, conservation, sustainability, self-efficacy, leadership, life-long learning, personal development and sport. There is a range of programme styles, from outdoor wilderness adventure to programmed active learning, and the learning intentions of these experiences can be recreational, educational, and developmental. However, some of the reasons why this outdoor medium is so often used in youth work are that the learning climate is often very personal, is significantly directed by the individual, and takes place within the real-life circumstances and perceptions of the learner. However, as much as such learning is clearly potentially transformative, it can also be potentially dangerous, which is why there are legal requirements and a great deal of advice and guidance around safety procedures which need to be followed. One way of managing these requirements successfully is to create a 'culture of safety' where the health and safety requirements are known through a regular engagement with policies, circulars and best practice guidance, clearly understood and conformed to processes and procedures, and exist within a primary climate of taking care of the self and each other.

Key Challenge – Literature Search

Conduct a search of the youth work literature, including academic journals, in order to ascertain the extent to which outdoor education has been recognised and promoted, over the past fifty years, as part of a youth work programme. For a contemporary example from youth work literature, consult Sapin (2009: 96–102) for a diagram of relevant games and sporting activities that are relevant to youth work, as well as some references for promoting the benefits of developing play and sporting activities.

Comment

Traditionally outdoor pursuits were strongly linked to youth work practice and indeed the environmental issues which lay within the promotion of the 'rejuvenating effects' of the great outdoors. In fact many youth movements, such as the Scout Association and the Boy's Brigade, were made up of serial campers who advocated use of the countryside as a communal resource for health and recreation. This led to the securing of national parks and rights of access. In more recent years this appears to have become more specialist, for example developing through the Duke of Edinburgh Award Scheme and outward bound experiences for those in youth justice programmes. Notwithstanding it still has an important part to play in youth work, especially in the socio/developmental understanding of the work (see Wilmington, J. (2011) Learning without walls, *Journal of Youth Work*, 7: 39–56: available at www.youthlinkscotland.org/webs/245/documents/JYWTextpgsandcoverIss7.pdf).

TRIPS AND VISITS

Trips and visits can be an excellent way of encouraging young people to make informed decisions, learn new skills, and take more control and responsibility for both themselves and others. This approach, with its emphasis on the process rather than the outcome, is sometimes traditionally referred to as social education (Davies and Gibson, 1967) and can help young people understand and name their world. The key reason for adopting this approach is that by planning and participating in a trip or event, the young person's (alternative learning 3Rs) developmental needs can be met, namely respect, responsibility and recognition. Also, taking control of organisational arrangements can encourage young people to be creative rather than compliant and ensures a relevant programme. Again, integrally involving young people in the preparation and planning will encourage an articulation of views and learning real-life skills and competencies. These aims will be successfully achieved only if the right level of preparation and planning has been undertaken and so the overall process needs to be proactively negotiated and supervised. This may include, for example, the development of a behaviour standards contract which all participants must agree and sign up to.

QUALITY PLANS

All quality plans for an outdoor excursion will have a number of key elements, including:

- a clear statement about the purpose and educational intent of the activity;
- a set of clear aims and objectives;
- the identification of costs, equipment and provisions;
- a risk assessment carried out by the most relevant people;
- a fact sheet about the trip with all relevant information;
- the provision of the fact sheet to parents and obtaining written parental consent (and medical consent);
- a clearly written and understood chain of responsibility;
- appropriate insurance;
- a clearly written and communicated set of emergency procedures;
- a clear system for reporting and the levels of accountability agreed;
- a list of participants with next of kin contact details;
- a separate copy of the master plan with a nominated third party who is available and contactable to act on the group's behalf when required;
- a debrief, an evaluation, and a written up report after the event.

PERMISSION FORMS

In law you are required to obtain a parental (or guardian) consent form for all young people under 18 years of age. Good practice suggests that this form should include:

- full details of the trip, including dates, times (outward and return), travelling mode and route, stops and destinations;
- leadership and other organisational arrangements;
- a full list of the activities, specifying the nature and extent of any activities deemed to be hazardous or strenuous;
- a request for information about any medical conditions (arrangements for any medication required to be taken must have an agreed system which is recorded and monitored by responsible adults who have volunteered to perform this function: see Appendix 2 for a sample form);
- permission for any treatment to be given if required;
- a list of appropriate clothing, money required and communication arrangements;
- contact numbers for further information before, during and after events;
- any other specific details that may be relevant to the particular trip and that a parent might reasonably be expected to know.

GROUP LEADER ROLE

Given that the group leader has overall responsibility for the group then that individual should make decisions about the delegation of responsibilities to other adults, ensure that both adults and young people are aware of their responsibilities, and make sure that appropriate communication and organisation systems are in place for a safe and enjoyable trip. The group leader should know the group members well, outline the supervisory arrangements for all different parts of the programme, and make regular checks (including head counts) to make sure all is going according to plan. If the group is sharing facilities with other groups, or operating in a public place, they may agree to wear some form of clothing which will help to identify them easily. Operating a buddy system could also be helpful with close supervision arrangements, while remote supervision will require a clear set of guidelines, assessed competences, detailed communication mechanisms, and agreed rendezvous points.

THE TEAM

It is vital to ensure that there is a sufficient number of staff and volunteer adults on a trip and that the team is sufficiently resourced to be able to act as any responsible parent would. Although there are no specific national regulations on the level of the adult/young person ratio, there is some advice available which may be helpful in determining the right level for your group. It is likely that your local LEA will have an appointed outdoor education advisor and specific guidance on this: it is worthwhile checking their requirements and advice. Decisions will be made based on the advice given and as part of the risk assessment process. Staffing ratios for visits are difficult to prescribe as these will vary according to the activity, age, make up and nature of the group, the location, and efficient use of resources. In relation to residential visits, the following advice has been adapted from HASPEV, paragraphs 195 and 196, for teachers and pupils: 'A good *rule of thumb ratio is 1 teacher for every 10 pupils'*. However, in youth work this could be much less depending on the type of group, the length of the trip, and the circumstances under which the activities will take place. Clearly age is a key factor, with higher levels of supervision for younger children and also when activities involve a water element (for example swimming, where the adult to young person ratio needs to be significantly lower than 1:10). Another danger time can be when there is a change of leader at different times during an elongated stay. This change in leadership arrangements should take place in an arranged way to make sure that all group members are made aware of these changes.

HIDDEN DANGERS

When undertaking trips and visits it is important that group leaders are aware that there are particular and hidden dangers when activities take place near coastal waters and cliff tops and in the sea. Potential hazards include tides, rip tides and sandbanks, and the group should be aware of warning signs and be conversant with the water flag system. There is also specified dangers and specific advice about swimming in the sea or other natural waters, as well as for farm visits, with particular recommendations about the level of adult supervision required. (Further advice on this is available through HASPEV: Chapter 8, 'Types of Visit', has advice on coastal visits at paragraphs 181–2).

Prepare a Plan

Devise a draft plan for a trip or visit using the information provided above. If you are currently employed then you could use the existing organisational forms to develop your draft information pack and plan. Alternatively you could ask your local authority for a copy of the forms and procedures that they recommend and use.

Comment

Use the issues to consider the section below and complete the pro formae provided in the appendices to this chapter which will provide you with a guide to the types of information required and some of the issues to be thought through.

RISK ASSESSMENTS

Risk assessments are a key tool in the process of ensuring that an activity is safe to undertake and the person conducting this assessment must be appropriately trained. There is a great deal of guidance around about what a risk assessment is and how to carry one out.

The current approach and advice on risk assessment is to adopt a commonsense approach and proportionate response to the extent of the risk. (For more information on this approach and direction see http://media.education.gov.uk/assets/files/pdf/h/ health%20and%20safety%20advice.pdf.)You should contact your local education authority (LEA) to obtain, read and action both their policies and circulars, and assimi- late the detailed guidelines about what to do when organising a trip with young people. Some LEAs offer a list of key questions to help you assess the viability of a given outdoor activity. There are a number of questions which you may find worthwhile considering, and successfully answering, before a particular activity is undertaken. For example:

- How well is the environment known?
- Are the staff members fully aware and conversant with the technical difficulties and demands of the activity?
- Does the leader have the proven competence to make on-site judgements related to the activity?
- Can the competence of staff and/or instructors be verified and assured?
- Is the quality and condition of the safety equipment acceptable, regularly checked, and certified?
- Is the time of year and weather conditions appropriate and predictably suitable for the intended activity?
- Have all the objective dangers been identified, mitigated, and prepared for?

THE PROCESS

Risk assessment is the process by which all participants are informed that a system- atic plan has been devised to manage the group's activities safely. A risk assessment is the currently recognised methodical and consistent examination of anything that could cause harm at a location or during an activity or excursion. In carrying out a risk assessment, a judgement has to be made about whether sufficient precautions have been put in place or whether more needs to be done so that the group can safely undertake the planned activities, including transportation, without anyone getting physically or emotionally injured or taking ill.

Risk assessment is principally about professional judgement, which is the ability to make sensible decisions based on education, experience and training. Although there are many types of risk assessments, it is necessary to recognise that the concept and formula for hazard management are straightforward to follow and can be cap- tured in six defined stages:

1. Identify the hazard(s).
2. Recognise who may be harmed from the hazard, in which way, and to what extent.
3. Make a judgement about the likelihood and severity of the potential harm.
4. Put in place the necessary control measures, through person or hazard management, to rectify the identified problem.
5. Record significant findings and implement them.
6. Monitor effectiveness, and review and update when necessary.

The HSE have produced an information leaflet on the five steps to risk assessment (which can be accessed at www.hse.gov.uk/pubns/indg163.pdf).

The group leader should also make continuous risk assessments to ensure the prevailing conditions and abilities of the group are appropriate, that first aid facilities are available, and that all group members have been briefed about the emergency procedures. The need for continuous risk assessments may be required due to a change in programme, adverse weather, illness, or unexpected difficulties with the task. It is recommended practice to hold regular briefings with both staff and young people to discuss any changing conditions and agree alternatives which would be subsequently risk assessed. It is important to keep an eye on the weather forecast which will help you to make judgements and offer advice about levels of clothing and any other precautions that may have to be taken.

ISSUES TO BE CONSIDERED

Issues for the group leader to consider include the following:

- The group should ideally have adjoining rooms with leaders' quarters next to the young people's: the leader should also obtain a floorplan of the rooms reserved for the group's use in advance.
- There must be at least one leader from each sex for mixed groups.
- There must be separate male and female sleeping/bathroom facilities for young people and adults.
- The immediate accommodation area should be exclusively for the group's use.
- There should be appropriate and safe heating and ventilation.
- The whole group must be aware of the layout of the accommodation, its fire precautions/exits (are instructions in English or otherwise clear?), its regulations and routine, and that everyone can identify key personnel: a fire drill should take place soon upon arrival, and before the first night if practical (late arrival).
- Where the reception is not staffed 24 hours a day, security arrangements should be in force to stop unauthorised visitors.
- The manager of the accommodation should be asked for assurances that the staff, including temporary workers, have been checked as suitable for working with young people.
- Locks on doors should work in the group's rooms but appropriate access should be available to leaders at all times; clear guidelines must be given to young people as to when to lock and open doors; staff will make sure the guidelines are being followed.
- There should be drying facilities.
- There should be adequate space for storing clothes, luggage, equipment, etc., and for the safe keeping of valuables.
- There should be adequate lighting (it is advisable to bring a torch).
- There should be provision for young people with special needs and those who fall sick.
- Balconies should be stable, windows secure, and electrical connections safe.
- Where possible young people should not be lodged in ground floor rooms.
- The fire alarm must be audible throughout the accommodation.
- There should be recreational accommodation/facilities for the group.

- The hotel/hostel should be able to meet any particular cultural or religious needs of the group.
- There should be an appropriate number of group supervisors on standby duty during the night.
- Before booking a hostel/hotel abroad, the group leader should confirm it has fire exits and lifts with inner doors and that it meets local regulations. After arriving at any accommodation it is advisable to carry out a fire drill as soon as possible (see Appendix 3 for the Accommodation Risk Assessment checklist).

Activities involving water need to be risk assessed to ensure that participants can swim appropriately for the activity, that ranges of safety measures are built in as routine practice, and that the appropriate staff are suitably trained (see the section below on training and certification for more information). The group leader can overcome some local omissions by carrying portable signs and a portable resuscitator if there are none in use and staff are trained to use such equipment appropriately.

Writing Task

Produce a 500-word statement about the relevance to your practice of risk assessment procedures. Also, utilise the questions above to ascertain any differences in approach to risk assessment depending on whether the activity was inside or outside a youth club.

Comment

For youth workers, risk assessment is an important process to be familiar with and adopt to ensure that young people are kept safe and protected. It is vital that recognisable, agreed processes are followed and standards maintained, but it is also about balance and judgement. There is a danger that if risk systems are employed which are overprotective and over safe then the fun can be taken out of challenge and young people can become risk averse. There are simple measures that can be taken to ensure that the right decisions are made about the safety of an activity, and these include what the participants feel, the experience and qualifications within the group, and any conditions including abilities and tiredness.

PUBLIC LIABILITY INSURANCE

From a legal and ethical standpoint, there are three types of insurance that will need to be considered: public liability, personal accident, and vehicle insurance. Public liability insurance is a policy which protects you against claims from anyone who has been caused harm by your actions. This is normally insurance that is taken out by an employing agency but you will need to check that this is indeed in place and who is covered (e.g., is it only employees or are volunteers and others covered?). It is also important to find out the extent and limitations of the cover so you can make informed judgements about undertaking reasonable activities. It is worthy of note that there will be specific, stated policy conditions which will need to be assured in advance of any activity, and it is therefore appropriate to obtain a copy of these so you can satisfy yourself of the ability to comply.

PERSONAL ACCIDENT INSURANCE

The second type is personal accident insurance which covers the workers and the group against personal loss or injury. This type of insurance can be taken out as an annual policy or directly pertaining to each excursion. Again, make sure that the personal protection policy suits the need and activities of you and each member of the group. In recent years particular activities, deemed to be high risk, have been less likely to be included in the standard insurance policy, and additional cover will be necessary if such activities are planned. Please check the terms and conditions of the insurance policy to ensure that you and the group are fully covered. It is good practice to give a copy of the insurance cover details to parents as part of the obtaining consent process.

VEHICLE INSURANCE

Vehicle insurance is the third source of insurance which may be relevant when organising outdoor activities. If a minibus is hired then the insurance is usually included in the hire agreement, but it is worthwhile checking the detailed terms to identify any restrictions and excesses. Again, if it is a local authority or community organisation vehicle that is being used, it would be prudent to verify the extent of the cover and ensure that it meets the needs and expectations of the group.

Key Challenge – Investigative Task

Having identified the three different types of insurance above, devise a way to obtain copies of each type of insurance, from an employer, insurance broker family or friend. Having obtained a copy, take time to read the details on the cover, paying attention to the limitations and exclusions. Reflect on whether such policies would be appropriate for group use or whether additional cover would be required for the type of activity that a youth work programme might involve.

Comment

Insurance cover is a key part of practice because it gives comfort and the assurance that if something goes wrong then the person(s) can seek compensation to help put things right. It is therefore important the most appropriate insurance is taken out and that the fullest amount of information is given about the nature of the activity and the participants. Pay particular attention to limitations and exclusions, and if in doubt ask for an explanation of the terms in writing.

MINI-BUS SAFETY

Unless transport is included in the package supplied by a commercial operator, all transport arrangements will need to be arranged by the youth worker or delegated person. The HSE guidelines, 'Driving at work', are very clear on this, and state that 'health and safety law applies to on-the-road work activities and the risks should be effectively managed within a health and safety system'. If mini-buses are to be used then only those people with an up-to-date appropriate licence with over two years' experience, and who are not being paid, will be allowed to drive mini-buses under 3.5 tonnes. If a member of staff or volunteer is driving the bus for the group, then it will be the group leader's responsibility to check and verify that the driver is qualified to drive and has the necessary documentation to prove it. If the proposed driver has a driving conviction then specific advice needs to be sought in order to judge whether the offence makes this person an unsafe driver or unfit person to drive the group members.

GROUP LEADER'S RESPONSIBILITY

It is the group leader's responsibility to ensure that the licence is valid and that refresher courses are undertaken as appropriate, and the driver has an obligation to report any accidents or offences since any permission was last granted. Transport in a private car needs to be subject to organisational safeguards and expressed written permission, with drivers ensuring that they are specifically insured for this purpose.

DRIVER RESPONSIBILITY

The driver is responsible for the vehicle and must ensure they complete a check before departure in order to comply with British and European Union standards marks. Check all lights and indicators, tyres, the spare tyre, brakes, doors, windscreen wipers, oil, water and fuel levels, the roof rack, safety belts, horn, mirrors, organisational paperwork, first aid kit, fire extinguisher and basic tools. Also check the height of the vehicle and avoid any low-level bridges (identified in the route-planning process), and check any height restrictions at campsites, car park entrances, and any other venues you plan to attend.

SEAT BELTS AND SUPERVISION

Since 1997 it has been illegal to carry any young person under 18 years old in mini-buses or coaches that are not fitted with seat belts. Also, there needs to be a separate seat belt for every person as it is illegal to carry more than one person per seat and belt. The leader should make sure that seat belts are worn, that emergency exits are kept clear, and that adequate supervisory arrangements are in place. Supervision tasks should not be expected of, nor allocated to, the driver whilst driving.

PROHIBITIONS, PRECAUTIONS AND PROCEDURES

When in charge of a vehicle and transporting young people, the driver should not drink any alcohol and also be aware that alcohol can remain in the body for up to 24 hours. If the driver is too tired, ill or affected by medicines that person should not drive the vehicle, which is one reason why there should be more than one driver in the group. Youth workers and volunteers must ensure they have sufficient rest during the hours preceding a journey which they judge to be very long or tiring. The arrangements prior to departure must be discussed well in advance and regular breaks built in to the organisation of the journey. The driver and leadership team should have access to a working mobile phone and check signal availability as part of the planning process, but must not use the phone while driving as it is illegal to do so.

The driver must also comply with the Highway Code, respecting all speed limits. Seat belts must be worn at all times, and passengers are not allowed to release their seat belt and/or move from their seat until the vehicle is at a standstill and the driver has given them permission to leave the bus. These instructions should be communicated on every journey, both prior to departure and again near to arrival at the destination. Drivers and/or passenger assistants should ensure that all passengers have been safely met. A post-trip vehicle check should be conducted and recorded on the documents provided in the vehicles.

For further and detailed guidance on the above (and on child restraints, techographs, and speed limiters for example) see *Minibus Safety: A Code of Practice* (RoSPA, 2008: available at www.rospa.com/roadsafety/advice/minibus/index.htm).

Organising a Trip with Young People

Devise a route map, including regular comfort breaks and timings, with a group of young people planning a three-day residential trip starting from Birmingham and travelling to a centre in Appleby in the Lake District. As far as you can, also prepare a back-up plan for alternative routes and timings in case of traffic delays, sickness or other emergencies. In addition buy a copy of the RoSPA (2008) booklet.

Comment

Route plans can be fun to do and can also be a good source of social education as young people research and investigate routes and resources across various parts of the country. This can be a particularly rewarding experience for a young person who has never or rarely been on holiday. You could also develop some role-play situations which include a variety of emergency scenarios for fun and interaction/team building, as well as for raising important 'what if' issues.

EMERGENCY PROCEDURES

It is important that as part of your preparation and planning processes that you have made sure that appropriate measures have been taken to act safely and efficiently when an accident occurs or an emergency arises. It is also good practice to have a back-up plan, for when circumstances alter significantly and a new programme has to be adopted (for example, because of adverse weather or illness).

EMERGENCY ACTION PLAN

To help ensure that emergencies can be dealt with successfully the group leader should agree an emergency action plan, which must include 24-hour cover, designated contact points, and specified roles for the group leader and identified members of the group. The group leader should also have a pre-planned communication strategy which will ensure that all stakeholders are kept fully informed of the facts and developments of the emergency or incident. During the emergency, the group leader should take control and seek to ensure that the group is safe, together, and looked after. It will be helpful to have a list of contacts and telephone numbers on a specified sheet for access and ease of reference which may include medical assistance contacts, the British Embassy/consulate if abroad and your organised contact, as well as the police, HSE and insurers. The group leader should also keep a full factual account of the emergency/incident, dates and time, along with the actions of all those involved. They must remember to preserve any relevant evidence and complete any necessary accident/incident forms as soon as possible.

PREVENTION IS BETTER THAN CURE

There should also be a preventative element to the emergency action plan which may involve ensuring that good standards of hygiene are kept, appropriate levels of nourishment, hydration and rest are taken, and the system for administering medication is robustly monitored. Other precautionary actions (such as high factor sunscreen, hats, light clothing and sunglasses for hot climates) are also advisable. In addition it would be prudent to ensure that members of the group are trained in first aid, as well as aware of local diseases and dangers and how these can be treated. Emergency drills should be practised to give group members experience of what to do in the event of an emergency.

Action Planning

Using the information above, develop a draft emergency action plan detailing any potential information that would be required in the event of an emergency experienced by a group on a hill walk.

Comment

An emergency action plan is a set of steps to follow when an emergency situation arises. Planning well in advance will mean that in the event of an emergency situation you will have already taken some steps to protect you and your group. There are a number of actions for you to consider when developing the emergency action plan. Make a list of emergency contacts, including the emergency services, your organisation, parents and any other stakeholder: when doing so make sure you have out-of-hours contact numbers as well as office ones. Review and update the evacuation procedures for the location of your activity. Make up an emergency kit which may include documents and items such as a torch, first aid kit, compass, portable radio, plastic bags and spare batteries. Your kit should be prominent and easily accessible in an emergency situation. Set up an emergency action and communication group, and make sure that each member is given a defined role or responsibility and are appropriately trained. Make certain that all angles are covered through testing and updating the plan.

TRAINING AND CERTIFICATION

When undertaking any activity, it is necessary to ensure that the activities are suitable for each member of a particular group. It is also necessary to ensure that the group leaders are appropriately experienced and suitably qualified for the intended tasks. There are many different types of outdoor activities, from canoeing, skiing and hill walking to mountaineering, and there is a range of qualifications which will qualify people to supervise these activities safely at predetermined levels. Qualifications are normally obtained through courses which offer the national governing body awards. For further and specific information see the relevant professional association or the Institute for Outdoor Learning (see www.outdoor-learning.org). There is also a range of universities which offer both undergraduate and postgraduate degrees in outdoor education.

The following list provides an indication of the types and range of national qualifications that are available and required to supervise defined levels of activities:

Swimming Lifeguard (Royal Life Saving Society)
RLSS UK National Pool Lifeguard Qualification (NPLQ)
RLSS UK National Pool Management Qualification (NPMQ)
RLSS UK National Beach Lifeguarding Qualification (NBLQ)
RLSS Bronze Medallion (General)
The Surf Life Saving Association Bronze Award
The Corps of Canoe Lifeguards Canoeing Safety Test
The Corps of Canoe Lifeguards Rescue Test
British Canoe Union
Level 1 Kayak
Kayak Level Two Training
Kayak Level Two Assessment

Kayak Level Three Training
Kayak Level Three Assessment
Canoe Level One
Canoe Level Two Training
Canoe Level Two Assessment
Canoe Level Three Training
Canoe Level Three Assessment
Sea Level Three Training
Sea Level Three Assessment
Surf Level Three Training
Surf Level Three Assessment
Coach Processes Course
White Water Safety and Rescue
The British Association of International Mountain Leaders (BAIML)
Mountain Walking Leader Award (MLA)
NGB Qualifications
BCU Level 1 and 2 coaches
Single Pitch Award
British Association of Snowsport Instructors
BASI Level I Instructor (Ski)
BASI Level 2 Instructor (Ski)
BASI Level I Instructor (Snowboard)
BASI Level 2 Instructor (Snowboard)

Key Challenge – Increase Your Knowledge

Choose any particular outdoor activity that you have a little knowledge of, but also a potential interest in, and investigate the level and range of qualifications that a person needs to have to instruct a group in that particular activity.

Comment

Qualifications are important not only to ensure safe and appropriate instruction for young people but also as a source of learning opportunities for those who show an interest and ability in a particular sport.

CONCLUSION

This chapter has offered some information and ideas about how to prepare and plan for outdoor activities in youth work programmes. It has not attempted to override or replace local or other professional guidance or regulations. I have tried to emphasise throughout that there is a range of sources for sound advice, including the HSE and the LEA, and community and voluntary youth groups should regard these as a reliable source of guidance. None of the statements made here should be accepted as an authoritative interpretation of the law as that is the duty of the courts. It should be noted that any contribution made in this format is necessarily partial and subject to change, so it is always advisable to ascertain the current legal position and best practice before taking any action. What is quintessentially important here is that young people are safeguarded in the processes and procedures adopted by the youth worker, and that no individual is harmed or put at risk due to negligence because of a lack of planning, training or robust operational systems.

In addition to the above, there are a number of useful sources of information, guidance and training opportunities whose website addresses I have included in the reference list. These include the Institute of Safety and Health who provide members with resources, guidance, events and training, the Suzy Lamplugh Trust which has produced a range of booklets, videos and training courses on personal safety, and the Safe and Responsible Expeditions and the Young Explorers' Trust which has produced guidelines for youth expeditions. In addition, the Royal Geographical Society Expedition Advisory Centre provides advice, information and training to anyone planning an overseas expedition and the Duke of Edinburgh's Award scheme.

Place yourself in Jay's situation and write up an account of what you would do if you found yourself in similar circumstances.

Jay is a qualified youth worker with ten years' experience who has just returned from maternity leave to find that she has a new boss who been transferred from a young people's counselling and advisory service. The new boss advises that one of her co-workers, a less experienced colleague, has been planning a residential trip with young people for the last few months. The trip is scheduled to leave in two days' time, namely this Friday at 5 pm. Her boss has asked her to act as the contact point while the group are away because she has heard that Jay is a very experienced youth worker who would know what is required because she has organised many trips with young people over the years.

Jay readily agrees to act as the contact point for the group and requests a copy of the full programme plan and pack to be made available to her as soon as possible. She is handed the pack at 3 pm on Friday, two hours before the group are due to leave.

As she reads through the documentation, she becomes concerned over three major points: that only eight members of the original group of twelve young people have signed parental consent forms; that in her opinion and based on her considerable experience, the staffing levels are too low for a two-day residential trip; that there has been no alternative programme devised which could be adopted if required.

Jay raises her concerns with her boss who says that the trip will need to be cancelled unless she offers to go along to 'shore up' the weaknesses. The boss offers to act as the contact point if Jay makes up the staffing ratio, and will get the other permission slips signed and use her experience to draft up an outline alternative programme.

(Continued)

Case Study 5

(Continued)

Jay refuses to become further involved because she states that it is too late in the day for such significant changes. She is concerned about the boss's lack of experience and ability to act as the group contact, she does not know the group members or the other worker, and she is also not familiar with the area and programme of activities that have been devised. The trip is cancelled and the young people feel let down and angry because they think that Jay should have stepped in to help save the trip.

In your opinion was Jay right to refuse to take part in the trip or is she being a 'stick in the mud' and hiding behind red tape? What would you do in similar circumstances? What could be done to avoid a similar occurrence? Who should debrief the young people, and what explanation should be given for the cancellation of their planned trip?

Summary of Key Points

- Be aware that attitudes to health and safety can change as part of social discourse, but that as group leader you will need to ensure the legal requirements are adhered to.
- Recognise that education in the outdoors is an important feature of informal learning with many potential benefits.
- Good planning and preparation facilitate a successful and enjoyable learning experience.
- Practise developing comprehensive quality plans which involve all stakeholders.
- Record all planning/preparation processes and decisions and keep full and up-to-date records.
- Get trained in, and be competent in, assessing, mitigating and recording risk.
- Comprehend the importance of route travel plans with alternatives and back-ups.
- Appreciate the value of insurance and ensure the level of cover is appropriate for the activity and the group members.
- Devise appropriate emergency information and make it accessible to all designated staff.
- When using other staff check that their qualifications are appropriate for the activity.
- Consult and take expert advice when you have gaps in your knowledge.
- Make sure that you are involved in and content with all the preparations and plans for a trip or visit.

REFERENCES

Activity Centres (Young Persons' Safety) Act 1995. Available at www.legislation.gov.uk/ukpga/1995/15/contents (last accessed 10.01.14).

Adventure Activities Licensing Regulations (AALR) 2004. Available at www.legislation.gov.uk/uksi/2004/1309/contents/made (last accessed 10.01.14).

Cooper, C. (ed.) (1983) *Theories of Group Process*. London: Wiley.

Davies, B. and Gibson, A. (1967) *The Social Education of the Adolescent*. London: University of London Press.

Dewey, J. (1938/1997) *Experience and Education*. New York: Macmillan.

Electricity at Work Regulations 1989. Available at www.legislation.gov.uk/uksi/1989/635/contents/made (last accessed 06.01. 2014).

Greenstein, D. (1993) *Backyards and Butterflies*. New York: New York State Rural Health & Safety Council.

Health and Safety at Work etc. Act 1974. Available at www.legislation.gov.uk/ukpga/1974/37/contents (last accessed 10.01.14).

Health and Safety Management Regulations 1999. Available at www.legislation.gov.uk/uksi/1999/3242/contents/made (last accessed 10.01.14).

Health and Safety of Pupils on Educational Visits: A Good Practice Guide: A Handbook for Group Leaders (HASPEV). Available at www.cfbt.com/lincs/PDF/Part%203%20of%20 3%20Haspev.pdf (last accessed 24.07.13).

Health and Safety: Responsibilities and Powers (HASPEV). Available at: http://media.education.gov.uk/assets/files/pdf/h/health%20and%20safety%20advice.pdf (last accessed 20.07.12).

Health and Safety Executive (2006) *Five Steps to Risk Assessment*, INDG163 (rev2). Available at www.hse.gov.uk/risk/fivesteps.htm (last accessed 06.12.2013).

HM Government (2010) *Common Sense Common Safety*. Available at www.cabinetoffice.gov.uk/sites/default/files/resources/402906_CommonSense_acc.pdf (last accessed 20.07.12).

Institute of Safety and Health (n.d.) Available at www.iosh.co.uk/ (last accessed 24.07.12).

Kolb, D.A. and Fry, R. (1975/1998) Toward an applied theory of experiential learning. In *Health and Safety of Pupils on Educational Visits (HASPEV)*. London: Department for Education and Skills.

Löfstedt, R.E. (2011) *Reclaiming Health and Safety for All: An Independent Review of Health and Safety Legislation*. Available at http://books.google.co.uk/books?hl=en&lr=&id=kk NzPHkNgscC&oi=fnd&pg=PA1&dq=lofstedt+2011+health+and+safety&ots=mLP5Fk vqFY&sig=a_mR6PgT2z2adt3bMu6ZcQRBcbk#v=onepage&q=lofstedt%202011%20 health%20and%20safety&f=false (last accessed 22.01.14).

Management of Health and Safety at Work Regulations 1999 (n.d.) Available at www.legislation.gov.uk/uksi/1999/3242/contents/made

Reporting of Injuries, Diseases and Dangerous Occurrences Regulations 1995. Available at www.legislation.gov.uk/uksi/1995/3163/contents/made (last accessed 10.01.14).

Royal Geographical Society Expedition Advisory Centre (n.d.) Available at www.rgs.org/eac (last accessed 24.07.12).

Royal Society for the Prevention of Accidents (2008) *Minibus Safety: A Code of Practice*. Middlesex: Author.

Sapin, K. (2009) *Essential Skills for Youth Work Practice*. London: Sage.

The Duke of Edinburgh's Award Scheme (n.d.) Available at www.theaward.org (last accessed 20.07.12).

The Suzy Lamplugh Trust (n.d.) Available at www.suzylamplugh.org (last accessed on 24.07.12).

The Work at Height Regulations 2005. Available at www.legislation.gov.uk/uksi/2005/735/contents/made (last accessed on 06.01.14).

Wilmington, J. (2011) Learning without walls: an exploratory journey, *Journal of Youth Work*, 7: 39–56.

Young Explorers Trust (n.d.) Available at http://2013.outlookexpeditions.com/safety/safety-structure/young-explorers-trust (last accessed 16.01.14).

6

DETACHED WORK WITH YOUNG PEOPLE

Chapter Aims

- Provide the legal background for practising youth work in the open environment
- Outline a range of practices which constitute 'external youth work'
- Provide an account of the history of detached youth work
- Explain the detached youth work process with reference to the practice and legal context
- Offer information on keeping safe and developing useful support systems to comply with the law and good practice
- Identify a number of main training requirements for effective detached practice

INTRODUCTION

Youth work takes place in many different settings and environments. It could be based in a local youth club, community centre, faith centre or school, or delivered as part of a detached youth work team on the streets in local estates. Each setting helps to indicate its purposes and shape its practices in relation to the needs and wants of young people.

Youth work that takes place in local neighbourhoods and across communities has been categorised under different headings, including detached, outreach and street work. Each of these terms has its own nuances and this chapter sets out to clarify the key terms by outlining the rationale and nature of the identified practises. It aims to present a history of detached youth work, outline some key operating principles, and provide advice on the types of support and operational systems required within a legislative and best practice framework.

There are a number of acts that are relevant to the operation of detached youth work, including the Children Act (2004), the Anti Social Behaviour Act (2003), the Crime and Disorder Act (1998), the Data Protection Act (1998), the Public Order Act (1986), the Health and Safety at Work etc Act (1974), and subsequent polices that have been developed by youth workers' employing agency to give advice on how to comply with these laws. This is within a practice context that seeks to promote access, equality, empowerment and social justice for young people.

More specifically, this chapter will help you understand the rationale and nature of outreach and detached youth work, explain the strategic importance of preparation and information gathering for the development of outreach/detached youth work, and offer guidance on how to conduct a community mapping/profile exercise. It will also emphasise the importance of safety and explain the legislative framework for conducting risk assessments, as well as help you analyse the working context with young people on the streets and suggest procedures and actions to handle potentially dangerous or illegal situations. It is worthwhile remembering that when you are working in an outside environment, there are a variety of legislative and good practice rules that must be adhered to.

FORMS OF 'EXTERNAL' YOUTH WORK

Work with young people in an 'outside environment' has been a part of youth work for more than a century. There are two different contexts to these outside operations: the first is a set of circumstances, described in the previous chapter, where young people and youth workers together create informal learning opportunities using the external environment; the second, both traditional and contemporary, is where young people congregate in an open space, 'the outside', in order to spend time with their peers. They do so because they want to be on their own to chat and experiment, without the interference of those adults who will largely control and direct their internal spaces, 'the inside'.

Adults (i.e., the societal discourse makers and power brokers) worry about young people when they are not under their control and concern themselves that the young people's peers may be adversely influencing each other. A youth worker, in their thinking and practice, needs to guard against being a 'friendly adult' who appears to be on the young person's side, but by their failing to recognise the complexity and tensions in youth work practice is actually, by default, doing the bidding of others.

OPERATIONAL TENSIONS

To avoid this inadvertent usury, and to be a successful practitioner, as youth workers we must recognise that there are some fundamental tensions in taking that role. One inherent dichotomy can be found between a youth worker operating with the over-riding interests of the young person at the core of practice (through a personal/socially oriented developmental youth work approach) and simultaneously attempting to satisfy the demands of adults who subscribe to, fund, and require a bureaucratised practice (Crimmens, 2004). The tension occurs with the latter's intent to deliver predetermined results to fit with the previously adult-diagnosed problem of young people. It could be argued that youth work practice generated in outside space takes place in a more equalised environment, and young people therefore feel more free to be themselves and enter into an honest and open dialogue.

There are a number of practice responses that can help youth workers to operate in an 'external' environment which will enable their practice to develop 'in the outside'. Over the years a number of different terms have emerged to describe particular aspects of youth work that are 'outside' and non-centre based, but these have largely been bureaucratic articulations rather than interpretations of practice that young people have coined.

'OUTSIDE' WORK

The first is known as *peripatetic work* where a youth worker operates out of different bases or across a number of different settings: this gives the impression of a generative practice that is not defined by a particular location, and suggests that both worker and practice may be flexible and not confined by a particular environment. *Outreach work* is a second bureaucratic response that takes place when a youth worker works from a centre but reaches outside of it to raise its profile and promote its use: additionally, work undertaken away from the base is designed to benefit the users of the centre. A third, and largely twenty-first century practice, is *mobile youth work*: this is where a youth worker uses a youth-bus, or other mobile provision, to engage with young people in their own locale and rotate the provision across a range of locations within a specified geographical area.

DETACHED YOUTH WORK

However, the main external youth work practice is *detached work*, which is also referred to as *street work* in different parts of the world. These international practices emanate from aligned traditions of concern and care and have similar operating principles. Detached work in the UK takes place when a youth worker operates in a particular area to connect with young people on the street, without any direction from another youth work organisation. This type of youth worker operates in places where young people themselves choose to congregate, and their practice respects and operates within the young people's own environment whether on a street corner or waste ground, or in parks and cafes. This is each young person's territory, and to a degree as the worker operates in their space this may help to alter the power balance between adult and young person in the latter's favour (McGinley and Watson, 2008).

Key Challenge – Reflective Questions

- Provide five good reasons for why you think 'external' youth work is relevant today.
- What would you hold to be the main differences between outside and inside youth work?
- What impact does outside youth work potentially have on the power relations between young people and the youth worker?
- Are mobile youth-bus/units a sustainable form of outside youth work?

Comment

Detached youth work is useful because youth workers get to experience firsthand the social environment experienced by young people. It can also help youth workers appreciate the strengths and constraints within the community and perhaps make contact with young people who are not engaged with other services. On the streets, relationships can perhaps more genuinely develop on young people's terms as they have the upper hand.

THE HISTORY OF DETACHED YOUTH WORK

Detached work, across different eras and to varying degrees, has long been an important feature of youth work practice. Detached youth work emanated out of early outreach practices such as district visiting in the latter half of the nineteenth century. Interestingly (and perhaps a capacity that is less encouraged in our young people today) some of the major developments were derived through young people's own initiative with support from farsighted adults. For example, the working lads clubs established by Charles Russell and the girls clubs developed by Ms Montague were both the work of visionaries who were clearly on the side of young people.

THE EARLY YEARS

While detached youth work operated in the early 1950s with teenage gangs in New York, it was not until later in that decade and into the 1960s that detached youth work became prominent in Britain. Detached youth work captured stakeholders' imagination through a combination of factors, including the recording and dissemination of written materials about the successes of detached youth work in America, a developing interest in practice experimentation by both workers and policy makers, and continuous moral panics (generated mainly by the press) concerning young people being viewed as 'unattached' on the streets and out of reach of adult influence. In this context, detached youth work provided some answers and presented an opportunity to contact young people in relevant, experimental and alternative ways.

The main approach developed at this time by youth workers was through a notion of project work based around local cafes and in local neighbourhoods.

It was these moral panics that precipitated the Albemarle report in 1960 and brought in new resourcing for youth work in England: although most of the resources were ploughed into buildings and traditional forms of youth work, there was some consideration and funding given to experimental ways of working (see para.187). As is the case with youth work as a whole, in these early days there was relatively little published about this new form of practice with the exception of those operating in the voluntary sector, for example the YMCA (see Goetschius and Tash, 1967) and the National Association of Youth Clubs (see Morse, 1965: this was a report based on the author's experience of a three-year project with young people on the streets).

ACTIONS NOT WORDS

Although there was a significantly increased number of young people in the 1970s and 1980s, detached youth workers spent most their time 'doing' rather than recording and publishing which is very understandable. There was an occasional publication in the 1980s (for example, Arnold et al., 1981) that detailed the management and processes of detached youth work. Also, in the following decade, there was a mini publishing revival in the early to mid 1990s which detailed specific circumstances for effective detached youth work (i.e., work with girls and young women, racism and prostitution: see Green, 1992; Smith, 1994; Dadzie, 1997; Benetello, 1996). Unfortunately this literary flourish did not last, even though it has since proved to be very useful in helping to provide a historic record of detached youth practice at a specific time in England. Notwithstanding, their contributions have lasted the test of time and remain relevant today. Smith (2004) in particular has had a lasting impact as he embedded and encapsulated the detached practice within the context of education in the community, offered a relevant way to structure and embed practice, and provided a reflective framework for evaluating practice in light of 'solidarity, cooperation and social responsibility' (Smith, 2004: 167).

In much of the current youth work literature there is little recognition of detached work, and where there is some cognisance it is often just a passing reference (see for example Tyler et al., 2009; Jeffs and Smith, 2010). The main exceptions to this situation include Crimmens (2004), who related the role of detached work to issues of exclusion from the education training and work; Sapin (2009), who articulates a good range of youth work settings and outlines different forms of outdoor youth work; and Rogers (2011), who has produced a resource for detached youth workers. Although there is a current re-emergence of, and broader interest in, the practice of detached youth work, it is largely partnership directed, and lacks significant sustainable resources which potentially taints and contains the potential of detached youth work. This recent type of practice, within the connexions service in England, has been questioned because it lacks some of the inherent principles attached to youth work practice, for example, voluntary participation and peer association. It appears that much of the current outside practice in England is targeted and outcome-based, aimed at solving the problem of young people rather than adopting a more universal approach where there is no agenda other than the young people themselves.

Key Challenge – Reading, Action and Reflective Writing Task

Obtain and read a copy of Rogers' *101 Things to Do on the Street* (2011, Jessica Kingsley Publishers). You will see that the book provides a range of innovative games for young people that are specifically designed with the nature, extent and purpose of street work in mind.

Your task is to identify and list ten games in the book that you think would be appropriate for the type of work you may do on the street in the future. After this select one game and practise using it on your student friends and/or colleagues. Reflect on and write up what you learn about yourself and the game as a result of running this exercise.

Comment

Street work and detached youth work offer many opportunities to develop work that cannot be developed elsewhere, and this is of particular importance to those who are vulnerable and/or disconnected. It is a practice which can appear to be accidental and organic but must be backed up with sound planning and disciplined execution. The art of detached youth work also requires confidence, good self knowledge, and an ability to reach out to others with their 'bag of tricks' or 'their rucksack of resources'.

PURPOSE, DEFINITION AND OPERATING PRINCIPLES OF DETACHED WORK

Detached youth work is a special and highly professional form of youth work which has been proven to succeed where other services have failed to meet the needs of young people. Detached youth work is not a quick fix, a cheap option, or an attempt to control young people by getting them off the streets. At its very best detached youth work is established with a clear set of values and principles, and developed with a strategic approach to preparation and information gathering and the routine operation of a robust system to evaluate the methods and approaches chosen. Such practice should be based on sound ethical and professional understandings of the rationale for engagement, and a clear articulation of the extent of the youth worker role to the young people involved. To successfully establish a detached youth work project, a worker needs to understand the safety considerations, including personal safety, inherent in the practice, and be familiar with the legislative background which requires risk assessments to be undertaken. They also need to operate a system which effectively analyses the street working context that identifies potentially dangerous or illegal situations as they occur, and demonstrate a variety of exit strategies for safely withdrawing in such circumstances. All of these purposes, procedures and processes should be developed in advance and operated within agreed organisational policies and procedures.

TARGET AUDIENCE

Detached youth work is a model of youth work practice aimed at young people who are often deemed by adult funders to be vulnerable, and which takes place in young people's own environment. While that vulnerability may be present (as it is present to a degree in all of us) a youth worker does not blame a young person for their circumstances or stage of development, but instead interprets the situation in its broader societal context and takes the opportunity to redress inequality and empower that person to realise their potential. Detached youth work can work best when there is a lack of infrastructure, such as poor or inappropriate local facilities, scant transport routes, and where a group of young people feel dislocated from their local community. This is essentially a democratic project which recognises the fundamental human dignity of the young person and values an interaction which is both positive and progressive for both the worker and young person involved. This relationship between the youth worker and young person is crucial to the practice and will need to germinate and take root over a period of time. It is only through a relationship based on trust that a detached worker can help to reduce any risky behaviours and promote positive valued alternatives.

DEMOCRATIC APPROACH

This democratic approach has to be developed with young people centrally involved in generating decisions about action to be taken. These decisions must be taken in a planned and educative way that enhances social skills through social learning experiences: these then promote equality by overcoming latent barriers to participation. Many of these detached young people will be vulnerable due to their difficult life circumstances and their exclusion from social and economic opportunities, resources and services. As detached workers we would aim to work with these young people to recognise the injustice of their situation, help to empower them to see their circumstances, and encourage them to embark on an educative journey of discovery that will allow them to protect themselves against the worst effects of exclusion.

As detached youth workers we will need to have an understanding of the social context which encourages and enables the young person to be empowered through owning the aspirations, direction and next steps in their lives.

A PRIVILEGED POSITION

Detached youth workers are often presented with excellent opportunities to help young people recognise the ways in which their behaviour can affect both their development and the perceptions of others in the community environment. Detached youth workers are in a privileged position, as they can be presented with the opportunity to influence young people in a way that no other professional will have open to them. Detached workers can be presented with an opportunity, which they need to be trained and prepared to deal with, to work with young people involved in risky actions such as drug and substance abuse, sexual promiscuity, and emotional problems such as self harming. Detached youth workers need to be aware of the potential range of responses in any given situation, ranging from proactively offering leaflets, advice and information on such matters as sexual health, to making a consented direct intervention to assist, for example, a suicidal young person.

INTRODUCING A FOUR-STAGE PROCESS

STAGE 1 – PRELIMINARY MAPPING AND OBSERVATION

This stage will be conducted to identify local resources, local geography and local organisations. It is sometimes referred to as reconnaissance, an area audit, or a community profile (see Burton, 1993; Hawtin et al., 1994). This is the time when workers need to become very familiar with the area, namely walking around at different times throughout the day and identifying the places where young people 'hang out'. Such local knowledge and recorded data are then used as part of the planning and preparation process to establish the detached project. Attention should be paid to local reports and statistics and to existing projects in the area to help build up knowledge about the potential issues in the community and the types of responses that have been made by local people and local services. Being around and chatting with people who live and work in the area (for example, other youth workers, volunteers, crossing patrollers, shopkeepers and those who deliver the post) is a good way of increasing local knowledge and becoming known within the community. Detached youth workers should also find out about the ways in which local services operate, such as health, police, leisure and social services, because the greater their local knowledge then the more young people will experience informed input from those workers.

Some of the skills that you will need to undertake an effective mapping exercise will include the ability to observe and record. You will also require the capacity to read the environment and accurately interpret what is going on and must be able to adjudicate and make appropriate decisions based on pre-determined, agreed processes. You will also be required to trust and rely on other workers and appreciate the importance of peer sharing and support, and it will help you to be effective if you have a sense of humour and a calm disposition as well as being agile in your approach. Of course, it goes without saying that it is advantageous if you like working with young people and believe in them by not prejudging them or their circumstances. These skills, abilities and commitments are necessary if as a youth worker you are to develop a robust, ethical practice that is based on tolerance and respect for fundamental human dignity and rights.

STAGE 2 – APPROACHING YOUNG PEOPLE

It is vital that as a detached youth worker you set out to establish a 'presence' in the area. This will be achieved by spending your time over a set period connecting with local organisations and establishing controlled, continuous, and increasing contact with young people. At this stage, you can use a range of tools and techniques to make contact with, work with, and build a relationship with young people. Note that making initial contact can be difficult, especially for the novice worker, and there is no magic formula to bring this about. It can often prove useful if as a novice worker you can be paired with a more experienced worker, as detached workers will often use their own personality, local knowledge, personal skills, abilities and interests to create an opening to make contact with young people, for example by using a sport like football (Jeffs and Smith, 2010: 22). Detached youth workers will also utilise local events, stories and situations in order to ascertain young people's views on issues and determine what is important to them in their daily lives. This approach can form the basis of a dialogue which will lead to a programme of commitments and actions that will encourage participation, the formation of views, and the development of personal responsibility. Many forms of informal learning techniques and experienced-based activities, such as drama and the arts, are used to help find expression and a voice (McGinley and Dunlop, 2011).

STAGE 3 – BUILDING AND MAINTAINING RELATIONSHIPS

The aim of this part in the process is to establish and develop sound positive relationships in which discussion, joint challenge and options can be a part of the development process. It is worthwhile noting that not all relationships are healthy and a young person's previous overriding experience of relationships could have been dysfunctional, unhealthy, or abusive. It is therefore vital that the relationship is built on trust, particularly in small things, and especially so at the beginning. For example, if a worker makes a commitment to meet a group at a specific location and time the following week then this commitment must be met, even if the young people have failed to turn up on previous occasions. Martin (2002:15) identifies relationships as a key feature of practice which delineates the role of the youth worker from other professionals and needs to be recognised and nourished. He posits that relationships are so pivotal to the practice that these actually define youth work. While other professionals will build relationships to deliver a service, the youth worker offers a service in order to build a relationship, and that service is judged by the quality of the relationships that are established through it. Thus it is the establishment, development and maintenance of youth work relationships that lie at the very heart of practice (and indeed research).

In the detached youth work process, this is a crucial phase which needs to be nourished by robust local research, an appropriate attitude, and a skills set that contributes to a positive introduction phase and successful initial engagements. Relationships are built and enhanced by creating the right environmental and operating conditions so that the detached worker is able, with confidence, to stand with young people and resist any attempt to be undermined by others. It would be fair to say that there will be power brokers and local community members who will neither understand nor approve of youth work in open spaces. The pervasive societal discourse that young people are either trouble or in trouble is so strong that local residents will often fail to see the potential and actual value of young people's and youth workers' contributions.

This is the social operating framework which needs to be challenged and overcome. It is only through establishing an environment of positivity that relationships will grow and become palpable. A productive relationship will enhance a sense of self worth and increase social participation. It will also build social confidence and potentially lead to societal recognition.

STAGE 4 – INFORMATION, SUPPORT AND ACTION

Gathering information is appropriate on a number of levels, including statistical analyses, local reports, and reflective accounts. Obviously it is important to remember that any personal and process information you access should be held in keeping with your employing organisation's information management systems. This recorded information will be subject to the Data Protection Act (1998) and the Freedom of Information Act (2000) which means that you should resist writing any comments that are unfair, untrue, or will not stand up to scrutiny by a third party.

It is worth noting that routine monitoring and evaluation processes are useful in providing the backcloth for making informed judgements about the effectiveness and value of the work undertaken. Enacting these information-based processes will help convince funders and mangers that the work undertaken is consistent with the aims, intentions and objectives set for the project. This type of information is also useful for local audits undertaken by management and national inspections by OFSTED.

Most importantly, every evaluation tool should integrally involve the young people at every stage in the process. Also, it is appropriate for this way of working to be continuously acted upon so that the work progresses knowingly and with consent. The evaluation system should not only identify what was achieved but also identify opportunities missed and future goals to achieve. Over time, the summation and interrogation of these evaluations should help you make a wider assessment of the impact that detached youth work is making within the gambit of other services and the value of this to community development.

In any relationship the ending is as important as the beginning. Exit strategies are needed when locally-formed peer groups begin to dissipate and young people's needs move away from detached work. This exit strategy should be positive and purposeful in celebrating the successes and recognising the next planned steps which may not have been possible without the intervention.

Key Challenge – Reflective Questions

- To give you an insight into conducting an initial area mapping in a familiar environment, list as many items as you can that you would be likely to encounter on a journey from your home to the local shops.
- Select one situation that you would look forward to when involved in a detached youth work situation and identify something that you have concerns about or require further information on. Discuss these concerns with a tutor, supervisor, or youth work mentor.
- Discuss with a colleague the reasons why mapping an area should be undertaken before working a patch.
- What skills and abilities do you possess that would help you make an initial contact with young people?
- Why is it important to keep accurate records?
- Indicate how important you feel positive relationships are to successful detached youth work.
- Why are monitoring and evaluation tools important in detached youth work practice?

Comment

Experienced youth workers will develop an enhanced social awareness and become able to read environments. Detached youth workers need to be open, friendly, approachable and engaging, as well as able to work with others, be flexible and emotionally literate, and to disengage sensitively. Detached work can be emotional and demanding and I would recommend appropriate levels of supervision. The work needs to be recorded not only as a record of practice situations but also as a mechanism for review and developing future plans. In modern practice, and especially in the integrated service environment, detached youth workers have to make sure that their work is not being usurped by other service objectives.

MANAGERIAL AND OPERATING SUPPORT SYSTEMS FOR KEEPING SAFE

In general terms, one of the principles of good youth work practice is that the work process is appropriately planned and safely executed. The legal framework that sets the context for safe working practises is made up of the Health & Safety at Work etc. Act 1974 and the Management of Health & Safety at Work Regulations 1992. There are also other pieces of legislation which a detached youth work project should be cognisant of and develop policies around to ensure compliance: these would include safeguarding procedures, children and young people substance use policy, sexual health guidelines, parental consent and emergency procedures. Further, detached youth workers should be aware of the Public Order Act 1986, the Criminal Justice and Public Order Act 1994, and the Racial and Religious Hatred Act 2006.

Obviously, no activity can be regarded as completely safe and we have seen in a previous chapter that there are risk management processes which need to be known and auctioned. It is therefore up to each detached youth work project to develop and implement their safe working practices, taking into account the legal and organisational policy framework.

RISK ASSESSMENTS AND OPERATING ROUTES

Clearly risk assessment and hazard management are the most obvious aspects of health and safety that demand a detailed and regularly reviewed risk assessment to be carried out in order to identify and control any potential risks to people's health and safety.

In order to ensure safe working practises, the detached workers' operating routes and an environmental audit should be undertaken and regularly assessed, at the operating times, to detect any dangers and hazards. Following this contextual assessment, a clear set of operating guidelines should be devised with staff and appropriate management systems developed to ensure compliance and safe operating practice. Staff should be routinely supported to advise managers of any circumstances where their safety has been actually or potentially compromised and managers should act on this information appropriately.

GENERAL PRINCIPLES

There are six general principles and health and safety guidelines for detached youth workers that have generated successful practice. The first is based on the principle of safety in numbers, so always work in pairs and keep together by being in plain sight of each other as you work. Secondly, effective managed systems are important so make sure the contact and control management systems work with accessible line manager contact numbers and clear, written operating routine in terms of locations, routes and timings. Thirdly, always have your operating toolkit, stick to the agreed routines, advise the line manager/ operating contact as soon as there is any alteration to the planned process, and have a sign-off procedure at the end of a shift. The fourth is about being known and accepted, so make sure that local organisations and services are aware of your work and at all times wear appropriate clothing that is identified with your role: always display your official identification badge. Fifthly, take care of yourself and your partner by setting clear boundaries for the professional relationship: do not condone any illegal activity and never procure goods or share personal data. Also, stay safe by keeping valuables locked in a safe place at your allocated office or base, do not take unplanned risks, and develop a way of communicating with your partner that will indicate to them if you feel uncomfortable and wish to withdraw. The sixth principle is to be prepared, as far as possible, for potential emergencies by being appropriately trained, having access to information, and knowing the expectations and requirements of your organisation.

Key Challenge – Order the Checklist to Reflect the Order of Importance

The list below suggests items that should provide a basic kit for each detached youth worker. This should include:

- a first aid kit, including surgical gloves;
- a torch;
- a detailed map of the area (highlighting phone box locations, doctors, etc.);
- a flask for hot drinks;
- a mobile phone (shared between the team);
- a personal alarm;
- proof of identity;
- an information card on the work safe system;
- advice and information leaflets for use with young people;
- a phone card;
- consent forms (if organising an activity/trip);
- a crisis line card;
- ID cards;
- a pen and notebook;
- project cards with contact phone numbers;
- waterproof clothing;
- QA monitoring sheets.

Consider the above items and rate these in order of importance from a safe practice perspective.

Comment

You should have a scenario in mind when conducting this exercise because the situation will dictate your decisions.

TRAINING

Initial and continuous training is necessary to help ensure a professional and effective approach to detached youth work practice. The induction training should be appropriate, well planned, experiential and interactive, and recorded with information about policies and procedures given for future reference. This is also a good time to conduct an initial training needs analysis. Many organisations produce an induction pack for new staff which includes a note of the systems operated, the process for obtaining and using identification badges, and information on the local area including agencies and other workers.

INITIAL STAGE

At this initial stage, health and safety procedures are articulated, support systems (e.g., supervision arrangements) are outlined, and practical kit items are issued. This is the time when new staff are given the time and guidance to become familiar with the organisation's policies and administrative procedures which are designed to help staff stay safe and operate within the law. It is important to remember that training should be continuous as policies will be reviewed regularly and changes introduced. It is only through appropriate initial and continuing training and professional developmental opportunities that high quality detached youth work practice can be assured. This applies to those who are supervising and managing the work as well as those on the frontline to ensure effectiveness.

For detached projects it vital that opportunities are created, and taken, to established networks and fora, and to develop conferences and training events which will help improve professional practice and enhance confidence through the sharing of good practice.

ORGANISATIONAL POLICY

An organisation that employs detached workers should have a detached youth work policy if it is engaged in this type of activity and you will need to be trained in and understand the operating procedures. Training and professional development should be a central feature on the agenda for supervision sessions. Notwithstanding those areas mentioned above, there are a number of other areas in which as a detached youth worker you may require training. These could be legislatively, organisationally and professionally based although these are not mutually exclusive. For example, it would be useful to know about child protection, sexual health, drugs and equal opportunities from all three perspectives. You may also wish to find out about and be trained in visits and outdoor activities, transport codes, first aid procedures, and any reporting requirements which have legal and operational significance. Again, you may require training in the youth work curriculum, the principles of detached work, and confidentiality limitations and arrangements. As a reminder, it is important that organisations, managers and detached youth workers stay informed about legislative, policy and practice developments.

Also, in relation to training, it is crucial that detached youth workers are aware of and comply with the employing agency's written policy for the prevention and reporting of crime, in keeping with the requirements of the Crime and Disorder Act 1998. This is an important area which requires careful thought and clear procedures, because while the work that detached workers undertake could in itself prevent crime, a main function of the act is to prevent crime and it places a *duty* on all individuals and agencies to share information for crime prevention purposes (section 115). Youth workers should never lie on young people's behalf, and young people should be made aware of the limitations to confidentiality in relation to crime and also be aware of the duty to cooperate under the Children Act (2004). Clearly, because of the nature and location of the work, detached youth workers will potentially find themselves in situations where they will gain information about potential crimes, both specifically and generally, and therefore they will require clear guidance and support to make sure they comply with the act. This is a key issue as there are potential conflicts of interest and a potential loss of trust between worker and young person. If this issue is left

Table 6.1

Statement	Strongly Agree	Mildly Agree	Strongly Disagree	Mildly Disagree
Young women are more vulnerable on the street than young men				
Detached workers must always work in pairs				
Detached workers should always carry condoms				
If you are a serious youth worker, you will work towards eventually moving the young people into a building				
Detached workers should never work with young people under the influence of drugs or alcohol				
If you overhear a young person refer to a shop by the race or religion of the owner then this must be challenged or reported on every occasion				
Young people who hang about the streets are generally up to 'no good'				
Graffiti is a good example of young people's freedom of expression and is a form of public art				
The ideal youth club is a street corner with a roof on it				
Detached youth workers should be in regular contact with the local police				
Detached youth workers may have to limit the times and locations where they meet with groups of young people				
It is acceptable for a young person to 'skin up' in front of a detached youth worker as long as the person does not smoke it				

unresolved it either makes the practice impotent or places the worker in an impossible position. Confidentiality is important to the trust inherent in a youth work relationship and while there needs to be compliance with the law, for example the Crime and Disorder Act 1998 and the Data Protection Act 1998, these requirements will be adjudicated in terms of what is best for the young person and society and thus should be clearly outlined in a confidentiality policy.

Both youth workers and employing organisations should be aware of, and make use of, the Federation of Detached Youth Work, which has been in existence since 1996 and aims to improve quality through supporting, promoting and developing practice. It holds conferences and has a very good range of publications which helps them to meet their other aim of improving the understanding of detached youth work in different policy arenas, professional fields, and wider society.

CONCLUSION

Detached youth work is an important feature of youth work practice but it needs to be well resourced and managed for it to be effective. This requires robust planning and operating processes which involve clear systems of work with enhanced and ongoing training and support. Detached youth work is a much needed service that does not get the credit it deserves and is vital for social development because society needs a set of professionals to work with young people who are or are potentially dislocated from society. This is a demanding service which needs to keep workers safe, informed and supported, and more attention should be paid to the wellbeing of staff involved in this area of work.

Society needs to recognise that the job they ask of detached youth workers is a big ask and not one readily carried out by other professionals. Although detached youth work is highly important it is not a straightforward practice, as there are tensions in the practice which need careful thought and the practice needs to recognise more the legal context of its operation. It would help to resolve some of these tensions if detached workers more routinely researched, recorded and published their practice, and this would also assist them in claiming their rightful professional space.

Min and Jax are two detached workers on the Ersham estate in Birmington. Min is an experienced worker whose usual partner Peete had called in sick. Jax, a newly appointed worker, has just recently completed the certificate in detached youth work and has limited experience.

The supervisor, Tot, introduced the pair to each other in the base and asked Min to 'pair up' with Jax to show a new person 'the ropes'. Min could see that Jax had not been issued with appropriate clothing and asked whether she had received any induction training.

Since this was Jax's first night, Min was told that no induction had been set up yet and the jacket and waterproofs would arrive before the end of the week. Although Tot initially disapproved, Min convinced him that it was neither safe nor appropriate for Jax to start work on the streets.

After making contact with the group he was supposed to meet up with to advise them that he would not be out working that night and agreeing another time, Min worked in the base with Jax informing

Case Study 6

(Continued)

(Continued)

her of the history of the project, its aims and objectives, its routes and networks, its routines and processes, and its successes and future plans.

Some weeks later, after considerable induction training covering the policies and procedures, the roles and expectations and personal strengths and weaknesses, all three workers ventured out to meet the young people of Ersham.

After a few weeks Tot moved to a less stressful office job, and eventually Min was appointed project supervisor by demonstrating a clear understanding of the detached process, and considerable reflective practice knowledge that put people first and successfully negotiated the practice tensions.

Summary of Key Points

- There is a full range of settings and situations in which youth work takes place.
- There are a number of Acts of Parliament that affect the operation of detached youth work.
- There are different forms of 'external' youth work.
- Detached workers must recognise and negotiate the tensions inherent in their work.
- Detached work can take place anywhere 'outside'.
- Detached youth work has been around for a long time but came to prominence in 1960s' Britain.
- Detached youth work is an under-researched practice.
- Detached work is a highly sophisticated practice which requires significant investment, robust preparation and planning, and supportive operational systems.
- Detached youth work is a democratic project which recognises the fundamental human dignity of the young person and values an interaction which is both positive and progressive.
- Detached youth work deals with real-life cutting edge issues.
- There is a distinct four-stage cycle to the practice.
- There are six general principles and health and safety guidelines for detached youth workers.
- Effective, agreed management includes support systems that are crucial for safe and successful practice.
- Initial and continuous training are central for professional development.
- Confidentiality is a big issue in this line of work, and requires some detailed and agreed operational protocols.

REFERENCES

Albemarle Report (1960) *The Youth Service in England and Wales*. London: HMSO.

Anti Social Behaviour Act 2003. Available at www.legislation.gov.uk/ukpga/2003/38/contents (last accessed 28.09.12).

Arnold, J., Askins, D., Davies, R., Evans, S., Rogers, A. and Taylor, T. (1981) *The Management of Detached Work: How and Why*. Leicester: National Association of Youth Clubs.

Benetello, D. (1996) *Invisible Women: Detached Youth Work with Girls and Young Women*. Leicester: Youth Work.

Burton, P. (1993) *Community Profiling: A Guide to Identifying Local Needs*. Bristol: School for Advanced Urban Studies.

Children Act 2004. Available at www.legislation.gov.uk/ukpga/2004/31/contents (last accessed 28.09.12).

Crime and Disorder Act 1998. Available at www.legislation.gov.uk/ukpga/1998/37/contents (last accessed 28.8.12).

Criminal Justice and Public Order Act 1994. Available at www.legislation.gov.uk/ukpga/1994/33/contents (last accessed 28.09.12).

Crimmens, D. (2004) 'The role of government in promoting youth participation in England'. In D. Crimmens and A. West (eds) *Having Their Say: Young People and Participation*. Dorset: Russell House Publishing. pp. 27–36.

Dadzie, S. (1997) *Blood, Sweat and Tears: A Report of the Bede Anti-racist Detached Youth Work Project*. Leicester: Youth Work.

Data Protection Act 1998. Available at www.legislation.gov.uk/ukpga/1998/29/contents (last accessed 13.04.12).

Federation of Detached Youth Work (n.d.) Available at www.detachedyouthwork.info/ (last accessed 01.06.12).

Freedom of Information Act 2000. Available at www.ico.gov.uk/for_organisations/freedom_of_information.aspx (last accessed 28.09.12).

Goetschius, G. and Tash, J. (1967) *Work with the Unattached*. London: Routledge & Kegan Paul.

Green, J. (1992) *It's No Game: Responding to the Needs of Young Women at Risk or Involved in Prostitution*. Leicester: National Youth Agency.

Hawtin, M., Hughes, G. and Percy-Smith, J. (1994) *Community Profiling: Auditing Social Needs*. Buckingham: Open University Press.

Health and Safety at Work etc. Act 1974. Available at www.legislation.gov.uk/ukpga/1974/37/contents (last accessed 03.04.12).

Jeffs, T. and Smith, K. (2010) *Youth Work Practice*. Hampshire: Palgrave Macmillan.

Martin, L. (2002) *The Invisible Table*. New Zealand: Dunmore.

McGinley, B. and Dunlop, T. (2011) It can be powerful in getting your message across: creating possibilities through community arts youth work, A *Journal of Youth Work*, 8: 47–62.

McGinley, B. and Watson, I. (2008) Can I have this dance? A perspective on the expectations and demands of current youth work practice in Scotland, *Scottish Youth Issues Journal*, 11: 23–37.

Morse, M. (1965) *The Unattached*. Harmondsworth: Penguin.

Public Order Act 1986. Available at www.legislation.gov.uk/ukpga/1986/64 (last accessed 28.09.12).

Racial and Religious Hatred Act 2006. Available at www.legislation.gov.uk/ukpga/2006/1/contents (last accessed 28.09.12).

Rogers, A. (1981) *Starting Out In Detached Youth Work*. Leicester: National Association of Youth Clubs.

Rogers, V. (2011) *101 Things to Do on the Street*. London: Jessica Kingsley.

Sapin, T. (2009) *Essential Skills for Youth Work Practice*. London: Sage.

Smith, M.K. (1994) *Local Education: Community, Conversation, Praxis*. Buckingham: Open University Press.

Tyler, M., Hoggarth, L. and Merton, B. (2009) *Managing Modern Youth Work*. Exeter: Learning Matters.

7

ESTABLISHING A COMMUNITY YOUTH ORGANISATION AND MANAGING PREMISES

Chapter Aims

- Outline some of the main legal considerations that need to be taken into account when securing and operating community premises
- Explicate the different ways of setting up and operating a community-based youth organisation.
- Articulate specific details on understanding and managing building-related matters
- Identify the four main sources of raising funds to help establish and operate a community-based youth organisation
- Describe the three basic ways in which property can be legally held
- Delineate possible legal structures and the nature of charitable status
- Relate some of the key issues involved in managing an organisation in terms of structures, processes and managing buildings
- Introduce some of the key aspects to ensure that children and young people are safeguarded

INTRODUCTION

As we have noted in earlier chapters, youth work takes place in a variety of external and internal settings which may involve open spaces and use of dedicated youth centres or shared premises with other community groups. There will also be circumstances where there will be a lack of facilities in an area for young people to meet, and youth workers will be required to work with those young people to secure and operate a community-based facility to meet their needs. In such circumstances many legal considerations will need to be taken into account when securing and operating community premises. Every effort should be made to link up with existing organisational structures in the community as this is often the simplest and most effective option in terms of time, effort, and cost. Another area that youth workers should consider is the appropriateness of taking up opportunities within the current government's developing policy area around community asset transfers, where local people can bid to take over a redundant building or run a local service under threat (see www.number10.gov. uk/take-part/your-neighbourhood/community-asset-transfer/). This new Community Right to Bid has been enshrined in the Localism Act 2011 in order to keep assets in local communities.

The legal issues explored in this chapter are deemed necessary, because setting up and operating a community-based youth organisation is still a key part of the skills and knowledge required by youth workers engaging with existing or new youth groups in local communities. This chapter complements and adds value to the advice outlined in other chapters, by providing specific details on understanding and managing building-related matters so that youth work can be carried out in a legal, safe, and enjoyable manner.

Effective management of buildings requires thoughtful consideration, good planning and a consistent application of structures and processes which are continually communicated, applied, and reviewed. As background you should be aware of the requirements of the Building Act 1984, which is a statute that consolidates previous legislation concerning buildings and related matters, as well as the Climate Change and Sustainable Energy Act 2006. Some of the main things to think about and organise are summarised here, for ease of reference, into five key sections which are defined and articulated below. Note that the following information is offered as a guide and has no legal standing. When setting up a local youth organisation it is vital to engage the services of a qualified and licensed legal practitioner, and also to use expert advice available through, for example, a Council for Voluntary Service or a Citizens Advice Bureau.

SOURCES OF FUNDING

Obtaining funding can be an onerous and continuous process for a local voluntary youth organisation. Funding can be secured from four main sources: fundraising; grants; sponsorship; and trusts and legacies.

FUNDRAISING

Fundraising is a very good source for a number of reasons, including that it is directly in your control, gets young people working together, and encourages them to work both for themselves and for one another. It can also be a good source of steady income, for example from regular donations, from which in certain circumstances, the tax can be reclaimed through schemes such as Gift Aid and payroll giving.

GRANTS

Grants can vary in size and conditions, and potential sources include European monies, the Lottery, and local council grants. There may also be partnership funds available under, for example, a community safety partnership. It is important to be aware of, and adhere to, the grant conditions set, and consider in advance whether the conditions can be met and if these are commensurate with the amount of money proposed. In terms of making a good grant application, it is positive to make sure that your application meets the stipulated criteria using the same sort of language and terms laid out in the information booklet. It is also good to start small and build up a track record over time, and to link in with local networks and strategies to build confidence in your organisation's ability to deliver.

SPONSORSHIP

Sponsorship can be secured from local businesses, medium-sized companies, and large corporations. Again, think about the ethical aspects of accepting sponsorship and make sure that their operations and practices are in keeping with your organisation's values and principles. A number of large corporations have charitable social responsibility structures that fund good works and are open to requests for support in cash or in kind.

TRUSTS

Trusts are a good source of income, and especially local ones, as these are not often well known and targeted at a specific cause, group, or area. Your local authority may have a list of trusts that it administers and could offer advice on how to access such funds. Legacies are money or property bequeathed to your organisation in a person's will.

The eligibility to access certain funds and the ways in which this income is treated will depend, to some degree, on the type of organisation you decide to become and the structure that is adopted. For example, many charitable foundations will only donate to registered charities. However, regardless of structure, it is vitally important that sufficient funds are identified and secured, as part of a robust business planning process, so that your organisation has the resources to set up and operate successfully to meet its undertakings and objectives. (For more information on writing a successful grant application see Reif-Lehrer, 2005).

Key Challenge – Questions and Tasks

Answer the following questions:

- What are the main sources of funding?
- What are the key benefits of fundraising other than raising money?
- What ethical issues might there be in seeking sponsorship for your youth group from a soft drinks company?

Complete the following tasks:

- Identify five local trusts in your area.
- Find and complete a funding application for a local grant.
- List ten activities that would be appropriate for a youth group to raise funds.

Comment

Youth work has a great tradition of fundraising which is helpful in developing organisational, planning and other skills, raising much needed cash, and developing team spirit. Many local authorities will have a full range of information and access to trust funds which should be called upon. Sponsorship needs to be handled sensitively to ensure that any ethical issues or subliminal messages are thought through and authorised.

ESTABLISHING THE ORGANISATION: SECURING THE OPERATIONAL BASE

Making a decision about which organisational structure to adopt is not to be taken lightly because this decision is not easily reversed and is likely to have lasting implications. Time and care should be taken to ensure that the right decision is made and based on the best legal advice and is the result of extensive consultations with all stakeholders. A new organisation should only be set up if there is no other one available and it is necessary for the intended purposes: it can be unincorporated if that is the most suitable arrangement. The main concerns when setting up a new youth work organisation are to make sure that the operational arrangements comply with the law, are flexible enough to suit the local circumstances, and best meet the needs of the young people they aim to serve. In essence, there are three basic legal ways to hold a property: freehold, leasehold, and with a licence to occupy.

FREEHOLD

Freehold exists when a 'real property' is bought outright and the purchaser therefore has outright ownership. This situation gives the owner the maximum opportunity to develop and use the site and property to best suit its purposes without recourse to a third party, subject to any planning considerations of course (see the Town and Country Planning Act 1990 which, although the principal act, also has had some subsequent alterations and revisions).

LEASEHOLD AGREEMENT

A leasehold agreement, on the other hand, is a time-limited possession where the land and all immovable structures revert back to the owner at the end of the lease period. A lease is a legal transaction which is governed by the Landlord and Tenant Act 1954, and this should be read in full and checked by a qualified solicitor before signing acceptance. This document sets out the terms and conditions on which a premise can be occupied for an agreed and specified period, and usually gives exclusive occupancy rights for the period of the lease agreement. It can be extended with the agreement of both parties, or it can be terminated at the end of the identified period when it reverts back to the freeholder. Clearly, the value of a property built on land that is leasehold decreases in value the closer it gets to the termination date. Consequently, adding years to the leasehold, which will incur additional costs, will also potentially add to the sell-on value of the property.

The terms and conditions of a lease can vary but long-term leases are usually established with a significant number of years, with low-cost ground rent and minimal restrictions on usage and management arrangements. Leases can apply to both residential and commercial properties but these are covered by different laws (i.e., the former is covered by tenancy laws). Also, if you consider the lease to be onerous or restrictive in meeting your needs then either walk away or ask your legal representative to renegotiate the terms of the lease. Unless it is an interim measure, it is unlikely that a lease of less than thirty years would be of sustainable value for a community facility. In general simple terms, the longer the lease the more the group has security of tenure which allows for longer-term planning.

LICENCE TO OCCUPY

The third way of securing access to a property is through a Licence to Occupy, which is a main practice for commercial businesses to rent property. This agreement outlines both landlord and tenant rights and responsibilities in occupying the premises and should be clear and specific about the terms. Such agreements tend to be short term, usually six months to a year, with multiple occupants and the landlord retaining rights of possession. The landlord normally retains responsibility for structural and external matters, whereas the responsibility of partial participation by the occupier normally demands the internal areas are to be kept clean and in a good state of repair.

In this relationship landlords will retain many of the property 'aces' in that they can decide on whether to renew the contract, may change the terms of the contract as part of the renewal process, and can terminate the contract early under certain circumstances. Also, the rights of occupation can be undermined if the property owner decides to sell the property or if it is foreclosed by a bank for example.

Key Challenge – Something to Think About

Is it always preferable to own your own premises or is it sometimes better to lease premises? Work out the merits and drawbacks of both situations for a community-based youth group.

Comment

The answer to this will depend on the organisation's circumstances and will vary depending on a number of factors, for example the history of the organisation, its financial turnover and access to loans, and the availability of suitable premises. If the lease is on very favourable terms and is an ideal size then there may be little reason to move elsewhere. On the other hand, if the existing premises are not suitable for current and future plans, and the organisation has a healthy bank balance, a robust business plan and a centre is available at a the right price, then the board may decide to move.

DECIDING ON LEGAL STRUCTURES AND SECURING CHARITABLE STATUS

Deciding on a legal structure is not a straightforward or simple matter. There will be many facts to be considered, and ultimately it will often be a balancing act between costs and bureaucracy against suitability to support objectives and the level of liability. There are various ways of establishing and constituting local bodies, including setting up a local community voluntary organisation with a basic constitution to outline the way it operates. However, should a local community organisation grow it may have to consider other options.

OTHER OPTIONS

When setting up a community organisation there are different legal structures that could be considered. The three main types are: Company Limited by Guarantee; Community Interest Company (CIC); or Industrial and Provident Societies (IPS).

Clearly there are advantages and disadvantages associated with each type, and it is important that due consideration is given to ensure that the structure chosen is best suited to the purposes and needs of the organisation and its members. This choice of structure is a crucial and fundamental decision which should be fully considered and investigated before opting for a particular form. A brief summary of the merits and demerits of each structure is provided below.

COMPANY LIMITED BY GUARANTEE

The first option available to youth workers to consider is to adopt a legal organisational structure known as a Company Limited by Guarantee. This is a flexible structure, with no shareholders, that has the advantage of limiting the liability of directors if the company faces insolvency. However, it does not remove the directors' onus to act responsibly as they will be potentially prosecuted if they act negligently or recklessly. Notwithstanding, this limited level of accountability is a key consideration for volunteers especially when their involvement and contribution are essentially an altruistic act. It is important to note that this type of organisation needs to comply with company law and also requires to be registered with Company's House, which brings with it some specified annual requirements.

COMMUNITY INTEREST COMPANY (CIC)

The second choice is to establish a Community Interest Company (CIC), which is an organisational form that has been recently created that has proved useful because it is a more flexible form of organisation that offers a clear focus on public benefit without the restrictions that come with charitable status. Its establishment comes under the remit of a CIC regulator who will demand a clear specification of the geographical area or people that are the intended beneficiaries of this organisation. This type of organisation has proved popular, with an average of around a 150 being established each year since its inception in 2005. A CIC can be a company limited by a guarantee or share issue with special conditions to detail a clear community interest, and can have assets locked on capital gains with a limit set on the dividends paid to shareholders and a cap on the amounts that private investors can take out of the organisation.

INDUSTRIAL AND PROVIDENT SOCIETY (IPS)

A third alternative would be to set up an Industrial and Provident Society (IPS) that is a co-operative trading organisation which exists for the benefit of its members or the wider community. These organisations are registered with the Financial Services

Authority (FSA), and those that are charities are regarded as 'exempt charities'. 'Exempt' charities are not allowed to register with the Charities Commission because they are regulated and supervised by a principal regulator through an agreed structure or system, although they are otherwise subject to charity law. Whether these organisations are eligible for tax relief is decided by Her Majesty's Revenue and Customs service (HMRC). However, this is a different case from 'excepted' charities that do not need to register with the Charities Commission but are still regulated by the commission, and these organisations will be held to account when there is due cause to demand information or conduct an investigation.

An IPS is normally funded by share capital, but is different from limited companies in that the shares are of fixed value and low cost based on a membership system of one-member-one-vote regardless of the number of shares held. There is also an upper limit on the cash value of shares that can be held by one person. Some IPSs are set up as cooperatives, which cannot be charities, but others are set up as community benefit societies, which can be charities where they meet certain criteria. At the time of writing, it is unclear how charitable IPSs will be regulated in the future (for further information on this see www.charitycommission.gov.uk/Start_up_a_charity/ Do_I_need_to_register/industrial_provident_societies.aspx).

CHARITABLE ORGANISATION

However, there is also a possibility of establishing a charitable organisation that can bring certain tax and other benefits but will restrict aspects of operation as charities face certain trading restrictions. It is possible for a charity to set up a subsidiary trading organisation to overcome some of the trading restrictions, but this can be a complex matter which would require expert advice. There is a set process for registering a charity and obligations that must be fulfilled to the Charity Regulator once the organisation is accepted and registered. Charities are established for the public benefit and not all voluntary organisations need to be registered as charities. Also small charities (i.e., those whose income is less than £5,000) don't need to register to prove that they are charities or benefit from charitable status. Another alternative to charities registration would be to apply to Her Majesty's Revenue and Customs (HMRC) for tax relief: the HMRC charity number can be used as evidence of charitable status.

CONSTITUTION OR ARTICLES OF ASSOCIATION

Once the overall organisational structure has been ascertained, attention should turn to establishing a constitution or Articles of Association to set out the principles and procedures that will shape the conduct and operation of the organisation. Such documents will delineate the roles and behaviours of directors and members. It is important that these documents are accurate, detailed, and relevant to the operation, so that those taking on positions (for example, a trustee or director) are fully aware of their responsibilities and obligations. There are model documents which can be used as a guide and these can be obtained from a range of sources including relevant regulators. More information on these matters can be obtained from the CIC Regulator, the Charity Commission, Companies House and the Financial Services Authority. There is also a range of model constitutions available from the Council of Voluntary Organisations and their websites.

Key Challenge – Question

Think about some of the advantages of keeping a local organisation small and the merits of growing the organisation more formally.

Comment

Some things to consider when making choices regarding structure and status will include whether to keep things simple or whether a more complex structure is required to help meet the growing undertakings. Also, make sure that the structure adopted is best suited to the aims and purposes of the organisation. Think both in the short and long term, and utilise both the actual and potential skills and resources of local people using, among other things, quality training, coaching and supervision. Weigh up the pros and cons of charitable status and seek professional advice when required.

MANAGING THE ORGANISATION: STRUCTURES, PROCESSES AND BUILDINGS

In order to operate an organisation successfully, a number of key strategic and operational functions should be put in place. These include the organisational structure, such as the establishment, recruitment and running of boards or committees to oversee the operation. These also involve a staffing and operating structure which deals with strategic planning, operational policies and procedures, and ensuring compliance with legal obligations such as employment law, insurance requirements and health and safety. Other duties will include the development of policies and procedures, such as human resources outlining a code of conduct, welfare policies, equal opportunities, operational duties and reporting procedures. Such policies will apply to paid staff and should specify employment rights, employment contracts and job descriptions (see Chapter 4). There may also be a need to develop polices for the recruitment, management and appraisal of volunteers. In addition, the management of finances is an important organisational area which starts with drawing an income, ensuring compliance with any conditions or restrictions on spending, establishing budgets, and laying out procedures for financial spending, monitoring and reporting.

MANAGING DAY TO DAY

Establishing an operational building and then managing its day-to-day activities can be a demanding part of a youth worker's remit that involves not just managing staff, young people and events but also ensuring that appropriate systems are established and adhered to. Such responsibilities may include making sure that leases are signed and up to date, the building is compliant with current building regulations and it is regularly maintained, rates and insurances are paid, and that safe user practices are in operation. In addition to this there are a number of licences and permissions that may need to be sought, for example alcohol and bingo licences for activities/fundraising events and permissions from the Performing Rights Society to play music. Note that the latter has a specified code of conduct which governs the way the society operates (see www.prsformusic.com/codeofconduct/Documents/PRS%20for%20Music%20 Code%20of%20Conduct%20Nov%202012.pdf).

OPERATIONAL DECISIONS

There are also a number of operational matters that will need some clear thought and agreed decisions which will include the opening and closing times of the building, the nature and level of access to the building, and the roles and responsibilities of those individuals operating in the building at any particular time. There will be requirements to operate a recording system to track all the users in a building at any given time. Other management issues that will need to be dealt with include developing a strategy for procurement to purchase equipment and secure energy requirements, and establishing sound cleaning and routine maintenance systems, as well as establishing ways of effectively managing waste by, for example, reducing use and promoting recycling. You may also need to establish a policy for priority and/or limited use of the building if the demand for space exceeds the accommodation available, which will need to be handled in keeping with your organisational values and principles that should include equity and fairness as well as being in keeping with the current drive for efficiency and best value.

PROCESSES AND PROCEDURES

In order to operate efficiently and transparently, there should be a clear policy on the delegated level of authority, and a defined code of practice to be followed for all those involved in the procurement of goods and services. These stipulated processes must be auditable and carried out in keeping with best accountancy practices, which will involve the establishment and regular updating of an inventory system. Seek professional help if you are unsure about the need for, or the operation of, these procedures.

All purchases ordered on the organisation's behalf should be made in keeping with its stated aims, objectives and policies. If the organisation has developed an ethical code then thought should be given to procuring ethical products such as Fairtrade goods and purchasing recycled products such as notepads made from recycled paper. When purchasing items for a centre, for example furniture, the decision on which goods to buy should not be based on cost or ethics alone. Other practical considerations (such as the intended purposes, types of usage, levels of durability and comfort, style, safety guarantees, storage, weight and size) should all be taken into account when deciding on the suitability of an item.

In addition, it should be borne in mind that all electrical equipment purchased, including electrified kitchen utensils and computers, are subject to separate and specific safety legislation (see the Health and Safety Executive website for the most frequently asked questions about Display Screen Equipment at www.hse.gov.uk/electricity/faq-portable-appliance-testing.htm). Also, you will need to note that 'The Health and Safety (Display Screen Equipment) Regulations 1992 implement an EC Directive and came into effect from January 1993 with some small changes ... made in 2002. The Regulations require employers to minimise the risks in VDU work by ensuring that workplaces and jobs are well designed' (see HSE, 'Working with VDU's', p. 4, at www.hse.gov.uk/pubns/indg36.pdf). Additional information covering other aspects of office management, potential hazards and the legal requirements post-1988 can be found at www.tuc.org.uk/workplace/tuc-15513-f0.cfm. There is more detail on these types of requirements in the next chapter.

SUSTAINABILITY AND COSTS

Allied to this issue of electrical safety is the type and amount of energy sources used to heat, light, and operate machinery in the building. The energy should be sourced at its best price which will mean a regular review of supplier charges, and controls must be put in place, both mechanical and human procedure, to ensure minimum wastage (for example, checking that stand-by lights are not left on and that lights are switched off after use). Also, heating the building at its optimum temperature and actively managing use reduction will save money and contribute to the sustainability of finite resources.

PROGRAMMING

Youth workers must also remember that young people are interested in a whole range of active, creative and participative activities, for example arts and crafts. Such activities may involve aspects of pottery making which may involve using a kiln: this will bring a range of health and safety issues, and use of such equipment is subject to specific additional legislative considerations (see www.hse.gov.uk/pubns/ceis3.pdf). For more comprehensive information about the relevant legislation in this area and guidance on the procedures and processes that will need to be adopted, see The National Society for Education in Art and Design (NSEAD) at /www.nsead.org/hsg/index.aspx

CLEANING MECHANISMS AND ROUTINES

The building also needs to be kept clean for the safety and comfort of the users. Cleaning staff (either dedicated or as part of other duties) should be identified and suitably trained to operate an appropriate cleaning schedule. The main statutory instruments for ensuring adequate cleaning come from the Factories Act, the Offices, Shops and Railway Premises Act, and the Food Hygiene Regulations. The building's users should be requested to use the facility with care and appropriate advice notices should be placed advising of any hazards, dangers, or limitations on access. Centre users should also be encouraged to use the facilities properly, look after and use the services with care, and maintain their own health and safety while in the premises.

Clear instructions should be issued to staff as part of their training to ensure that the issued cleaning materials are used in accordance with the manufacturer's instructions, that they are appraised of any health and safety issues, and advised of what action to take if an accident occurs. If your organisation uses chemicals then you must protect your workers from harm. A Chemical and Hazardous Substances document should be drawn up and maintained which will be required as part of the health and safety documentation: this will need to be made available for an annual health and safety visit by the inspector. Consideration should be given to the necessity of using any chemical cleaning product or other substance which is listed in Table 3.2 of part 3 of Annex VI of the CLP Regulation, denoted as very toxic, toxic, harmful, corrosive or irritant (see www.hse.gov.uk/coshh/detail/substances.htm), and appropriate controls put in place where necessary.

LOCAL ENVIRONMENT

Attention should also be given to the condition of the area immediately surrounding the building and this must ensure safe access and egress for all centre users. A quid pro quo arrangement may be negotiated with the local council where an identified area surrounding the centre is kept clear, by staff and/or volunteers, as part of a mutual waste management agreement.

Key Challenge – Strategy, Policies and Procedures

Write a paragraph, in your own words, stating why it is important to have clearly written policies and procedures which will outline the roles and responsibilities of the people involved in purchasing resources and services on behalf of an organisation.

Comment

Policies and procedures are needed to provide the organisation's direction of travel and to detail the systems and processes that will bring about their aims. Well thought-out policies and

(Continued)

(Continued)

procedures will make sure there is transparency in the operation. These also help staff to know what they should be doing and alerts management if there is any deviation from the norm. They provide a process of authorisation and paper trail that can be investigated to establish who made decisions and at what point should something go wrong. They also help to demonstrate to users of the service that the organisation is well organised, will keep them safe, and is prepared to prevent and act in an emergency.

SAFEGUARDING CHILDREN AND YOUNG PEOPLE IN CENTRES

This issue is significant enough to have a chapter of its own (see Chapter 9), but it is also relevant to locate this issue within the context of buildings management which is the focus of this section. There will be activities that youth workers organise themselves, or are organised on their behalf, which will require a working knowledge of making sure that young and vulnerable people are safeguarded. There may also be groups using the centre (such as parent and toddler groups, disability groups and out-of-school clubs) which will all need to operate with appropriate protection procedures.

LEGAL BACKGROUND

In relation to the law, the Children Act 1989 introduced the welfare principle and gave the framework for investigation into a child's situation. The Children Act 2004 outlines the duty to cooperate in promoting children's wellbeing, and places the accountability for their welfare firmly on the shoulders of directors of children's services and a lead councillor under sections 18 and 19.

DISCLOSURE AND BARRING SERVICE (DBS)

It is important to know that the Disclosure and Barring Service (DBS) was created under the Protection of Freedoms Act 2012, and brings together the functions formerly carried out by the Criminal Records Bureau (CRB) and Independent Safeguarding Authority (ISA). This organisation provides services both for those individuals who need to apply for a DBS check and for employers, or an organisation, that has concerns that an individual has caused harm or poses a future risk of harm to vulnerable groups including children. In this latter case a DBS referral form should be completed (see www.gov.uk/government/publications/dbs-referrals-form-and-guidance).

PROTECTION SCHEME

The child sex offender disclosure scheme was established in 2008 and is applicable across the whole of England and Wales. It enables those who look after young people to find out if a person has a record for child sexual offences, and also allows parents, carers and guardians to make a formal request to the police to tell them if someone has a record for child sexual offences.

While the aim of such schemes is to put operations in place to help keep children safer, it is worth remembering that 80 per cent of child sexual offences are committed by a person known to the child around the family unit. This is not, in any way, to undermine the importance of looking after and protecting children when in your care by ensuring that robust protective procedures are in place and enacted, however, it is vital to note that state intervention alone will not in itself prevent the ill treatment of children, and therefore youth workers should work beyond the legislative requirements to advocate that all children are respected in society and treated with fairness and justice by all adults.

PERSON IN CHARGE

If as a youth worker you are the designated person in charge of a building then you will need to satisfy yourself that all user groups are complying with the current legislation around child protection. You must also be proactive in ensuring that the use of new technology is supervised and used for appropriate activities to avoid some of the abuses that can be associated with new media. As an overriding principle, all professionals, volunteers and visitors should be encouraged to report any concerns about the safety of vulnerable people, including children, to the appropriate authorities in accordance with policy and in keeping with advice received in training.

There is a range of information and support services available and these should be promoted to raise awareness about child sexual abuse, to answer questions, and to give parents and carers information to help inform and alley fears. For example, the Lucy Faithfull Foundation has resources available in this area and operates a free and confidential helpline on 0808 1000 900.

Key Challenge – Applying the Knowledge

- Locate and read the main sections of the Children's Act 1989 and 2004.
- Research best practice around keeping vulnerable people, including children and young people, safe.
- Identify five sources of useful information on child abuse and disseminate this information.
- Start to collect information and resources around the issue of child protection.

CONCLUSION

In this chapter we have seen that establishing and running a local youth organisation is not straightforward and therefore it is important to investigate other options, like joining an existing organisation or getting an existing organisation, from within or outwith the area, to develop the service that is needed.

We have also identified the potentially different ways of setting up a legal organisation and holding property, and detailed the importance of and range of sources for securing appropriate funds. Again, we have considered the range of legal and operational issues that need to be considered when operating a building and keeping young people safe with appropriate safeguards and secure ways of working.

Of course, we must not lose sight of the reasons why we need to conduct our affairs properly and transparently which is for the direct benefit of the young people that we serve. They deserve good quality services and highly-trained effective youth workers because the social economic and cultural barriers that hold them back are insidious. However, this work with young people is no longer a 'voluntary goodwill mission' as was the case in the past, but a professional social practice based on an economic and moral argument as well as, most importantly, on a legislative case based on an enactment of the provisions of the UNCRC, the Children Act 1989, 2004, and the ECHR.

Case Study 7

Tim grew up in a former mining town named Filbex: he had left it four years ago to go to university in London. Increasingly, during his time away, Tim became determined to make a new life elsewhere and never return to Filbex.

However, although he had qualified with an honours degree in youth work Tim had been unable to secure a job after university. As a result, he had decided to return to stay with his gran until he could successfully move on.

On returning to the town Tim was shocked at the extent of the adverse impact that the economic downturn had had on the local area. He also realised that many of the local services had closed and numerous young people were hanging about the streets. He was convinced, given what he had read at university, that this lack of infrastructure and services for children and young people was adversely affecting the UNCRC.

After a week Tim met Jet, a friend he had grown up with and attended the local school with. Jet asked Tim to help start up a youth organisation for the young people in the town who had little to do.

He was eager to put his new found learning and skills to the test. The first thing they agreed on was that he could not do it on his own and would need many volunteers to help, and that the young people should be directly involved from the start to shape the project.

Tim called a public meeting and gained full support from the community to do something for the young people, receiving offers of help from a range of different local people. At the public meeting, which the young people helped organise, many individuals and local groups attended as a result of the open invitation that was issued around the town.

Tim had planned to set up a new organisation, but one of the local community associations that had local premises, systems and resources in place offered to support the initiative and take them under its organisational umbrella so that there was no need to set up a new organisation.

From this, they set up a working committee to develop their project but as a subgroup with the community association. This meant that they adopted the main organisation's incorporation, policies, procedures, minutes, funds and other resources at little extra expense. The main organisation also provided support systems and vetting procedures that were required, which meant the subgroup could focus on meeting young people's needs and sustaining a programme that was literally life-saving for those young people.

Since all the structural elements were in place, and the organisation had a good track record and in-house expertise, the youth development project found it straightforward to secure funds and develop the project. The initiative operated for five years in that way before a regeneration initiative revamped the area and the community association formed itself into an Industrial and Provident Society (IPS) to take advantage of the emerging local economic development opportunities in the community.

Although the initiative was a great success for the time that it was needed, Tim had left after two years when he secured a senior youth worker post in Plymouth.

Summary of Key Points

- Only establish a new organisation and open up new premises if there is a real local need and these actions will bring identifiable added benefits.
- Establishing an organisation with premises has to be carried out thoughtfully, systematically, and with access to expert advice when necessary.
- There are at least four good sources of fundraising which should be maximised to achieve the organisation's stated objectives.
- It is important to take time and establish the most appropriate legal structure to fit the purposes of the organisation.
- There are three basic legal ways to hold a property: freehold; leasehold; and with a licence to occupy.
- There are three main types of company structure: Company Limited by Guarantee; Community Interest Company (CIC); or an Industrial and Provident Society (IPS).
- There is an option to register as a charity if the organisation is for the public benefit. There is a separate registration process but not all voluntary organisations will need to register as charities.
- In order to operate an organisation successfully a number of key strategic and operational arrangements will need to be put in place.
- Children and vulnerable people will need to be safeguarded, via robust procedures and adequate training, when they are in contact with the organisation.

REFERENCES

Building Act 1984. Available at www.legislation.gov.uk/ukpga/1984/55 (last accessed 10.01.12).

Building (Amendment) Regulations 2011 (SI 2011/1515). Available at www.legislation.gov.uk/uksi/2011/1515/contents/made (last accessed 03.12.12).

Building (Amendment) Regulations 2012 (SI 2012/718). Available at www.legislation.gov.uk/uksi/2012/718/contents/made (last accessed 03.12.12).

Building (Approved Inspectors etc.) Regulations 2012. Available at www.legislation.gov.uk/uksi/2010/2215/contents/made (last accessed 03.12.12).

Building Regulations (2010). Available at www.legislation.gov.uk/uksi/2010/2214/contents/made (last accessed 03.12.12).

Charities Act 2006: What Trustees Need to Know (2007) Available at http://webarchive.nationalarchives.gov.uk/20100304041448/http:/www.cabinetoffice.gov.uk/media/cabinetoffice/third_sector/assets/charities_act_web.pdf (last accessed 09.12.12).

Charities Act 2011. Available at www.legislation.gov.uk/ukpga/2011/25 (last accessed 10.11.12).

Children Act 1989. London: HMSO.

Children Act 2004. London: HMSO.

Climate Change and Sustainable Energy Act 2006. Available at www.legislation.gov.uk/ukpga/2006/19/contents (last accessed 10.01.13).

Disclosure and Barring Service. Available at www.homeoffice.gov.uk/agencies-public-bodies/dbs/ (last accessed 25.02.13).

Factories Act 1961. Available at www.legislation.gov.uk/ukpga/Eliz2/9-10/34/contents (last accessed 10.02.13).

The Food Hygiene (England) Amendment Regulations 2006. Available at www.legislation.gov.uk/uksi/2006/14/contents/made (last accessed 10.02.13).

The Food Hygiene (England) Amendment Regulations 2007. Available at www.legislation.gov.uk/uksi/2007/56/contents/made (last accessed 20.02.13).

The Food Hygiene (England) Amendment Regulations 2012. Available at www.legislation.gov.uk/uksi/2012/1742/made (last accessed 08.07.13).

The Food Hygiene (England) Amendment Regulations 2012. Available at www.legislation.gov.uk/uksi/2012/1742/schedule/1/made (last accessed 15.02.13).

Health and Safety Executive (Computers). Available at www.hse.gov.uk/pubns/computers.htm

Health and Safety Executive (Electrical Appliances). Available at www.hse.gov.uk/electricity/faq-portable-appliance-testing.htm

Health and Safety Executive (First Aid). Available at www.hse.gov.uk/firstaid/legislation.htm

Health and Safety Executive (1995) RIDDOR - Reporting of Injuries, Diseases and Dangerous Occurrences Regulations 1995. Available at www.hse.gov.uk/riddor/ (last accessed 10.11.12).

Health and Safety Executive (2002) COSSH. Available at www.materials.ox.ac.uk/uploads/file/COSHHRegulations.pdf (last accessed 23.12.12).

Landlord and Jenant Act 1954. Available at www.legislation.gov.uk/ukpga/Eliz2/23/56/contents (last accessed 16.01.2014).

Localism Act 2011. Available at www.legislation.gov.uk/ukpga/2011/20/contents (last accessed 12.11.12).

Lucy Faithfull Foundation. Available at www.lucyfaithfull.org.uk/home.htm (last accessed 10.01.13).

Offices, Shops and Railway Premises Act 1963. Available at www.legislation.gov.uk/ukpga/1963/41/contents (last accessed 10.02.13).

Protection of Freedoms Act 2012. Available at www.legislation.gov.uk/ukpga/2012/9/contents/enacted (last accessed 04.02.13).

Reif-Lehrer, L. (2005) Grant Application Writer's Handbook. London: Jones and Bartlett.

The National Society for Education in Art and Design (NSEAD). Available at www.nsead.org/hsg/index.aspx (last accessed 06.12.2013).

Town and Country Planning Act 1990. Available at www.legislation.gov.uk/ukpga/1990/8/contents (last accessed 21.11.12).

Trade Union Congress (2008) Available at www.tuc.org.uk/workplace/tuc-15513-f0.cfm (last accessed 06.12.2013).

FURTHER INFORMATION AND CONTACTS

The Charity Commission
Website: www.charitycommission.gov.uk/
Tel: 020 7674 2463
CIC Regulator,
Room 3.68,
Companies House,
Crown Way,
Cardiff, CF14 3UZ.
Tel: +44 (0)29 2034 6228 (a 24-hour voicemail service)
Email: cicregulator@companieshouse.gov.uk

Companies House
Crown Way,
Cardiff, CF14 3UZ,
DX 33050, Cardiff.

Companies House,
4th Floor,
Quay 2,
139 Fountainbridge,
Edinburgh, EH3 9FF.
LP - 4 Edinburgh 2 (Legal Post) or
DX ED235 Edinburgh 1

Companies House,
2nd Floor,
The Linenhall,
32–38 Linenhall Street,
Belfast,
Northern Ireland, BT2 8BG.
Or
DX 481 N.R. Belfast 1

Companies House,
4 Abbey Orchard Street,
Westminster,
London,
SW1P 2HT.

The Financial Services Authority
Write to: Mutual Societies Registration,
Financial Services Authority,
25 The North Colonnade,

Canary Wharf,
London, E14 5HS.

Mutual Societies Registration Team
Email: mutual.societies@fsa.gov.uk
Phone: 0845 606 9966
www.fsa.gov.uk/Pages/Doing/small_firms/MSR/index.shtml

8

HAZARDS AND PROTECTION AT WORK AND IN THE COMMUNITY

Chapter Aims

- Provide information about the nature of negligence and the duty of care
- Outline the legal background to occupiers' liability
- Provide a context for understanding health and safety compliance
- Explain the need to be aware of health and safety legislation when managing a building
- Offer information on the requirement to provide safe systems of work, and ensure that equipment, procedures and process are safe
- Detail the legal requirements for recording and reporting accidents and dangerous occurrences

INTRODUCTION

We have seen in previous chapters that the Health and Safety at Work etc. Act 1974, together with subsequent regulations, employment law and equality laws, overarch and guide much of the expectations and standards of behaviour required in the working environment. In this chapter we consider the Law of Tort and the legal context which affects a range of operational issues and employment situations that may not be immediately obvious to the youth worker unless attention is drawn to these. The main thrust of the chapter will be to provide information on negligence and the duty of care, exploring the levels of care expected under the occupiers' liability legislation. More specifically, we will look at the principles around being health and safety compliant and managing buildings and people safely. Generally speaking everyone expects to attend their work and be safe and free from harm, but when something does go wrong then the law provides the framework to determine who was negligent, and adjudicate on the level of duty of care and the extent of the liability.

NEGLIGENCE AND THE DUTY OF CARE

Responsible employers will put operating processes and procedures in place to avoid being negligent under the law. In order for negligence to be proven it needs to be shown that a person owes a duty of care, that a breach of that care has taken place, and that damage to a person or property has been caused.

As a common law duty, an employer needs to take reasonable care of employees. In 1938, the House of Lords in the case *Wilson and Clyde Cola versus English* first stated that an employer has a duty of care to all employees. This duty is to provide safe and competent working colleagues, safe plant and equipment, safe premises to work in, and a safe system of work. In relation to the safe system of work, this needs to be both created and enacted. If any of these are breached, an employee can take action under the tort of negligence.

The tort of negligence has been developed through case law over the last century which established the circumstances whereby a duty of care was owed. In modern times the criteria for deciding whether a duty of care is owed are based on what are known as 'the Caparo tests' (i.e., if there was foreseeable damage, if there is a sufficient 'proximate' relationship between the parties, and if it is just and reasonable to impose a duty).

Once the duty of care is established, it is still up to the claimant to demonstrate that the duty has been broken in order to establish negligence. It is worth noting here that the defendant also has a responsibility to take reasonable care of themselves, otherwise contributory negligence could be established, and that the level of care expected will vary depending on the situation and the reasonably anticipated level of expertise. And added to this, for a breach of the duty of care to be properly established the risk must have been known and reasonably significant. In terms of proving that damage occurred as a result of a breach in the duty of care, it must be proven that it was a direct result of the defendant's action or lack of action, directly linked in causal terms, and that it was foreseeable.

Key Challenge – A Case in Point

One summer evening, a young man called John Walker was attending a peer education session on bullying at his local youth centre. As John made his way to the room where the event was to take place, he noticed a cleaner mopping the floor at the end of the corridor. As he approached, John slipped on the wet floor and fell, breaking his wrist. Just at that moment, the youth worker came out of her office, administered first aid, phoned for an ambulance, and recorded the incident in the accident book.

The youth worker also undertook an investigation of the incident and reported her findings to the youth manager. As a result the cleaner was clearly instructed to have signs placed on the floor when she was cleaning. Also, the cleaning of corridors and public areas was changed so that it took place first thing in the morning, in the hour before the public came into the building.

- Who do you think is responsible for the incident: the cleaner, the youth worker, or another person?
- Do you think that this incident could have been avoided?
- Do you think that the youth worker acted responsibly both during and after the event?
- Does John have grounds for compensation?

OCCUPIERS' LIABILITY

The Occupiers' Liability Act 1957 and the Occupiers' Liability Act 1984 are the two Acts of Parliament which provide the legal basis for determining the level of duty of care to a person entering your land. The first act legislates for lawful visitors while the second is an update act that recognises the rights of a 'non-visitor'. The first states that the occupier has a duty to take such care, as is reasonable, to ensure that visitors will be reasonably safe while using the premises on the basis for which they were invited. For this purpose, the lawful visitor would include an invitee, a purchasing customer of a service, a person who has implied permission to be there, and anyone on official business. It is worthy of note that whereas it may be enough to provide warning notices for adult visitors, case law recognises that young child visitors must be treated with greater care as they are more prone to dangerous situations because, for example, they may not be able to read or pay heed to warning signs.

INDEPENDENT CONTRACTOR

Further, the occupier is not usually liable for danger created by an independent contractor if they are specialists in their work, but would be liable if the danger was caused by a contractor who did not have any expert knowledge to carry out the task, for example cleaning steps. However, employers could be liable if they authorise a contractor to commit a tort where the work is extra hazardous, where the work is being carried out over a highway, and where the law states that an employer must provide a safe system of work and cannot transfer the responsibility to a contractor.

The Occupiers' Liability Act 1984 states that the occupier owes a duty of care to non-visitors (e.g., trespassers and thieves) but is limited in that the occupier needs to be aware of the danger, has reasonable grounds to believe that there are non-visitors in the vicinity of the danger, and that the risk is one against which he may be reasonably expected to offer some protection.

More specifically, in relation to employment situations an employer can be vicariously liable for the actions taken by employees when they are acting on the employer's behalf. The employer will be liable when the employee is acting in the course of their employment, and even when that employee acts carelessly and carries out work in a way that is expressly forbidden. However, the employer will not usually be liable if the employee is doing something that is not part of their employment, even if it happens in the workplace, is not acting within the scope of the agreed employment terms, or is using the employer's facilities for their own purposes.

In addition, the employer is not usually liable for the torts of employees when travelling to or from work unless during working hours and for the benefit of the employer.

Case Study

Liability and Duty of Care

Jax was the centre manager and designated responsible person at Goahead Youth Centre which was run by the local council. One summer day both Jax and Mar, a youth worker, were playing a game of mixed football with a group of 14 to 16 year olds on the patch of land outside the youth centre.

After half an hour, one of the players hit the ball onto the centre roof and was encouraged by the others to go and retrieve it. However, Jax stepped in and said that the player should not go onto the roof because she was not insured.

Jax, as the senior worker, then asked Mar to go and retrieve the ball from the roof of the centre because 'you are a fit and strong youth worker and an insured council employee'. Mar expressed some concern about undertaking this task to Jax, but the crowd of young people drowned out her protestations by urging her to go and retrieve the ball so they could resume the game.

Mar said to Jax that there was no obvious way to get onto the roof and that height was an issue. Jax laughed this off and explained that there was a ladder in the storeroom which was readily available.

Mar retrieved the ladder, set it up, climbed up it, retrieved the ball, and kicked it from the roof onto the ground where the young people were waiting. As Mar came off the roof and stepped onto the ladder it slide sideways. Mar was knocked onto the ground.

First aid was administered, an ambulance was called, and the accident was recorded in the accident book. Mar suffered a broken leg and was off work for six months.

- Who was at fault?
- Was Mar responsible for the incident because the ladder was not made secure?
- Was Jax at fault for instructing a member of staff to carry out a task that was not in the job remit and for which there was no training?
- Do you think that Mar would be entitled to sue the council for compensation because Jax was acting on its behalf?

HEALTH AND SAFETY COMPLIANCE

The Health and Safety at Work etc. Act 1974, under section 2, states that an employer is under a general duty to ensure, as far as practicable, the health, safety and welfare at work of all employees. The act specifies four main duties: to provide and maintain a safe plant, systems of work and workplace; ensure safety in the handling, storage and transport of articles and substances; provide such information, instruction, training and supervision as is necessary to ensure health and safety at work; and provide a safe working environment.

Health and safety is an important area of activity for any organisation and it can be overseen by a general manager or a youth worker in charge, but it can also be designated to a health and safety manager if the demands warrant it and resources permit. In applying health and safety law, there is a balance to be struck between the employer providing a safe system of work and employees being required to look after themselves. It is important to note that many safety laws are written as general duties which require an agreed interpretation about the ways in which these apply in practice in particular circumstances. Also, legal standards vary in their strictness, ranging from absolute compliance to 'apply if practicable'. This is often a decision based on the degree of risk compared to the level of cost.

It is necessary to be aware that there is provision for independent trade unions to appoint safety reps and committees whose job it will be to identify and advise on safety hazards. They will require facilities to carry out these duties, including time off work to do so, as these are legal safety functions under the Safety Representatives and Safety Committee Regulations 1977.

Key Challenge – Activity

- Make a list of actions, processes and procedures that would help to make any workplace a safe working environment.
- List three reasons explaining why you think that it is important for trade unions to have a key role in health and safety.

Comment

Health and safety is important for all workers and the law recognises the role of trade unions who want to make sure that their members are safe at work. They also help to make sure that protective agreements are carried out by members and that, as far as possible, there are no long-term adverse health effects for their members.

MANAGING HEALTH AND SAFETY IN BUILDINGS

There are a number of main health and safety regulations that are vital to know about and deal with when managing a building. The most obvious are building regulations, electrical safety, fire procedures, risk assessments, reporting accidents, first aid, maintaining efficient and clean premises, maintaining plant and equipment, maintaining personal protection equipment, manual handling, safe use of VDUs, and general health and safety procedures. There are also issue such as noise, stress and the use of personal equipment which are also relevant. An introduction is provided here in relation to these specific requirements.

BUILDING REGULATIONS

The main aims of building regulations are to set the rules to make new and altered buildings safe and accessible and to limit waste and environmental damage. The current set of building regulations has recently been updated. The Building (Amendment) Regulations 2012 (SI 2012/718) came into force on 6 April 2012, and the Building (Amendment) Regulations 2011 (SI 2011/1515) came into force on 15 July 2011: both of these should be read in conjunction with the Building Regulations 2010.

WORKING ENVIRONMENT

In terms of planning and developing the work, as an employer you would wish to ensure that there is adequate space to carry out the task and that there is no potential cause of injury through overcrowding or poor workstation layout.

You would also wish to make sure that the working environment is suitable through the provision of adequate heating and lighting with sufficient sanitary and welfare facilities. You would have to make certain that all workers are adequately trained and supervised where appropriate, as well as ensuring a safe and practicable system of work. While the building regulations should help ensure that stairs, gangways, floors and passageways are soundly built, it should also be your responsibility to make sure that these areas are well maintained, free from obstructions, and fitted with suitable non-slip flooring.

SUPPORT DOCUMENTS

To operate successfully in terms of general health and safety procedures, as a youth worker you will need support documents that must be signed by staff and volunteers to demonstrate that there is a working health and safety protocol supported by guidance that explains how to use the forms and what the significance is of signing such forms. The type of documents you will require include health and safety policy statements, risk assessment forms, environmental forms, and fire safety procedure records. You will also require first aid, accident and disease forms, as well as smoke free, drug free and alcohol policies. One of the most comprehensive documents will be the risk assessment forms. A manual must be kept by the organisation and made available for any audits you might have. The health and safety manual will help to assess risk and develop a plan for dealing with that risk, as well as provide the rationale for the adoption of safety policies. You should also be aware that the four most common sources of injury are bad posture, manual handling, repetitive work and vibration, and action should be taken to minimise the risks and make improvements through training for example.

PLANT EQUIPMENT

In relation to the maintenance of plant and equipment, this must be suitable and maintained, kept in good working order, and compliant with European legislation and standards. Employees must be given information on the equipment they use and effective steps must be taken to ensure non-access to dangerous part of the machinery. All machines must also have adequate controls for access, and must possess the ability to stop and isolate when required.

If the organisation has equipment that is operated by employees then procedures need to be put in place to secure a personal protection equipment document before use. This document highlights and details the risks involved to the employee in operating the machinery, and also asks the employee to acknowledge that they have been appropriately trained and know how the machine works: it also specifies all those who have the capability to run that machinery.

CLEANING

Under the regulations regarding the maintenance of efficient and clean premises, the employer needs to maintain, repair and clean their premises effectively. They must also provide pure air, reasonable temperatures, and adequate lighting in the workplace. Again, they must provide seats for employees when work can be performed sitting down, control the construction of doors, ladders and other work access arrangements, and provide adequate sanitary arrangements for all employees.

It is also worthwhile noting that cleaning materials may contain chemicals and toxic substances and the advice contained in the labelling must always be read, understood and adhered to. Staff using such products should also be provided with information, instructions and training in their proper use, and appropriately supervised as required. Under the Health and Safety at Work etc. Act 1974, manufacturers and suppliers must conduct research into the potential harm that could be caused before making these available for sale. However, this is no guarantee that a product does not cause harm and work practices should minimise the potential for inhalation, skin absorption and ingestion.

DANGEROUS SUBSTANCES

It should be noted that dangerous substances will have to be labelled under the Classifications, Packaging and Labelling of Dangerous Substances Regulations 1984 (SI No 1244), and data sheets should also be provided which, while a good potential source of information, may not be complete. The Control of Substances Hazardous to Health (COSSH) Regulations 2004 is the main legislative framework for controlling risks from chemicals and toxic substances. If you are using chemicals then you should make sure that the contents of the first aid box will enable any remedial advice to be carried out by a qualified first aider.

ELECTRICAL SAFETY

Electricity is a useful, efficient source of energy, but it needs to be treated with respect as it has the potential to cause shocks, burns, fires and even explosions. Even though a small electrical shock may not in itself cause a known harm, this may have disastrous consequences if it happens at height or the sudden reaction causes another accident to occur. Electrical shock can generally be prevented by good design, regular certified maintenance, and authorised repairs by a competent certified electrical engineer.

EMPLOYER RESPONSIBILITY

In legal terms, it is the employers' responsibility to satisfy themselves that in normal operation all live parts are inaccessible, that protection is built in against dual current by use of an earthing device that reduces the voltage, that systems are used for portable tools, and that all tools are insulated or double insulated. Also, if an electrical system is being maintained or repaired then it must have a 'permit to work' approved by an experienced and competent person to ensure that the system is dead and cannot become live inadvertently.

ELECTRICAL SAFETY REGULATIONS

The main regulations for electrical safety are: the Electricity at Work Regulations 1989; the Electrical Equipment (Safety) Regulations 1994; and the Electrical Safety, Quality and Continuity Regulations 2002 (amended in 2006 to exempt the requirement for an electricity generation licence, and in 2009 to incorporate the latest revision to the British Standard Requirements for electrical installations (BS 7671) into the ESQCR).

FIRE SAFETY

The law on fire safety in England and Wales was simplified when the Regulatory Reform (Fire Safety) Order 2005 came into force on 1 October 2006. The Order repealed the Fire Precautions Act 1971 and the Fire Precautions (Workplace) Regulations 1997 to create a simplified fire safety system. Under the order, fire and rescue authorities have the power of enforcement and can serve prohibition or improvement notices: the need to apply for a fire certificate has been removed but the requirements placed on employers remain largely the same.

FIRE PREVENTION

The system in place should ensure that all personnel are aware of, and comply with, the law relating to fire prevention and control. There are eight main elements that should be in place to help prevent fire and protect centre users: that fire policy and procedure is part of the local health and safety policy, and that fire detection and fire-fighting equipment should be regularly maintained by qualified personnel and tested by trained staff. It is also important that appropriate fire exit routes are provided and kept clear along with appropriate signage and instructions about the routes to follow and roll-call points: emergency lighting should also be checked and maintained regularly. This may involve operating a centre register that records everyone entering and leaving the building, as well as ensuring that fire safety precautions must also be brought to the attention of all new staff, volunteers, contractors or visitors. Again, a chief fire marshal, and fire marshals to cover all areas of the building, should be appointed and trained and regarded as competent persons under the law.

STAFF TRAINING

A coordinated staff training programme should be in place to ensure that everyone is trained in their respective duties and that regular evacuation drills are conducted to give staff and users practice, with the outcomes recorded to ensure that they are effective. Also, it is important to prepare and plan for any fire and security emergency, such as bomb alerts, by developing a policy which outlines the roles of key staff, their responsibilities, and the actions to be taken in the event of a major incident. Further, it is essential that flammable and easily combustible materials are appropriately stored in keeping with the Control of Substances Hazardous to Health (COSHH) Regulations 2002. Finally, all of these procedures and systems should be underpinned by a comprehensive series of risk assessments, for all areas and all activities, which must be carried out by trained personnel (note that the technical aspects of fire safety need to be conducted by trained competent persons).

ACCIDENTS AND REPORTING REQUIREMENTS

An accident can be described as an unplanned happening. In this definition the emphasis is on an occurrence that could not be reasonably predicted or measures should have been put in place to stop it from happening. There are hundreds of thousands of accidents and injuries reported every year across the UK, and hundreds of people are killed by accidents each year.

RIDDOR (the Reporting of Injuries, Diseases and Dangerous Occurrences Regulations 1995) puts duties on employers, the self-employed and people in control of work premises (the responsible person) to report serious workplace accidents, occupational diseases and specified dangerous occurrences (i.e., near misses). Youth workers should be aware of RIDDOR and comply with the stated requirements (see www.hse.gov.uk/riddor/).

The reporting of accidents is a detailed and involved procedure and should be known about by the 'responsible person' (e.g., employer, self-employed or person designated in charge, in advance of any accident happening. Information on what types of accidents and dangerous occurrences need to be reported, by whom and in what way is contained in an HSE document (A Guide to the Reporting of Injuries, Diseases and Dangerous Occurrences Regulations 1995: RIDDOR) which is available to download free from www.hse.gov.uk/pubns/priced/l73.pdf

Something to note is that one major change has recently happened: as of 6 April 2012, RIDDOR's over-three-day injury reporting requirement has increased to over seven days' incapacitation. This does not include the day on which the accident happened. The interpretation of incapacitation is 'that the worker is absent or is unable to do work that they would reasonably be expected to do as part of their normal work' (HSE, 2012).

FIRST AID

In relation to first aid requirements, there are five clear legal duties placed upon employers under the Health and Safety (First Aid) Regulations 1981. These are: to provide adequate and appropriate first aid equipment and facilities (regulation 3 (1)); to provide an adequate number of trained and qualified first aiders (regulation 3 (2)); to provide an 'appointed person' if the first aider is absent (regulation 3 (3)); in some smaller workplaces to provide an 'appointed person' in place of a first aider; and to provide information to all workers about the provision and location of first aid equipment, facilities and personnel (regulation 4) (see: www.hse.gov.uk/firstaid/legislation.htm).

FOOD HYGIENE

Where a community youth centre offers catering facilities to members and/or the general public, then food hygiene and safety legislation will need to be taken into account and adhered to. The Food Hygiene (England) Regulations apply, as do EU regulations, to premises where food is prepared, handled, cooked or stored, and which are subject to inspection by a local authority's environmental health inspector.

PROTECTIVE EQUIPMENT

Also, it is important to ensure that protective equipment including protective clothing is fit for purpose (i.e., the right type for a specific job, fits the person properly, and is regularly maintained). It is also important to remember that protective clothing is only a barrier against a hazard and does not in itself take away the danger, which means that appropriate uses and monitoring arrangements should be part of the work system. Again, the various elements of protective clothing should be compatible and this should be recognised and compensated for when protective clothing creates other problems (such as a loss of hearing for ear muffs and a lack of mobility for heavier clothing). Another series of factors which should be considered when using protective clothing includes an appropriate process for cleaning/laundering, a system of regular inspection to ensure good condition or replacement as necessary, and the systematic storing, drying and issuing of protective gear.

NOISE

Noise may not be an immediately obvious concern for the manager of a community youth centre, but there are many potential sources of noise and there are codes of practice about managing the frequency and intensity of noise. Such sources could include internal and external noise emanating from a woodwork machine (see the Provision and Use of Work Equipment Regulations 1998: Regulation 15, Stop Controls – Application to Woodworking Machinery) or the level of noise coming from a disco unit.

The external affect of noise on the area around the centre would be treated as neighbourhood noise, and it may cause what is known as a statutory nuisance which is managed by the local authority under the Environmental Protection Act 1990. There is a requirement to carry out a noise assessment. Basically, there are four ways to combat noise over and above turning a machine's volume down. These are: redesign the noise source or use an alternative method; make modifications to the existing source; block the noise transmission path; or protect the workers through reduced noise levels and limit the number of those exposed.

ARTIFICIAL LIGHT

However, it is not just noise that may prove a problem, it is also the artificial light which may form part of young people's entertainment and shows. The Royal Commission on Environmental Pollution (RCEP), in their 2009 report, expressed concern about the potential for artificial light to have an adverse ecological impact and called for further research to be undertaken.

MANUAL HANDLING

The Manual Handling Operations Regulations 1992 (as amended) outlined three main control measures to avoid hazardous manual handling by either redesigning the task to avoid moving the load or by automating or mechanising the process, or if unavoidable, by making a suitable and sufficient assessment of any hazardous manual handling operations and/or by reducing the risk of injury through mechanical assistance or changing the task, load and working environment.

ERGONOMIC ASSESSMENT

The modern-day approach is based on the idea of ergonomic assessment which takes in a holistic range of factors and options in an effort to remove or reduce the level of risk by putting the person first and at the heart of the process. Schedule 1 to the regulations posits a number of questions to help ensure that assessments are carried out in a structured manner. These five interrelated categories are: the task; the load; the working environment; individual capability (this category is discussed in more detail under regulation 4 (3) and its guidance); and other factors such as the use of protective clothing.

As manual handling can cause many long- and short-term injuries, staff should be trained in manual handling techniques if these are required as part of their job, regardless of the weight of the item to be carried, as the regulations do not state a lower or upper limit. It is also worthy of note that items of a relatively light weight can cause injury if not lifted properly, for example over-stretching to lift an item just out of reach (see Manual Handling Assessment Charts (INDG383)). All appropriate training should cover such elements as identifying manual handling risk factors and explaining with understanding the ways in which injuries can occur; practical experience of carrying out safe manual handling, including good handling techniques; outlining appropriate systems of work for the individual's task and environment; and exploring the safe use of mechanical aids. Practical demonstrable exercises will allow a suitably qualified trainer to identify and rectify anything a trainee is not doing safely. The training should also be tested and certified to demonstrate that the person is competent in safely operating manual handling procedures.

In relation to training, the guidance to the regulations states that 'Section 2 of the Health and Safety at Work Act 1974 and regulations 10 and 13 of the Management of Health and Safety at Work Regulations 1999 require employers to provide their employees with health and safety information and training. This should be supplemented as necessary with more specific information and training on manual handling injury risks and prevention, as part of the steps to reduce risk required by regulation 4(1) (b) (ii) of the Regulations' (HSE, 2012).

OFFICE PROTOCOLS (VDUS)

An office environment can quickly become a second home to a person who is using it every day and for lengthy periods of time. Office workers can become so familiar with this environment that some of the operational dangers are easily overlooked. So it is necessary to remember that the office location is a working environment and subject to general health and safety as well as specific work-based laws. The main injuries in an office environment include falls, trips and slipping, but also for example pulling muscles when reaching, bending or lifting. Hazards include cramped conditions, poor work systems, inadequate lighting, and unventilated spaces.

OFFICE MACHINERY

When planning to install office machines, consideration should be given to the noise, space and heat generated as well as making sure that maintenance processes are carried out safely. Also think about the safe use of electrical equipment, the effects of artificial lighting, and the heat levels at different times of the day. In addition, new technologies (such as computers, mobile phones and other hand-held devices) have become commonplace and integrally embedded in work practices. These devices are so handy, powerful and easy to use that doing so can become 'automatic', which may then encourage safety procedures and applications to be overlooked. In relation to the law on VDU work (the Health and Safety (Display Screen Equipment) Regulations 1992), this requires employers to analyse workstations and assess and reduce risks, and to look at the whole workstation including equipment, furniture, and the work environment, the job being done, and any special needs for individual staff.

Employees and safety representatives should be encouraged to take part in risk assessments (e.g., by reporting health problems). Where risks are identified, the employer must take steps to reduce them (see HSE Leaflet INDG136 (rev3), revised 12/06). Regular breaks should be considered as well as alternative work away from VDU screens: regular eye tests should also be offered.

STRESS

Stress is very much a modern phenomenon which is recognised as a serious work condition that needs to be prevented and dealt with appropriately when it arises. Stress can be very harmful to the physical and mental wellbeing of employees. There is little doubt that stress is more prevalent among certain groups of workers. Information taken from the 2011/12 Labour Force Survey (LFS) shows that the total number of stress cases, which has maintained similar levels over the past ten years, was recorded as 428,000, which is (40 per cent) of all work-related illnesses.

The industries that reported the highest rates of total cases of work-related stress, over a three-year average, were health, social work, education, public administration, and defence. The main work activities identified as causing or contributing to work-related stress were work pressure, a lack of managerial support, and work-related violence and bullying. Clearly steps should be taken to make sure that this does not happen in youth work settings. The sources of work stress can also be down to the work environment (e.g., noise and overcrowding), contractual issues (e.g., low pay and the unsocial hours worked), the job design (e.g., isolation, a lack of supervision), and relationships (e.g., poor relations with a supervisor or poor communication).

Although there is no direct law dealing with work-related stress, there are a number of laws and regulations that can be used to deal with its causes including an employer's requirement for a duty of care.

Scenarios: Consider the following situations and consider what action you would take.

1. You are a youth worker and you walk into a room in the youth centre and notice that a CD player is plugged into the wall with wires showing from the base of the plug.
2. You are a centre manager and a worker comes to you and says that he gets daily headaches after working on the computer for a couple of hours.
3. As the centre manager, on a routine safety inspection you note that three fire extinguishers have been let off and are empty, safety notices have been pulled from doors and walls, and the accident book is missing.
4. You think that your colleague may be suffering from stress because she lacks her usual commitment level, is fearful of doing detached youth work, and feels she cannot connect with the young people any more.

Comment

Health and Safety is an important area of practice which is sometimes overlooked or minimised. It covers so many areas that there is a mountain of information guidance and duties. There are also many myths and excuses for inaction attributed to health and safety concerns. It would be worthwhile for youth workers to undertake a NEBOSH qualification to help ensure an increase in knowledge and their ability to assess health and safety implications. Details and advice on health and safety matters may be obtained from www.hse.gov.uk/guidance/index.htm

---

CONCLUSION

In this chapter we have identified the nature of negligence in law and explored the employer's duty of care towards employees and service users. You have also received information about the nature and extent of occupiers' liability as well as an explanation about the importance of being health and safety compliant. This chapter explained the need to be aware of health and safety legislation, especially in terms of managing a building, and offered information on the requirement to provide safe systems of work. It also drew out a range of legal requirements for recording and reporting accidents and dangerous occurrences, and specified ways of looking after people.

The information provided in this chapter is of a general nature and does not cover every aspect of operation that may be required when managing a community facility. There may be a need, for example, to ensure that young people are protected from the hazards associated with hand tools if the centre has a woodwork shop that they use, and similarly you would need to comply with machinery guarding which requires compliance with a number of acts.

Again, issues like violence may need to be addressed as part of the proper management of the youth service. It should be an established benchmark that no one should be subject to violence at work, and procedures should be put in place to ensure that this does not happen, and where it does, action should be taken. Remember that, under the Health and Safety at Work Act, employers need to provide safe methods of working, safe workplaces, a safe working environment, and information, instruction and training for staff.

Finally, there may be times when hosting celebratory events that fireworks may be used. In this case you should make sure that safety advice is followed in the purchase, storage and lighting of fireworks in keeping with the Firework Legislation 2004. For example, 'adult' fireworks (category 2 and 3, not sparklers and party poppers) cannot be bought or used by those under the age of 18, and it's against the law for anyone to set off fireworks between 11 pm and 7 am (except on Bonfire Night when the cut-off is midnight, and New Year's Eve, Diwali and Chinese New Year when the cut-off is 1 am).

The National Organisation of Local Voluntary Youth Centres (NOLVYC) is an organisation which has been based in London since its inception in 1926.

The organisation appointed a new chief executive last year who replaced Sir Jasper Coldneck who had held the office for over forty years. The board were impressed with the energetic plans that the new appointee outlined at interview, which spoke of member involvement, change management, and challenging the status quo.

Some of the early actions that the chief executive has undertaken were to conduct an internal management review, establish a monthly member newsletter, and host a series of events for politicians, the public sector, business leaders and the chairs of local associations.

In addition to these developments the organisation has held a comprehensive series of local seminars across England to determine how effectively it is representing its members and establish the basis of a strategic plan that will direct and focus the organisation's activities over the next five years.

Overwhelmingly the main issue to emerge from the consultation was that organisations did not feel they got valued support for their annual subscription fee, and they have been asking, for a number of years, for direct support from the organisation to ensure that their youth centres are operating legally and efficiently.

You are a youth worker who has recently been employed by the new chief executive, and you have been asked to respond to this concern by devising a robust plan to resolve this issue.

Questions

Given what you now know:

- What would your approach be?
- What are the main actions you would take?
- Who would your main targets be?
- What timescale would you operate to?

Case Study 8

Summary of Key Points

- The Law of Tort affects a range of operational issues and employment situations.
- An employer has a duty of care to provide safe, competent working colleagues, safe plant and equipment, safe premises to work in, and a safe system of work.
- Occupiers' Liability refers to the level of duty of care to a person entering your land or premises.
- The Health and Safety at Work etc. Act 1974, under section 2, states that an employer is under a general duty to ensure that, as far as practicable, the health, safety and welfare at work of all employees.
- There are a number of main health and safety regulations that are important to know about and deal with when managing a building, including fire procedures, electrical safety, risk assessments, reporting accidents, first aid, maintaining efficient and clean premises, maintaining plant and equipment, maintaining personal protection equipment, manual handling, the safe use of VDUs, and general health and safety procedures for specific activities.
- There are also issues like noise, stress and the use of personal equipment which are also relevant, as well as managing specific activities like woodwork and metalwork and other concerns, for example, violence and fireworks.

REFERENCES

All of the publications referred to below are available from HSE Books, PO Box 1999, Sudbury, Suffolk CO10 2WA (Tel: 01787 881165 Fax: 01787 313995)

Building (Amendment) Regulations 2011. Available at www.legislation.gov.uk/uksi/2011/1515/contents/made (last accessed 06.01.14).

Building (Amendment) Regulations 2012. Available at www.legislation.gov.uk/uksi/2012/718/contents/made (last accessed 06.01.14).

Cleaner Neighbourhoods and Environment Act 2005

Control of Pollution Act 1974

COSHH Regulations 2004. Available at www.legislation.gov.uk/uksi/2004/3386/contents/made (last accessed 16.01.14).

Directive 2002/49/EC relating to the assessment and management of environmental noise: *The Environmental Noise Directive* (END)

Electricity at Work Regulations 1989. Available at www.hse.gov.uk/lau/lacs/19-3.htm

Electrical Equipment (Safety) Regulations 1994. Available at www.legislation.gov.uk/uksi/1994/3260/contents/made

Electrical Safety, Quality and Continuity Regulations 2002. Available at www.legislation.gov.uk/uksi/2002/2665/contents/made (last accessed 06.01.13).

Electricity Act 1989 (Exemption from the Requirement for a Generation Licence) (England and Wales) Order 2006. Available at www.legislation.gov.uk/uksi/2006/2978/memorandum/contents (last accessed 06.12.13).

Electricity Safety, Quality and Continuity (Amendment Regulations) 2009. Available at www.legislation.gov.uk/uksi/2009/639/note/made (last accessed 10.12.12).

Environmental Noise (England) Regulations 2006

Environmental Protection Act 1990

Fireworks Legislation 2004. Available at www.legislation.gov.uk/uksi/2004/1836/contents/made

Food Hygiene Regulations 2006. Available at www.legislation.gov.uk/uksi/2006/14/contents/made (last accessed 15.01.13).

Full Regulatory Impact Assessment (PDF 200 KB) for Environmental Noise (England) Regulations 2006, SI 2006.2238.

Health and Safety at Work etc. Act 1974. Available at www.legislation.gov.uk/ukpga/1974/37 (last accessed 06.06.13).

Health and Safety (First Aid) Regulations 1981. Available at www.hse.gov.uk/pubns/priced/l74.pdf (last accessed 24.01.2014).

HSE www.hse.gov.uk/guidance/index.htm (last accessed 06.12.2013).

HSE: A Guide to the Reporting of Injuries, Diseases and Dangerous Occurrences Regulations 1995. Available at www.hse.gov.uk/pubns/priced/l73.pdf (last accessed 10.02.13).

HSE leaflet INDG136 (rev3), revised 12/06. Available at www.hse.gov.uk/pubns/indg36.pdf (last accessed 15.02.13).

HSE (2004) *Manual Handling: Manual Handling Operations Regulations 1992 (as amended): Guidance on Regulations* L23 (third edition). (ISBN 0 7176 2823 X, Manual handling assessment charts (INDG383)).

Noise Act 1996, amended in 2008 by The Environmental Noise (England) (Amendment) Regulations 2008, amended in 2009 by The Environmental Noise (England) (Amendment) Regulations 2009, amended in 2010 by The Environmental Noise (England) (Amendment) Regulations 2010.

Noise and Statutory Nuisance Act 1993

Occupiers' Liability Act 1957. Available at www.legislation.gov.uk/ukpga/Eliz2/5-6/31/contents (last accessed 10.01.14).

Occupiers' Liability Act 1984. Available at www.legislation.gov.uk/ukpga/1984/3/contents (last accessed 10.01.14).

Provision and Use of Work Equipment Regulations 1998: Regulation 15, Stop Controls – Application to Woodworking Machinery.

Regulatory Reform (Fire Safety) Order 2005. Available at www.legislation.gov.uk/uksi/2005/1541/contents/made (last accessed 12.01.14).

Safety Representatives and Safety Committee Regulations1977. Available at www.legislation.gov.uk/uksi/1977/500/contents/made (last accessed 20.02.13).

9

CHILD PROTECTION

Chapter Aims

- Provide an introduction to the historical background about concern for children and the prevalence of child abuse
- Outline the significance of international agencies in establishing the rights and protection of children
- Denote the changing understandings in society about the nature of childhood and expectations of children
- Place the legislative framework on safeguarding children within a UK and devolved context
- Articulate the roles, procedures and knowledge that a youth worker should be aware of to carry out their work with young people successfully
- Provide information around the different definitions, explanations and categories of abuse
- Draw out a range of safeguarding principles, procedures and systems to ensure effective youth work practice

INTRODUCTION

The Prevention of Cruelty to, and Protection of, Children Act of 1889, the Children's Charter, was England's first comprehensive law to protect the welfare of children. The law established legal penalties for the mistreatment and abandonment of girls under the age of 16 and boys under the age of 14 (note the gender variance). This law restricted the employment of children in taverns and banned them from begging. It also gave power to local magistrates to issue warrants to search premises where mistreatment of children was suspected.

Thus it could be argued that across the UK, throughout the last century and before, in certain quarters of society at least, concern for the welfare of children was recorded in literature and more recently, and increasingly, in domestic and international legislation. This progeny angst, recognised and acted upon mainly by adults motivated by Christian values, led to the establishment of such organisations as the YMCA by Sir George Williams in 1844, the Save the Children fund by Eglantyne Jebb in 1909, and the Scout Movement by Robert Baden-Powell in 1916.

FOUNDATIONS OF YOUTH WORK

In fact, the foundations of youth work were established out of a concern for the plight of children as they grew into young people and their needs and treatment changed, which was recognised and met through innovative work by concerned adults running Sunday schools, ragged schools and youth's institutes which all developed towards the end of the nineteenth century and into the beginning of the twentieth century. Such leaders, and their subsequent movements, helped to influence the changing discourse, over a substantial period of time, about the expectations placed on children and the ways in which they were valued and viewed by families, institutions and society. All countries across the UK have a legislative history of attempting to protect children, although such attempts are generally reactionary, partial and incremental.

THE UK RECORD

Although England's history of child protection laws dates back to the 1889 Children's Charter, this does not denote any sort of elongated pedigree in prioritising children's welfare and rights. In fact, in international terms the UK has a poor record of protecting children's rights and a joint House of Lords and Commons Committee looking at children's rights in the UK 2008–09 expressed a range of continued concerns about the government's ability to protect children's rights. The committee reported on both UNICEF and Child Poverty Action Group (CPAG) research which 'suggests that children's rights are not being adequately respected and promoted in the UK' (HL Paper 157, HC 318, 2009) due to the extremely low levels of wellbeing and poverty experienced by children. The committee also noted that the UNCRC found that the society in the UK was generally intolerant and negative towards children and this was evident in the way that many vulnerable children were treated in the criminal justice system which, for example, leads to questioning the effectiveness of legislation such as ASBOs.

THE PREVALENCE OF CHILD ABUSE

As a reader and practitioner you would be right to question, at the outset, how prevalent child abuse is and whether this focus on prevention is necessary. While it is difficult to assess accurately, given the circumstances of secrecy and power in which such crimes take place, at the turn of the twenty-first century it was estimated that 750,000 children would have suffered from abuse by the time they reach 18 years of age, and of that number 400,000 will have been sexually abused; 72 per cent of sexually abused children did not tell anyone about the abuse at the time, although 27 per cent told someone later. Approximately a third had still not told anyone about their experience(s) by early adulthood (Cawson, 2000). In 2011, for example, almost 21,000 allegations of children suffering abuse were passed from the NSPCC to police or children's services (NSPCC, 2012).

AWARENESS OF CHILDREN'S RIGHTS

In today's society, it is important that professional youth workers have a developed awareness of children's' rights, are familiar with what constitutes abuse, and demonstrate a practice which is informed, healthy and protection-based along a series of safeguarding principles. All organisations that work with children should be familiar with their local child protection procedures, have policies that state what staff and volunteers should do if they are worried about a child's wellbeing, and follow best practice in keeping children safe. A key part of a youth worker's job is to possess the appropriate attitudes, values and knowledge which will help to protect and empower young people to make informed decisions about their lives, and will also help to ensure that their voice is heard as enshrined in the UN International Treaty, adopted as the Convention of the Rights of Children 1991 in the UK.

Over and above the role of youth workers, it is surely the responsibility of parents and all adults in society to help ensure that children and young people receive the support and encouragement to achieve their potential and to be all they can be. It should be recognised that all children must be protected from all forms of violence as to physically hurt a child deliberately, for any purpose, is not acceptable. Parental disciplining is a case in point, where we need to break the cycle of dominance by supporting parents to apply positive methods of sanctions, so that children and young people are treated with dignity and respect and given the same legal protection from assault that adults possess and in keeping with section 58 of the Children Act 2004. These issues of maltreatment are international issues that are being made more obvious through mass communication, and which will only be resolved by international agreement to set the standards and expectations of the way children should be treated, ensuring that intentions and commitments are transformed into positive and lasting action.

LEGISLATIVE FRAMEWORK

Internationally, the first formal Declaration of the Rights of the Child, in 1924, was endorsed by the League of Nations which was the predecessor of the United Nations, which went on to establish the UN Declaration of Rights of the Child in 1959 and the

International Year of the Child in 1979. However, it was the Convention on the Rights of the Child adopted, in 1989, by the General Assembly that was unquestionably the most significant milestone in the development of child policies across the world. Only ten months after its adoption, the convention had obtained the 20 ratifications from member states that were required for it to come into force as international law. Its importance as a foundation for modern human rights law was later emphasised at the 1993 World Conference on Human Rights in Vienna. This legislation was a watershed in shifting the focus away from adults' responsibility to providing protection for children, and moving to a recognition of their own civil and political rights through, inter alia, article 12. Much of the thinking and action taken in child protection processes are based on this legislation.

INTERNATIONAL LEGISLATION

Due to this international legalisation the systemisation of child protection, with its defined terminology and processes, has become a more recognisable issue in recent decades as children's rights are progressively recognised and their wellbeing is given greater consideration socially and culturally. However, this is not true in every country and culture as many children, in many parts of the word, still suffer horrendous conditions of poverty, have no access to education, and have little familial or community protection from human traffickers and other forms of abuse. Notwithstanding, mainly due to the UN Convention on Children's Rights for example, adopted in the UK in 1991, there is a more general acceptance of children's rights not only to care and protection but in ensuring that their best interests, as rights, should be protected and promoted. Given this relatively recent sea change in approach, there is still room for improvement in terms of the ways in which society effectively and holistically supports children's development and potential. The fact remains that in spite of an increased awareness of child protection, supported by continuous review with increased specified standards and procedures for inter-agency working, there continues to be significant examples of children being abused and children killed. On average, every week in England and Wales at least one child is killed at the hands of another person (Smith et al., 2011).

THE UNITED NATIONS CONVENTION ON THE RIGHTS OF THE CHILD

As treaties go, the UN Convention on the Rights of the Child (CRC) is the most popularly sanctioned accord of all the United Nations' human rights treaties. The treaty establishes the fundamental human rights of all children who are less than 18 years of age. It has proven to be a very useful agreement because the CRC provides a complete and acknowledged international standard on children's rights and provides the operating structure for the actions of UNICEF, the UN children's agency.

Important as this document is, there is also a range of other UN documents, covenants and instruments which internationally protect children's rights. Some of these are, for example, the Universal Declaration of Human Rights, the International Covenant of Economic, Social and Cultural Rights, the International Covenant on Civil and Political Rights, and the International Labour Organisation Conventions.

It is recognised that signing the treaty is not an end in itself and will not, on its own, improve the protection of children. Therefore, the monitoring and evaluation of the undertakings and obligations as given by member states when ratifying this treaty are carried out by the United Nations Committee on the Rights of the Child. This adjudication process includes a requirement for countries that have ratified the treaty, to present regular reports to the committee, stating the extent to which children's rights are being advanced and put into practice. This system recognises that understandings and practices around work with children are influenced by history and culture, as well as social and economic conditions, which is why actions need to be monitored and promoted in light of children's rights.

THE CHANGING PERCEPTIONS OF CHILDHOOD

It is significant to note that the notion of childhood is a social construct which has changed, and continues to change over time. (For a discussion around the origins and construction and position of childhood see Coster, 2007.) Youth workers should also recognise that childhood is a concept that relates strongly to the way society is organised and contextualised in relation to the historical, socio-economic and cultural dimensions of society.

In the eighteenth century, for example, children were regarded mainly as family possessions who were dependent on adults and 'should be seen but not heard'. Aries (1962) argued that children were viewed as small adults, and that the notion of childhood was absent from people's language and therefore only later became a concept that was used in the modern period. In more recent times children have been viewed as people with rights (UNCRC, 1989; UN, 1989) who have a voice to be heard and a role to participate in citizenship matters.

This positive change in the way that children and young people are viewed has brought with it a language and terminology which describe the processes, systems and intentions in place to help ensure that children and young people are treated appropriately. The process of *safeguarding* has been defined as a way of *'protecting children from maltreatment, preventing the impairment of children's health and development and ensuring that children grow up in circumstances consistent with safe, effective care'* (DCSF, 2010: 34). Also, child protection is viewed as *'a part of safeguarding and promoting welfare and refers to activities which protect those suffering or at risk of significant harm'* (DCSF, 2010: 35). Under the Children Act 1989, section 31, significant harm is *'the ill treatment or the impairment of health and development'*, and where this occurs there is a requirement to start child protection procedures in keeping with the employer's procedures that have been made clear during training.

CHANGING EXPECTATIONS

It is also the case that work with children and families has changed over the past twenty years, moving from managing risk to early intervention and prevention (Cronin and Smith, 2010), and that the role and expectation of the youth worker are to help ensure that, as part of universal children's services, the communication routes are strengthened to support early intervention practices. This proactive change could be viewed as an approach concomitant with the duty to safeguard and promote welfare outlined in the Children's Act 2004, section 11.

Reflective Questions

Having read the first section in this chapter, answer the following questions.

1. Why do you think that international and domestic legislation is needed to protect children?
2. Do you think that legislation alone will ensure that children's rights are respected?
3. In what ways does this legislation affect the way in which youth workers deliver services?

Comment

You are thinking along the right lines if you have identified that the world is becoming closer through mass communication and globalisation and that constructions of childhood have taken on international dimensions. Historically, the record of promoting the wellbeing of children is generally poor in both advanced and developing countries. Legislation is required internationally to articulate the principles and set the standards that countries should aspire to meet, and domestic legislation is needed to translate these into practice by holding people to account when this does not happen. Also, legislation alone is not enough and it will require all professionals to work together, improve communication, and intervene early on so that children and young people are able to be all that they can be. Youth workers hold young people at the heart of the process, being aware of their environmental circumstances, and work with other professionals to ensure that each young person's rights are recognised, articulated and honoured.

UK LEGISLATION

This section on the UK legislative situation around child protection matters has not been easy to construct for three main reasons. The first is that legislation concerning children in the UK is largely a devolved matter which comes under the jurisdiction of the respective Scottish Parliament and the Welsh and Northern Ireland Assemblies. The second reason is that Scotland has always operated its own separate and independent legal system, and the third is that the legislation around child protection has continuously mushroomed before and since devolution, and the legislation, policies and practice frameworks have increasingly reflected the political power and local circumstances that have brought in variance in the direction, approaches and emphases in different parts of the UK.

Within the past twenty years or so, there has been a range of publications and guidance notes around the issues of child protection. These include legislative requirements, commissions, research advice, and information from Government departments (the Home Office, DHSS, and DfES/DOH).

LEGISLATIVE BACKGROUND

Therefore there is no single piece of legislation that provides for all child protection procedures. Instead, there is a range of historic and more recent pieces of legislation which have aimed to protect children from harm, for example, the various factories acts (1802–1961) which increasingly improved conditions and limited working hours for children. However, one of the older pieces of child protection legislation that still has relevance today is the Children and Young Persons Act 1933 which, for the first time, outlined a list of Schedule One offences against children. However, in the current debate on child protection matters, readers in England would want to be familiar with the foundational Children Act 1989 and the Children Act 2004 ('Every Child Matters') which outlines what action to take on suspicion that a child is being abused: *Working Together to Safeguard Children: A Guide to Inter-agency Working to Safeguard and promote the Welfare of Children* (DCSF, 2010) is also the coalition government's most recent statement on child protection.

CHILDREN ACT 1989

The current child protection system in England is founded on the Children Act 1989, which aimed to bring clarity and consistency to the different laws concerning children's welfare. At its introduction, it was claimed to be both an important and extensive reform based on a set of principles which promoted the centrality of the child's welfare in decision making, took into account the child's wishes and feelings, and recognised the importance of defending the child's home and family relationships.

This 1989 law also brought in the idea of parental responsibility in relation to 'the child and his property' (section 3) and outlined specifically the action required by both local authorities and the courts to protect children's welfare. Local authorities had a 'duty to investigate if they have reasonable cause to suspect that a child in their area is suffering, or is likely to suffer, significant harm' (section 47) and also a duty to provide 'services for children in need, their families and others' (section 17).

This act also provided, in section 31, the basis of definitions for such terms as what constitutes 'harm'(which includes sexual abuse and other forms of ill-treatment) or the impairment of physical or mental health or a lack of development involving the physical, intellectual, emotional, social or behavioural.

What was not been defined in this law was the term 'significant' which meant that the court must decide what is significant based on the merits of each case and such judgements will be subsequently be used by forming case law.

Under this act case reviews need to be conducted following the death or serious injury of a child, and although local authorities have a mandatory duty to investigate if they are informed a child may be at risk, there are no specific mandatory child abuse reporting laws in the UK, except for Northern Ireland, that require professionals to report their suspicions to the authorities.

CHILDREN ACT 2004

Since the Children Act 1989 many new laws have been passed to strengthen the ways in which children are protected, including the Children Act 2004 which came about following the death of 8-year-old Victoria Climbié in 2000 and the government's response to Lord Laming's report in 2003. Other pieces of legislation include laws to recognise the rights of children, protect victims, monitor offenders, improve structures and processes, and tackle domestic violence. In addition to the civil laws that outline the obligations of public bodies to protect children, there are also laws that protect children by monitoring adults who pose a risk to children by making specific the offences with which such people can be charged, as well as preventing them from working with children.

RECENT REVIEW

Although much of this legislation is still relevant there has been a change in thinking and approach following the election of a Conservative/Liberal Democrat coalition government in May 2010. One of this government's earliest actions was to ask Professor Eileen Munro to conduct an independent review of children's social work and child protection practice in England. It was said at the time that the aim of the review was to tackle a bureaucratic operational culture which prioritised ticking boxes over effectively dealing with children's needs and circumstances. The subsequent Munro review of child protection in May 2011 saw faults on many sides, and argued for a more child-focused system and a reduction in prescriptive timescales and targets from central government. 'A child-centred system: the government's response to the Munro review' (DfE, July 2011) accepted all but one of Munro's recommendations, and laid out a programme of changes over the coming years.

ENGLISH AND UK WIDER LEGISLATION

In 1991 the United Kingdom ratified the UNCRC (Convention on the Rights of a Child). In 1997 the Sex Offenders Act 1997 created the sex offenders' notification arrangements through a series of monitoring and reporting requirements. The following year, the Human Rights Act 1998 enshrined the principles of the European Convention of Human Rights in UK law. This does not explicitly refer to the protection of children, but it does recognise that children are classed as persons and should therefore be given the same protection as adults. In 2003 the Sexual Offences Act made changes to the sexual crimes' laws in England and Wales, and to some extent other parts of the UK, bringing in a series of alterations to sex offender notification arrangements. Scotland has its own Sexual Offences (Scotland) Act 2009. The Safeguarding Vulnerable Groups Act 2006 was also passed to establish vetting and barring arrangements for England and Wales, and established the remit of the Independent Safeguarding Authority which works in Northern Ireland to prevent unsuitable adults working with children and makes barring decisions. The Protection of Freedoms Act 2012 (UK-wide) became law in the UK. It will see the scrapping of the vetting and barring scheme and the creation of a new Disclosure and Barring Service to oversee a streamlined barring regime that will restrict the scope of the 'vetting and barring' scheme for protecting vulnerable groups, as well as make changes to the system for criminal record checks. It will also bring in a new framework for police retention of fingerprints and DNA data, and require schools to get parents' consent before processing children's biometric information.

SCOTLAND

The main recent acts pertaining to protecting children in Scotland are the Children (Scotland) Act 1995 and the Protection of Children (Scotland) Act 2003. Interestingly, the Children (Scotland) Act 1995 and the Children (Northern Ireland) Order 1995 share the same principles but have their own guidance (i.e., 'Co-operating to safeguard children', DHSSPS, 2003).

GETTING OUR PRIORITIES RIGHT

One of the latest activities by the Scottish government in protecting children's rights in Scotland has been the updating and publication of *Getting Our Priorities Right* (GOPR), which is a good practice framework for child and adult service practitioners working with vulnerable children affected by problematic parental alcohol and/or drug use. The document has been revised in keeping with the Getting it Right for Every Child (GIRFEC) approach which focuses on early intervention and 'whole family recovery'.

As the Scottish government has responsibility for child protection in Scotland, it has published the national guidance for child protection in Scotland ([C9Q3]Scottish

Government, 2010). This guidance is in four parts, providing a section on definitions and concepts, principles and standard for child protection, information sharing and recording protocols, and references to relevant legislation. The second part describes the roles and responsibilities for child protection, including collective responsibility, single and shared responsibilities, and wider planning links including a range of partnerships. The third part details the way in which concerns about children are identified and responded to, including the assessment and management of risk and the process of assessment, investigation and management. The final part deals with a range of specific issues including domestic abuse and parental alcohol and drug misuse, as well as unexpected death, mental health, forced marriages and bullying.

WHAT TO DO?

In Scotland, anyone who has a concern about the welfare of a child should report this through one of five channels: their local authority child protection team (a telephone number including an out-of-hours contact should be made publicly available); the National Child Protection Line in Scotland on 0800 022 3222; the NSPCC by phone on 0808 800 5000; the Children's Reporter local office or by emailing childrensservices@ scra.gsi.gov.uk; or in case of an emergency the Scottish Police Service.

PUBLICATION

In addition, some recent activity in Scotland has seen the publication of the *National Framework for Child Protection Learning and Development in Scotland 2012*, which sets out a common set of skills and standards for workers to ensure the delivery of a consistently high standard of support to children and young people across the country. The main aim is to strengthen the skills and training of professionals and improve the advice and tools available when assessing, managing and minimising the risks faced by some of our most vulnerable children and young people. You may find this useful resource and it is available for download from: www.scotland.gov.uk/Topics/People/ Young-People/protecting/child-protection/national-framework-cp-learning-2012

WALES

The current guidance for protecting children in Wales is the *NAFWC12/07 Safeguarding Children: Working Together under the Children Act 2004* (Welsh Assembly Government, 2006/2007). The Welsh Assembly government has issued guidance for the bodies named in Sections 28 and 31 of the Children Act 2004, and it is intended to assist these organisations to review their current policies, procedures and practices and decide on the appropriate steps to take in order to implement the guidance.

This is aimed at all levels of officers involved in protecting children, from chief officers to front-line practitioners. The Welsh Assembly government has adopted seven core aims which are intended to ensure that children and young people have access to quality services and that their rights are respected.

One of the most recent pieces of guidance on child protection by the Welsh government has been the *Child Sexual Exploitation Safeguarding Guidance 2011*.

NORTHERN IRELAND

Northern Ireland has a range of orders and acts which govern its child protection operations. The Children (Northern Ireland) Order 1995 came into law in Northern Ireland and was enabled a year later in 1996. The order set out the responsibilities of authorities to provide services to children in need and their families, to provide for and support looked-after children, and to investigate children who were at risk and take appropriate action. Also, the Safeguarding Vulnerable Groups (Northern Ireland) Order 2007 replaced the Protection of Children and Vulnerable Adults (Northern Ireland) Order 2003, while the Sexual Offences (Northern Ireland) Order 2008 modernised sexual offences' legislation in Northern Ireland, bringing it largely into line with that in England and Wales, including lowering the age of consent from 17 to 16.

The Criminal Justice (Northern Ireland) Order 2008 initiated the introduction of statutory Public Protection Arrangements on a statutory basis to enhance the quality and improve the effectiveness of managing the risks posed by sexual and violent offenders released back into the community. In 2011 the Safeguarding Board Act (Northern Ireland) 2011 became law and provided the legal basis for the establishment of a new regional Safeguarding Board for Northern Ireland (SBNI), along with the establishment of safeguarding panels and committees to assist board operations.

Key Challenge – Selective Research

Choose one of the four parts that make up the UK, England, Wales, Scotland or Northern Ireland. Make a list of the most recent relevant legislation, policies or guidance that relate to child protection, sexual offences and safeguarding arrangements.

Comments

It may prove useful to choose the place where you are currently working or where you plan to work. You will know by now that there are differences in emphasis and approach across the various parts of the UK. Although there is some evidence of respective governments sharing information and having consistent approaches, especially when applying laws to people moving across the various parts, it is still important for social practitioners to be familiar with the legal framework, operating policies and guidance in their respective area.

DEFINITIONS AND CATEGORIES OF ABUSE

In today's society many different forms of abuse are recognised, including physical, emotional, sexual, neglect, and a failure to thrive. In definitional terms, *physical abuse* is the actual or attempted physical injury to a child. *Emotional abuse* takes place when a child's basic emotional needs are not met which is likely to have a negative effect on that child's behaviour and development. Examples of emotional abuse include ridiculing, threatening behaviour, constant unwarranted criticism, bullying and intimidation. *Sexual abuse* is deemed to have taken place when any person or persons, by design or neglect, exploits a child, directly or indirectly, in any activity that is intended to lead to the sexual gratification of that person or persons. *Neglect* happens when a child's basic needs (food, warmth, clothing, safety and wellbeing) are not met sufficiently to enable their secure and safe development. *Failure to thrive* occurs when a child fails to meet expected growth and development targets due to a lack of nutrition, poor physical care and a lack of emotional support.

UNDERSTANDING ABUSE

It is important to recognise that there are no acceptable reasons for the abuse of children, but in order to deal with it successfully we need to have some understanding of the causes so that we can identify risk situations, look to mitigate the circumstances, and deal effectively with the problems. No one can state with any certainty why abuse occurs, or how to prevent it, as explanations are dependent on the author's view of the world. Explanations are mainly offered around issues of poor experiences, limited capacities, poor choices and/or social conditions, but abuse continues to happen around the world and across cultures and conditions.

THEORETICAL POSITIONS

Drawing from the academic literature (Corby, 2000; Wilson and James, 2007) there are three main hypotheses about why abuse happens. However, we need to remember that theories are not revealed truth and will change over time and depending on the circumstances and purpose (Mintzberg, 2005).

The first theory, based on a psychological perspective, suggests that abuse may have something to do a person's instinctive and psychological wellbeing which is linked to a biological or innate way of behaving. Also, it may be partly due to the inability of the abuser's main carer to control and manage that person's behaviour during childhood.

The second theory, drawn from a social psychological perspective, concentrates on the way in which the person relates to the immediate environment. This theoretical viewpoint holds that it has something to do with the poor quality of family relationships and that the individual's behaviour seems to be separate from social norms and understandings of acceptable behaviour.

The third hypothesis, emanating out of the feminist tradition within sociology (although functionalist or structuralist standpoints would offer different ideas), highlights the prevailing social and political circumstances which include the patriarchal nature of society and the subsequent use of power which disadvantages both women and children. It is argued that the inequality within society shows itself in other social issues like domestic abuse which has received some increased recognition in social policy.

For professional practice in youth work, it is necessary to recognise that there are many different situations in which children are reared and not all of these will be healthy and protective environments. For example, abusive familial settings are often characterised in the literature by collapsed boundaries where the child may feel, or actually be, responsible for the welfare of parents (see Harris, 2011). In such circumstances children and young people themselves, along with their professional helpers, need to find ways of understanding and working effectively in these challenging conditions.

RISK FACTORS

Risk factors are crucial to identify in order that we can recognise the potential situations in which families and communities are unable to safeguard their children and young people. As a background to this we need to recognise that abuse can be carried out within the family, by members or friends, that abuse can be perpetrated by peers, that the young person themself may be an abuser, and that a young person can put themself in danger by engaging in risky behaviour.

Therefore we can identify a range of risk factors that may make abuse more likely to happen. Based on the work of academics (e.g., Finkelhor et al., 1990; Gregg, 1995) it may prove useful to categorise these risk factors into the five dimensions of family, parenting, child, health, and environment.

PROTECTIVE/RESILIENCE FACTORS

To balance against the risk factors, a range of protective factors are also recognised in work done by Garmezy et al. (1984) that was based on the three notions of compensation, challenge and immunity. These ideas are that a person can protect themself from the negative effects of circumstances by having personal qualities or support which negate the stress. Alternatively, the individual is able to use the situation as a challenge and then build competence from it, and/or the child is able to adapt to the uncertain and changing circumstances with apparent ease. For youth workers to build protective factors into their practice then they would aim to create opportunities for developing a greater sense of self-worth, thereby enhancing proactive self-help skills, promoting healthy attitudes with helpful thinking routines, and ensuring appropriate and empowering levels of support.

Reflection/Action — How Would You Respond?

1. A colleague comes up to you and states that all these safeguarding processes are undermining professional trust and are only relevant for managers trying to catch those who abuse children.
2. A child comes up to you and tells you, for the first time, that his best friend has called him bad names.

Comment

It could be argued that an effective youth worker is a person who has good self knowledge, an awareness and appreciation of others, and an understanding of how the ways that society is organised can limit some people's opportunities and adversely affect their ability to make the most of their potential. Such knowledge would be translated into practice by recognising that good safeguarding systems and processes can help to protect and value both children and youth workers. It is also about ensuring that the operating environment is safe, challenging, fun and nourishing, where harm is minimised, and where harm has occurred that the person is listened to and believed and appropriate action is taken.

In answer to the second question, as in any situation the circumstances and context will be important, but the fact that they are friends, and that this is the first time, may influence the way you handle the situation. However, what is important is that the young person is affirmed in his action to tell (i.e., he is believed and it will be dealt with appropriately). You may then wish to have a quiet word with the culprit, check out the circumstances from their perspective, and advise that such a course of action (i.e., calling people names) is not acceptable. If the person does not act positively to the advice or if it happens again then it will need to be discussed with colleagues and addressed within the group. The incident should be recorded appropriately within the organisation's guidelines in case the situation escalates.

SAFEGUARDING PRINCIPLES, PROCEDURES AND SYSTEMS FOR YOUTH WORK

In youth work practice, sound safeguarding principles will need to be consistent with recognised management and organisational procedures. This starts with a robust set of recruitment procedures which will ensure that the most suitable candidates are appointed to work with those at risk. From the start of employment, a youth worker should receive a thorough induction programme that should include being given in writing, by an appropriately responsible person in the organisation, a list of clear job roles and a note on work expectations and standards of behaviour, along with a defined communication and reporting structure. As a youth worker you should be made aware of the organisation's policies and procedures and should receive regular support and supervision as well as regular and appropriate training for the roles undertaken.

SAFEGUARDING CODE OF GOOD PRACTICE

In addition to legally and operationally robust organisational and management practices, the employing organisation should also have a specified written Safeguarding Code of Good Practice. Such a code should seek to safeguard the welfare, safety and wellbeing of people of all ages who are involved in any capacity (employed, volunteers or service users) within the organisation. The organisation should also articulate and accept the responsibility for everyone to work together to prevent the physical, sexual, or emotional abuse or neglect of children, young people and adults at risk. Under the law it must also be able to demonstrate that all reasonable steps have been taken to create a safe environment for all.

The safeguarding code should specify the ways in which a safe environment is being created by providing the necessary information for anyone to act appropriately should they be concerned about the safety of a child, young person or vulnerable adult, and outlining clear referral processes. The code should also recognise the necessity of building open and trusting relationships which are based on listening to children's and young peoples' concerns, acting as a reliable role model, demonstrating consistent respect in practice, and referring them to other professionals when appropriate for further specialist help or guidance.

HOLISTIC APPROACH TO YOUTH WORK

As all youth workers will know, young people need to be both challenged and kept safe in order to grow and thrive through their successful engagement in development opportunities. Therefore it is important to know that in youth work settings safeguarding young people is a much more comprehensive approach than child protection, one which requires a holistic approach that will protect young people from potential sources of harm.

Effective youth work practice is not just about focusing on preventing and acting upon abuse crimes, it is also concerned with treating children and young people with respect by recognising and valuing their human dignity. In this regard youth workers have a responsibility to treat young people well but also to help parents and other professionals recognise children's rights and engage with them in a way that is central, positive and developmental rather than detrimental, inconsistent and dismissive. Quality youth work is about making sure that the best people are recruited as employees and volunteers to work with young people in all settings, creating a culture of openness and honesty, and protecting young people from harm and danger without thwarting their potential for, and need of, appropriate challenge, stimulation and animation.

EDUCATION AND TRAINING

For youth workers to carry out these responsibilities successfully they should be educated and trained, not only to adhere to set organisational policies, but also to develop and enhance safeguarding policies and procedures in their own operating circumstances when working with young people. This is key because protecting young people is not just about following pre-set safety standards and guidelines, it is also about creating an operating environment which takes young people's understandings, needs and desires as the starting point and developing a young person-centred approach to the practice. This means that youth workers must be appropriately trained in 'thinking through practice' which informs the writing and implementing policies and procedures in all aspects of safeguarding within the context of national policy. Organisations like NCVYS can help in this regard, providing training and resources to enable youth workers to practise safeguarding effectively.

NETWORKS AND AGENCIES

In the current social practices arena, youth workers will be acutely aware that youth work is neither a singular nor a stand-alone practice. They will also appreciate the way in which the changing integrative patterns of service delivery will affect professional relationships that is being driven by the legislation, policy and guidance on safeguarding. Such national drivers of social practices taken together aim to promote the principles of integrated working and achieve multi-agency effectiveness for the benefit of children and young people.

In this new dawn, children and young people become the focus of the service through collaborative and integrated practice recognising and supporting their needs and assessment tools, development theories and models of practice, all of which will lead to effectively providing therapeutic care, supporting wellbeing, and enhancing the quality of life. However, this is not a panacea that can be established and then ignored: it is a proactive approach where the systems and processes need to be regularly built, developed and reviewed through clear planning and co-ordination, in keeping with the provisions of the various Children Acts and the Human Rights Act 1998 to support the welfare of children and young people. This youth work practice also needs to understand the reasons for and the effects of risk-taking behaviour in young people, as well as being prepared and able to support them in their transitions. It must also take the opportunities for communication and reflection on situations, and develop a practice which is culturally competent that meets the needs of a diverse population.

A NEW PHASE FOR YOUTH WORK?

It could be argued that youth work is entering a new phase of practice by operating in a social context which increasingly acknowledges the rights and voice of children and young people and where there is increased interest in society to promote their physical, psychological and social wellbeing: this is potentially a very significant development for youth work.

This youth work practice needs to be holistic in its approach, with youth workers being appropriately trained and competent in safeguarding requirements, and appropriately informed about local networks, forums and developments, as well as confidently drawing on the expertise of other professionals and agencies such as relevant national associations, the NSPPC, and access to legal advice.

PROFESSIONAL ROLES AND RESPONSIBILITIES

It is vital that youth workers act responsibly and professionally at all times by knowing what is expected of them and making sound judgements based on reliable values, principles and ethics. Youth workers should know the importance of taking appropriate action and be aware of any reasons that may prevent them from taking action such as their latent beliefs. Dingwall et al. (1995) state that practitioners can be prevented from recognising and acting on abuse because of a 'rule of optimism' that makes them think that abuse will never happen in their situation. A second factor is known as 'cultural relativism', where the wrong is recognised but excused as being normal within that culture or community (for example, genital mutilation). Professional youth workers must also have appropriate and continuous supervision so that they can talk about and develop effective practice.

Questions

1. Do you think that abuse mainly happens in poor families and areas?
2. Who is more likely to harm a child: a stranger, an acquaintance, or a person who is trusted and known to the child?
3. Should you always share concerns of abuse that you have with the child's parents?

Comment

Beliefs and knowledge about children, their situation and abuse are crucial in making sensible judgements and taking appropriate actions. You will be on the right lines if you are thinking that children are harmed by people from across the social classes, although there might be something about people in social stress being more susceptible, that abusers will usually be known to the child (NSPCC, 2000), that the abuse will normally take place in a familiar environment (for example, home, school or local community), and that telling the parents could put the child at greater risk.

CONCLUSION

The issue of child protection is not easy to deal with in practice. One of the most important features to remember is that the child comes first. Children and young people must be listened to and taken seriously when they express their needs and situations to adults. Procedures and protocols must be followed and staff should be fully trained and conversant with what is expected.

The laws around child protection have increased exponentially over the last thirty years, but these alone will not provide all the answers and ethical judgements will still have to be made by practioners. Experienced youth workers will know that when a young person is upset for example that physical contact can be stress reducing, emotionally containing, soothing and healing, and can also be helpful for relationship building. However, at such times, there is a range of guiding principles that would need to come into force:

1. The physical contact should meet the child's/young person's needs, not the adult's.
2. Everything should be kept public.
3. The child/young person should be asked if being comforted would help them.
4. The type of comfort will depend on the person's age, need and situation.
5. The contact should seek to demonstrate care, understanding and reassurance.
6. Inappropriate and unwanted physical contact should be avoided.
7. The person's dignity must be protected at all times.

Staff must therefore protect themselves as well as the children and young people in their care. Over and above a registration scheme, there should be a recognised supervision and support scheme where professional youth workers can talk about practice issues in a supportive and therapeutic environment.

Obviously children and young people must be safeguarded from harm, but this must also be balanced with the freedom to develop and take some risks as they carve out a growing sense of themselves. They need freedom to develop away from adult supervision when they want to, and youth workers should help to make sure that they have the information and skills they need to keep themselves safe when they are on their own or with peers.

Also, adults in the community must also learn to accept the presence of children and young people on our streets and give them the 'freedom to be' based on the same level of respect that adults want from young people. In short, it is less likely that children and young people will be abused if they are truly valued and respected across every level of society.

Lesley is a young youth worker who was working part-time at a youth club operated by the Valedal Community Association while studying at university for a youth and community/CLD degree.

Following a successful interview, as part of the induction process, Lesley had been given a role description which was agreed and signed together with clear reporting lines. The supplied references had been taken up and the appropriate checks and clearance had been given through the organisation's child protection policy. Lesley had been given a copy of the safeguarding policies and procedures, the code of good practice, and this is an item for discussion at the regular supervision sessions.

Case Study 9

(Continued)

(Continued)

One night, after three months in the post, a young person came up behind Lesley, who was busy tidying up the cafe area, and said that he had something he wanted to say. Immediately, Lesley felt panicked inside but was composed enough to indicate a move to a more private but still open space in the club. Lesley also wanted to be mentally present and alert to the young person and listened clearly to what they had to say.

The young person told Lesley that he was suffering from an abusive situation.

Lesley listened attentively and gave the young person time and space to speak. She did not ask any leading questions, share any personal experiences, or use any phrase that would indicate disbelief or judgement. Lesley rightly did not ask for further details, make comments, or question in any way what was being said. She also did not give a guarantee of confidentiality or secrecy, but stated that the only people who would be told were those whose job it was to keep young people/children safe. Lesley found that the most helpful responses were those that affirmed and reassured the person in their right to tell, recognising the courage that it takes to talk about this, reaffirmed the person in their feelings, and asked the open question if there was anything else that the individual wanted to tell.

Other main points that Lesley could remember from the training were to follow the procedure of listen, respond, and record and refer. She was clear from the training that it was not the youth workers' role to investigate child protection enquiries because that was the statutory responsibility of social services and the police. It was also understood that, legally and organisationally, Lesley did not have the authority, training or skills to investigate and that her role was to follow the agreed guidelines.

She also remembered that there should be no delay in referral because this would allow for the potential of subsequent abuse to occur by giving time for the abuser to devise a false alibi or disappear. In addition, confronting the alleged abuser would alert them to the fact that a report had been given which would give them time to destroy any physical evidence and potentially put untold pressure on the victim.

Lesley's approach, in keeping with the organisation's stated policy, was to listen to, acknowledge and take seriously the young person's concerns and allegations. As soon as it was practical she wrote up a full record, using the young person's own words, of what had been said and heard. The record was duly signed and dated. In writing up the record Lesley tried very hard to be accurate, concise and objective, as well as recognising and treating confidentially the information supplied.

Lesley also made it a priority to ensure the young person's immediate safety. After speaking with the safeguarding adviser, emergency action was taken to ensure that the young person was not put back into the alleged abusive situation by making direct contact with social work, police and medical services.

After the incident, Lesley sought and received help, guidance and support from a line manager and occupational health services.

Summary of Key Points

- Child protection laws have been around for a long time but with limited effectiveness.
- The foundations of youth work grew out of a concern for children and young people's welfare.
- UNICEF and the CPAG do not think that the UK looks after its children well.
- Child abuse is very prevalent across the world and we think that much of it goes unreported.

- There is a more significant degree of awareness of children's rights through international treaties and domestic legislation.
- It is only relatively recently that processes and procedures have been formalised for the identification and investigation of abuse and neglect through Safeguarding Boards.
- There is a raft of legislation across the UK which sets out child protection aims, sexual offences and safeguarding policies.
- There are a number of reasons put forward for the existence of child abuse: whilst none are definitive, we do know that there are both risk and protective factors which can help us to deal with it.
- Safeguarding principles and procedures in youth work are concomitant with good youth work practice where young people are valued, respected and challenged.
- This is potentially a good time for youth work where the rights of children and young people are increasingly being recognised in society and youth work can work with them to ensure that their voice is heard.

REFERENCES

Aries, P. (1962) *Centuries of Childhood*. London: Penguin.

Cawson, P. et al. (2000) *Child Maltreatment in the UK: A Study of Child Abuse and Neglect*. London: NSPPC.

Children Act 2004. Available at www.legislation.gov.uk/ukpga/2004/31/contents (last accessed 10.05.13).

Children and Young Persons Act 1933. Available at www.legislation.gov.uk/ukpga/Geo5/23-24/12/contents (last accessed 05.05.13).

Children (Northern Ireland) Order 1995. Available at www.legislation.gov.uk/nisr/1996/297/contents/made (last accessed 18.06.13).

Children (Scotland) Act 1995. Available at www.legislation.gov.uk/ukpga/1995/36/contents (last accessed 03.03.13).

Convention on the Rights of a Child (UNCRC) 1991. Available at www.education.gov.uk/childrenandyoungpeople/healthandwellbeing/b0074766/uncrc/ (last accessed 20.06.13).

Corby, B. (2000) *Child Abuse: Towards a Knowledge Base*. Milton Keynes: Open University.

Coster, W. (2007) Social constructions of childhood. In P. Zwozdiak-Myers (ed.), *Childhood and Youth Studies*. Exeter: Learning Matters.

Criminal Justice (Northern Ireland) Order 2008. Available at www.legislation.gov.uk/nisi/2008/1216/contents (last accessed 25.05.13).

Cronin, M. and Smith, C. (2010) 'From safeguarding to safeguarding'. In G. Brotherton and G. McGillvray (eds) *Working with Children, Young People and Families*. London: Sage. pp. 97-117.

DCSF (2010) *Working together to Safeguard Children: A Guide to Inter Agency Working to Safeguard and Promote the Welfare of Children*. Nottingham: DCSF.

Dingwall, R., Eekelar, J. and Murray, T. (1995) *The Protection of Children: State Interventions and Family Life*. Oxford: Basil Blackwell.

Department of Health (2004) Children Act 2004: *Every Child Matters*. London: DoH.

Finkelhor, D. et al. (1990) 'Sexual abuse in a national survey of adult men and women: Prevalence, characteristics, and risk factors', *Child Abuse & Neglect*, 14 (1): 19–28.

Garmezy, N., Masten, A.S. and Tellegen, A. (1984) 'A study of stress and competence in children: A building block for developmental psychopathology', *Child Development*, 55: 97–111.

Gregg, S. (1995) *Preventing Anti Social Behaviour in At-Risk Students*. New York: OERI.

Harris, B. (2011) *Working with Distressed Young People*. Exeter: Learning Matters.

House of Lords, House of Commons: Joint Committee on Human Rights (2009). *Children's Rights: Twenty-fifth Report of Session 2008–09*. London: HMSO.

Human Rights Act 1998. Available at www.legislation.gov.uk/ukpga/1998/42/contents (last accessed 21.06.13).

Mintzberg, H. (2005) Developing theory about the development of theory. In K.G. Smith and M.A. Hitt (eds), *Great Minds in Management*. Oxford: OUP.

Munro, E. (2011) *The Munro Review of Child Protection: A Child Centred Approach*. Available at www.official-documents.gov.uk/document/cm80/8062/8062.pdf (last accessed 20/05.13).

National Guidance for Child Protection in Scotland 2010. Available at www.scotland.gov.uk/Publications/2010/12/09134441/0 (last accessed 06.12.13)

NSPCC (2012) *Helpline Highlight: A Year in Review*. London: NSPCC.

Protection of Children (Scotland) Act 2003. Available at www.legislation.gov.uk/asp/2003/5/contents (last accessed 05.05.13).

Protection of Children and Vulnerable Adults (Northern Ireland) Order 2003. Available at www.legislation.gov.uk/nisi/2003/417/contents (last accessed 15.06.13).

Protection of Freedoms Act (2012). Available at www.legislation.gov.uk/ukpga/2012/9/contents (last accessed 08.07.13).

Safeguarding Board Act (Northern Ireland) 2011. Available at www.legislation.gov.uk/nia/2011/7/contents (last accessed 10.06.13).

Safeguarding Vulnerable Groups Act 2006. Available at www.legislation.gov.uk/ukpga/2006/47/contents (last accessed 06.07.13).

Safeguarding Vulnerable Groups (Northern Ireland) Order 2007. Available at www.legislation.gov.uk/nisi/2007/1351/contents/made (last accessed 05.06.13).

Scottish Government (2010) *National Guidance for Child Protection in Scotland* 2010. EdinburghL Scottish Government.

Sex Offenders Act 1997. Available at www.legislation.gov.uk/ukpga/1997/51/contents (last accessed 10.06.13).

Sexual Offences Act 2003. Available at www.legislation.gov.uk/ukpga/2003/42/contents (last accessed 10.06.13).

Sexual Offences (Scotland) Act 2009. Available at www.legislation.gov.uk/asp/2009/9/contents (last accessed 08.07.13).

Smith, K. et al. (eds) (2011) *Homicides, Firearms Offences and Intimate Violence 2009/10: Supplementary Volume 2 to Crime in England and Wales 2009/2010*. London: Home Office.

United Nations (1989) *United Nations Declaration on The Rights of The Child* (UNCRC). Geneva: United Nations.

United Nations (1989) *United Nations Convention on the Rights of the Child*. Geneva: United Nations.

Welsh Assembly Government (2006/ 2007) *NAFWC12/07 Safeguarding Children: Working Together under the Children Act 2004*. Cardiff: WAG.

Wilson, K. and James, A. (eds) (2007) *The Child Protection Handbook*, 3rd edition. Philadelphia: Elsevier.

USEFUL CONTACTS

Bullying online
Helpline: 0808 800 2222
www.bullying.co.uk

Child Exploitation & Online Protection Centre
33 Vauxhall Bridge Road,
London, SW1V 2WG.
Tel: 0870 000 3344
www.ceop.police.uk

ChildLine
Floor 2,
50 Studd Street,
London, N1 0QW.
Office: 020 7239 1000
Helpline: 0800 1111
www.childline.org.uk

Children's Rights Office
City Road,
London, EC1V 1LJ.
Tel: 020 7278 8222
www.cro.org.uk

Children's Society
Edward Rudolf House,
Margery Street,
London, WC1X 0JL.
Tel: 020 7841 4436
www. the-childrens-society.org.uk

Kidscape
2 Grosvenor Gardens,
London, SW1 0DG.
Helpline: 0845 1205 204
Tel: 020 7730 7081
www. kidscape.org.uk

National Children's Bureau
8 Wakley Street,
London, EC1V 7QE.
Tel: 020 7843 6000
www.ncb.org.uk

NCH Action for Children
85 Highbury Road,
London, N5 1UD.
Tel: 020 7704 7000
www.nchafc.org.uk

NSPCC
42 Curtain Road,
London, EC2 3NH.
Tel: 020 7825 2500
www.nspcc.org.uk

Save the Children
17 Grove Lane,
London, SE5 8RD.
Tel: 020 7703 5400
www.savethechildren.org.uk

10

PRACTISING BEYOND THE LAW

Chapter Aims

- Outline some differences and similarities between law making and youth work practice
- Explore the need for youth work in relation to the social treatment of children and young people
- Identify and discuss the existence of a youth category
- Recognise the roots and tensions inherent in youth policy
- Articulate a developing youth work practice based on participation, social justice and critical actions through critical informal learning

INTRODUCTION

In Chapter 1 of this book I outlined the communal importance and similarities of the law and youth work practice. In this chapter, I will develop some of these points and identify some of the differences, as well as arguing for developing a youth work practice that operates within the law but is not limited by it since young people are treated unfairly by society.

From the outset let us be clear that no one is above the law, but practice with people cannot simply use compliance with the law as a benchmark for good practice. Complying with the law is, in some sense, a minimal standard where legislation is used to keep people safe and protect their rights. However, we must recognise that lawmaking is not a revealed truth and like government policy and intervention is a part of the current social and economic discourse (Considine, 2005). This is why some laws become either irrelevant or unacceptable as society's position changes, which then requires laws to be repealed (for example, the penal and slavery laws of the past). Similarly, this is why new laws are instituted (for example, the latest equality laws) because as circumstances and situations change laws need to be articulated to reflect the changing social conditions. As with youth work practice lawmaking is ever-changing, as both are tied up with political ideas of society and the role of the state, open to interpretation, dialogue and representation, and with notions of participation at their heart.

Of course, what lies at the heart of the debate about the role of law and the need for youth work is where one stands on the nature versus nurture debate which is often politically aligned. If you think that human beings are inherently lazy and self-ish by nature, a position concomitant with largely right-wing political thinking, then it would follow that you would see the need for a strictly ordered law-based society to encourage compliance and provide the motivation to act judiciously through fear of the consequences. If, on the other hand, you subscribe to the ideas, supported mainly by political thinkers on the left, that people are naturally good and that they will cooperate and help one another if the society is egalitarian and just, then this would generate a more egalitarian approach to lawmaking. It also begs the question about how you understand the nature of society, how it perpetuates inequality, and what can be done about it.

LAW AND YOUTH WORK: SIMILARITIES AND DIFFERENCES

Both the law and youth work provide important social functions but play separate roles in different ways for the benefit of human development. The law has an overt and well-defined function in society to set standards of behaviour and protect people's rights, based on a judicial system which adjudicates on the application of the law (i.e., case law). The law has a very public function which is readily understood and recognised, however it is also limited in that while there are explicit legal standards to be met (for example, at work) there will be other times (for example, around some equality issues) when a person would need to undertake litigation (Roberts, 2009: 43) at their own expense and personal cost to receive justice.

Youth work, on the other hand, is an important social practice but is not as easily understood in concept or practice and is also not effortlessly captured in the public 'mind'. Spence et al. (2006) identify the presence of both a public and private discourse, which suggests that youth work provides both expressed and latent functions. The public position aligns with a practice that delivers informal education programmes in a way that is acceptable to politicians and funders by placing young people within a social policy of perceived need, control and development. The private discourse is what these researchers classify as an understanding of 'interpersonal friendliness' based upon a dialogue through which the young person can dictate the pace, time, extent and achievements of the encounter. Thus, they conclude that there are significant features of the practice which are 'repressed or silenced' (Spence et al., 2006: 49) and could prove counterproductive when attempting to identify the need and potential for youth work practice and secure sustainable resources for its application.

This research may have uncovered the heart of the problem in that youth work is operating to two different agendas (the government's and young people's) which may be doing a disservice to both. By analysing the government's agenda, outlined through policy development, Tett (2010: 73) articulates three discreet typologies of policy on young people. The first identifies young people as being at risk, which signifies that they are deficit beings in need of social care and protection. The second type identifies young people as a problem, which indicates that they are deviant and in need of programmes which can control them and provide diversions. Lastly, young people are viewed as active citizens with a focus on development with promotion of the capacity for participation and social change. In thinking about these three policy streams, it could be argued that the first two typologies are dominant in practice through the discourse of a risk society and the need for community safety programmes. The third element, the active citizen, remains largely rhetoric-based because politicians are inherently reticent about encouraging young people to become politically active, as they do not have a vote and may potentially challenge their power and disrupt the adult alliances to which the elected representatives are bound. So if youth workers are not aware of, and actively work to combat, the structural restrains that prevent this third policy dimension from happening to any degree of significance, then it is unlikely that the young people they work with will feel empowered to act politically.

Yet politics and activism is where it is at because youth work, as with lawmaking, has never been a stagnant practice: it has always been a changing practice, within a currently rapidly changing societal environment, one which includes a transient society and globalised world. One of the differences is that the judiciary aim to uphold and interpret the law which may also point out deficiencies which require further lawmaking, whereas youth work has the potential to advocate and campaign for changes in the law for a more equal society.

Reflective Challenge – Questions

- Why do you think that youth work is not easily defined or understood by the public?
- What functions do you think youth work usefully serves in society?
- Is legal compliance enough or should youth work challenge the status quo when there is inequality?

THE NEED FOR YOUTH WORK AND THE YOUTH CATEGORY

Youth work has long had a tradition that has successfully survived and negotiated a number of ideological impositions, policy constraints, new public management demands, and limited resourcing. Yet the practice continues and develops in spite of these changing circumstances because it serves useful functions in society. However, the functions it serves are both latent and publically expressed, and by giving consideration to the ways in which young people are regarded by society at large will provide some insight into the need for youth work.

From the youth work literature it is clear that dominant social discourse is of limited value to young people (Jeffs and Smith, 1999). Given this, an understanding of how young people are held in society is important to youth work as it can be used as a barometer for the health of a given society. The youth category is a social construct rather than a biological state that is sandwiched between childhood and adulthood (Fulcher and Scott, 1999: 369), which means it can be changed. However, it is tied up with a notion of adolescence based on the work of Stanley Hall, who developed a theory of four stages of human development of which adolescence was the stormy phase before adulthood (Mauss, 1962: 13).

This youth category, across the UK, has strong overtones of dependency and control for young people, as well as economic and transition factors as the state expands and contracts both the meaning and terms of the youth category. For example, the category can be extended through enacting a social policy which increases the leaving age for exiting compulsory education due to the needs of the economy (Baldrock et al., 1999: 287). Again, the ability of a young person to leave home is dependent on social policies which determine the nature and shape of the education system, as well as the employment and housing markets (Jones, 1993, cited in Morrow and Richards, 1996: 50). However, not only do the policy makers provide the operating context they also ignore the impact of these policies on young people and find ways of excluding those who fail to conform to the policy (Dwyer and Wyn, 1999: 41).

Mizen (2004) argues that youth is not a straightforward category but is rather ambiguously constructed to determine legal rights and responsibilities. This increasingly complex transition process of adolescent development involves changing relations between the individual and the multiple levels of the young person's embedded environment. Significant variations in the substance and timing of these interactions present sources of risk or protective factors at this period in their life.

The key risk factors of the contemporary adolescent period involve drug, alcohol, and substance use and abuse; unsafe sex, teenage pregnancy, and teenage parenting; school underachievement, failure, and dropout; and delinquency, crime, and violence. Poverty among young people exacerbates these risks, as verified in study conducted by MacDonald (2002) who developed a theory of 'differentiated normalisation' in relation to drug use. This expounded the position that drug use was being normalised but not everyone was involved in it or agreed with it.

In light of this, it could be argued that the age of modernity, with its stable environments and defined social patterns, has passed, and this postmodernity period is dominated by a capitalist globalised economy (Denney, 2005: 28, 33) which is uncertain and increasingly inequitable. These changes are significant for young people and particularly in the western world which is witnessing a historical transformation, one in which the law finds it difficult to keep pace. Industrial society is being replaced by a new modernity in which the old 'scientific' world view is challenged: predictabilities and certainties that were characteristic of the industrial era are being threatened by a new set of risks and opportunities are brought into existence (Furlong and Cartmel, 2007: 3).

This changing societal situation provides the setting in which youth work takes place and has implications for the experiences of young people in terms of family relations

(Coles, 1995), choice biographies (Henderson et al., 2007), risk factors (Denney, 2005), and the type and extent of independence (Holdsworth and Morgan, 2005).

It is widely accepted that the dominant social discourse around young people is largely negative. This is evident in the media where, for example, a MORI research project identified that three out of four newspaper reports about young people were essentially negative, and only a small fraction gave a voice to the young person. Therefore youth, both as a term and a concept, should be used with care as it is a generic tag which does not often reflect the experiences and realties of young people (Spence, 2004). In essence, it is a label which is often used as a pejorative term that is synonymous with instability, risky behaviour, a lack of control and deficit beings.

The reality is that the very existence of the youth category is recognisable in the exclusion paradigm (Silver, 1994). Young people are excluded from full partici-pation in society because of a perception of age-based risk. This means that exclu-sion is not accidental when it comes to young people: it is the rationale for the creation of the youth category. During this period of high modernity (France, 2007), the scope, impact and length of exclusion for young people have been increasing exponentially. In the previous era, at the turn of the last century, the gap between biological adulthood and social adulthood was approximately five years. Now the difference has tripled and is estimated to be closer to fifteen years. This means that young people currently experience a ludicrous and interminable elongation of adolescence and dependency, with a resulting infantilisation which is made evident by increasing restrictions on their movements and a violation of their fundamental human rights. Thus our current generation of young adults, who in any other time and place would have been parents, are classified and treated ever more rigidly as children.

However, there are inherent dangers in this strategy that society has adopted. The main risk of excluding a population cohort, in this way, is that it could become not only excluded but also disengaged. If a population becomes disengaged then this can become socially dangerous and individually destructive. Since the industrial revolution youth work has responded to this risk, mostly by connecting with young people and engaging them on their own terms. Youth policy has responded to this risk mostly by being concerned with the potential for social disruption: this is the core of the tension.

Reflective Questions

- Are you convinced that the youth category exists and is it harmful to the development of young people?
- Do you think that the government has the same or different intentions?
- Should youth workers be more political?
- Are young people potentially disengaged across the UK today?

(Continued)

(Continued)

Comment

Hopefully, I have convinced you that young people get a raw deal from society and that this is getting potentially worse through globalisation and it won't get better unless we take positive action. Politics is too important to leave just to the politicians. I think what youth workers need to do is to be part of the solution not the problem. This means helping young people to think for themselves but using a critical appraisal of their circumstances and helping them to act politically in a way that adds value to the current political debate.

UK YOUTH WORK POLICY

The earliest traditions and roots of youth work emanated from the vision and work of volunteers who created structures through the setting up of voluntary organisations. In more recent times the beginnings of state intervention in youth work with the creation of a youth service can be traced to three core policy documents produced by Albemarle (1960), Milson-Fairbairn (1970), and Thompson (1982). Interestingly, government policies and attempts at defining the role of youth work have been largely nebulous, and ever-changing definitions can be contradicted by further attempts over time and often emphasise the political expediency of the era. The Albemarle Report (1960) was significant in that it marked a clear and direct relationship with policy aspirations. It was advantageous to youth work through building a universal service for 14 to 20 year olds, resourcing a youth work infrastructure through training and funding for youth workers, and encouraging partnership work with the voluntary sector through experimental ways of working which led to the introduction of detached youth work. It also had elements of equality and respect at its core by recognising that young people coming from different social economic and class backgrounds could demonstrate 'mutual respect and tolerance' by being in fellowship. However, it is thought that the lack of success for these policies may have been due to a failure to recognise the political dimensions of the social revolution that was taking place.

THE TENSION IN YOUTH POLICY

France and Wiles (1997) contrasted the role and structure of youth work in modern and late modern societies. In their assessment, modern societies linked citizenship to inclusion in production and youth work helped the transition of young people from childhood to inclusion into the labour market and citizenship. When post-war full employment eased these transition processes then youth work concentrated on leisure provision and dealing with the small numbers of excluded young people. However, they argued that late modern societies redefined citizenship in terms of market choices but also created increasing risks, which a declining state could no longer manage, which would lead to a growing use of social exclusion as a form of social control. In their opinion such changes demand a new role and structure for youth work (France and Wiles, 1997: 60).

In more recent times, youth work practice has been incorporated by the state sector and has put its own defining features on youth work to help deliver a governmental policy agenda. For example, the National Occupational Standards for Youth Work in the UK's identification of the role of a youth worker is to engage with young people in ways that are educative, participative, empowering, and promote equality of opportunity and social inclusion (Lifelong Learning UK, 2008).

The competing ideologies of the voluntary and state sectors have contributed to the difficulty in practitioners being able to define and articulate their practice. Ingram and Harris (2001:16) point out that youth workers will often use phrases that mean very little to the general public, using words like empowerment and citizenship. Thus we need to articulate practice which is reflective of its current status and easily understood by workers, participants and funders.

Spence (2004) identifies the tensions between generic youth work and contemporary policy initiatives. She argues that there are fundamental and distinguishing aspects of youth work practice in terms of relationships, partnerships and time, which enable youth workers to undertake successful interventions with groups of young people who are defined as 'socially excluded'. Therefore, the demands of government policy in relation to targeting and accountability are in tension with practice in these key areas. Spence calls for a clearly articulated and specific language of youth work practice to avoid the very aspects of youth work which make it attractive to policy makers being undermined by policy.

If youth work is to claim its rightful role in society, it needs to vociferously contest with three key policy dimensions. The first is that there is a strong link between success in education and the ability to negotiate into the labour market. The fact that this is not a straightforward process raises issues of latent forces and inequalities, and the variances of market demands also need to be raised. Second, policy assumes that it assists in the transition process from child to adulthood. This whole notion of transition is problematic and contestable, especially when it is a period which is starting earlier and lasting longer at a time when resources are being diminished. Third, that young people are discriminated against and society needs youth work which is not closely tied to the state agenda but is a free practice that holds each young person at the centre of practice.

Activity

Take five or ten minutes, in a quiet space, to think through and then make a columned list of the pros and cons for youth work being state sponsored or voluntary and free.

Comment

You might think about using Tett's (2010) typologies above to determine which type of practice may be more prevalent under either of the two given settings.

DEVELOPING YOUTH WORK PRACTICE: THROUGH MEANINGFUL PARTICIPATION

Participation is a major theme in studies on youth and a major plank of youth work practice. Over the past twenty years or so, the idea and implementation of youth participation have become one of the most important issues with regard to participation and active citizenship. However, there is a problem here which is particularly relevant today as young people continue to be viewed as 'part citizen and part villain' by both seeking their involvement and also regarding them as a threat (McCulloch, 2007). Added to this, there is not a culture of participation in the UK with a lack of effective structures which creates major barriers to young people being meaningfully involved to any significant degree. This lack of infrastructure is indicative of the poor regard society has for young people, thus the fact that they are denied genuine participatory rights is symptomatic of their inadequate social, cultural, and personal recognition. The need for change is clear and this should be advocated for by youth workers and young people alike to enable our current young people to be meaningfully recognised and involved in civic affairs.

However, this will only happen if youth workers are able to reflect and act on their own personal understandings of themselves and society in a way that overcomes the powerful socialisation messages we all receive, as very young children, about the ways in which we regard people who are different from us. We, as youth workers, need to examine and reflect on those powerful early messages we were given that translate into our beliefs, stereotypes and behaviours towards other individual and groups of people. We need to recognise and act upon those manifested discriminations on the individual, institutional and cultural levels of society

Participation cannot take place in isolation and there is a strong rationale for ensuring the consistent involvement of all citizens in civic processes. This involvement is central to the operation of democracy (Parry et al., 1992). The successful operation of democratic structures needs the involvement of the hoi polloi to ensure that power is not held in too few hands. Thus the effective involvement of all young people in participatory structures is necessary for the exercise of full rights as active citizens. The practice of participatory action needs to be nurtured as part of a conscious-raising relationship which transcends current political debates and convinces people of the benefits of sustained participation to make a significant impact.

The opportunities to make such arguments will vary at different points in history. However, democratic possibilities can only be opened up by entering into current debates within the existing political structures: the case for change to create participation spaces and structures still needs to be made.

Historically, the participation mechanisms across the UK have been based on an understanding and promotion of informal education and volunteering. The systems and processes have been developed as structural responses based on policy directives influenced by political positions. As a result, the meaning and context for participation are strongly influenced by this political discourse, and ultimately politicians have the power to create or remove rights for ordinary citizens.

Participation is generally regarded as a good if not an essential notion. This is based on the assumption that participation is the best way to unlock human potential and the cultural capacity. This thinking should then lead to a bottom-up approach which focuses on the natural assets of a given locality. The rationale for promoting partici-pation is based on notions of social justice to facilitate young people's development and gain a voice in society. However, political rhetoric and policies are not enough since local representative participation is dependent on the capacity of local people and the opportunities they encounter to have their voice listened to.

In effect, the governmental policies affecting young people have been mixed with a combination of positive developments through enhanced consultation arrangements with young people and the creation of a Children's Rights Commissioner (Children Act 2004). However, young people continue to suffer from a discourse which promotes increased surveillance, stop and search, and anti social behaviour orders. These contra-dictory messages have helped to sustain the conditions whereby generations of young are disadvantaged and blamed. In spite of having a legislative back-up to ensure that public bodies consult with young people and others, the research indicates that not all young people, local authority workers and public partners are ready and willing to engage in this level of dialogue (Barber and Naulty, 2005: 49).

Reflective Challenge – Questions

- Do young people think that the idea and practice of participation does any good for those involved and youth in general?
- Have you come across any participation initiatives that you would consider empowering?
- Do you think that the government felt forced to create a Children's Commissioner because of children's rights being more recognised through international law?

Comment

I think that participation has great potential which it has yet to realise. There are some good examples of participation projects but they remain just that, and significant progress will only be made when it is integrated into the daily way of thinking and working by every social professional in the UK. I think also that the time is right, due partly to international law, for children and young people to be more aware of this potential and act to lay the foundations of a world worth inheriting.

DEVELOPING YOUTH WORK PRACTICE: POWER AND SOCIAL JUSTICE

Stuart (2006) examined the impact of a 'Gandhian' approach to effective youth practice. Based on the life and work of Mahatma Gandhi, he identified three main implications on youth practice. First, is the need for integrity within the work, nurturing non-manipulative environments, free from exploitation. Second, is the realisation that youth work practice goes beyond the individual young person and the immediate group. Third, is a commitment to 'power-with' relationships rather than 'power-over'. In addition, he highlights the danger of the practitioner focusing on the 'immediate needs of the young people that they have little time or energy for social change' and that 'although youth workers and young people are not equals, working from a position of "power-with" encourages youth workers to recognize the insights of young people and adopt strategies that are empowering' (Stuart, 2006: 86).

This recognition of power is one of the more crucial aspects in which informal youth work differs from formal work with young people. For example, other professionals take young people through a process to achieve a pre-determined goal based on where those in power think those young people should be at the end of the experience. Youth work is different as it starts from where the young people are at and not from where adults perceive them to be. Identifying differing needs among young people is crucial, along with negotiating and developing the various paths and goals that will meet those articulated needs.

Thus social justice lies at the heart of youth work practice because of this inherent inequality built into the youth category, along with the inconsistent and contradictory development of policies (Crooks, 1992). Also the understanding of conducting 'professional' youth work practice should be based on professional ethics, and a 'new radicalism' which stresses the worker's own personal or political commitment and individual moral responsibility (see Banks, 2005).

DEVELOPING YOUTH WORK PRACTICE: DEVELOPING CRITICAL ACTIONS THROUGH INFORMAL LEARNING

One of the main reasons for conducting youth work is a recognition of young people's disadvantaged status, which has led to a practice of participation through which young people can express their views. The route that many youth workers choose to develop personal agency is to engage in a process of informal learning which is based on purposeful conversations and dialogue. This section will look at the role of the youth worker as a critical informal educator, consider the relevance to notions of active citizenship, and explore the traits of inclusive and representative practice.

Youth work in the UK is based on the notion of informal education. This has strong roots in the UK youth work discourse and a coherent set of principles, values and approaches that inform practice. Within the social policy context we have seen a significant movement in youth work from its original voluntary, philanthropic roots to efforts by the state to intervene and control. Alongside this there has been a strong tradition for local people to get involved in local communities, as it is held that they are best placed to come up with solutions to local problems.

It has been argued that the roles of the informal educator are principally three-fold although some of the terms and emphasis differ: the first aim is to create space for association and conversation; the second, to encourage self-directed learning with action taken based on the new knowledge; and the third, to utilise a critical perspective on society and circumstances which helps to focus the participation (Ord, 2007; Packham, 2008).

The relationship of democratic values to the process of informal education is identified in the academic literature (Jeffs and Smith, 1999: 25) where the conversations and ontological orientations are 'central to democracy'. In policy terms this is often referred to as a process of engagement. It is within this context that youth workers need to see beyond the current political discourses and take a longer-term, higher-principled view when conducting 'democratic audits' (Smith and Jeffs, 2007).

The approaches adopted by the youth worker in the critical informal education context are drawn from a range of sources, including the work of Paulo Freire which is located in the 'popular education' tradition. His work has provided both the philosophy and practice which inform youth work across many parts of the UK. The thinking and approaches are based on three key texts (Freire, 1972, 1992, 1998) which identify and explain five key concepts of dialogue, conscientisation, problem posing, experiential learning, and praxis.

Dialogue is the intentional process of engaging others in conversation with the purpose of developing a joint worker and young person critical understanding of the world. *Conscientisation* is an awareness process, with the oppressed, to identify the ways in which the paradoxical, economic, social and political forces integrate to maintain inequality as a disadvantaged reality. Third, *problem posing* is the joint critical exploration of reality that leads to a 'committed involvement' based on understanding the need to act to improve the status quo. The fourth major idea is *experiential learning* which is the lens through which an egalitarian teacher/learner interaction uses previous and current experience, problem posing and enquiry skills as a framework for developing literacy in its widest sense. The notion of *praxis* provides a route through which reflection, based on theoretical understanding and personal values, enables political action to be taken on an informed and continuous basis.

While this aim of inclusive practice is often levied at youth work, the ways in which it is achieved are not always evident. In order for the practice to achieve inclusion and participation within youth work, a youth worker would need to find ways to achieve the three major aims of informal education. This relies on the worker demonstrating the skills to create the space using the group work process, to promote self-direction through problem identification, involvement and action, and to develop the critical perspective using a reflexive starting point that interventions are not value free.

The creation of space can be generated through group work to develop the potential for growth, as a support mechanism to develop ideas and agree on collective action. Another approach to developing critical consciousness work with the learner is to use the concept of communities of practice (Wenger, 2006), which provide a sense of belonging and a context to learn from the previous experience of others. Informal education will only take place if the worker recognises the central role of the participant young person in both identifying and naming their situation and seeing a commitment to action as part of the change process. The essential point here is the recognition of how power is executed, and ultimately how decisions are made about problem identification, resource allocation and effective action. Also, the youth worker, as an informal educator, needs to be self-aware and articulate ideological and critical perceptions. Youth workers also need a planning process such as Lewin's planning spiral, which involves the five stages of research, planning, action, evaluation and continuity.

Batsleer (2008:151) suggests that a potential starting point for critical educational practices to combat unequal dominant constructions is to 'explore common ground and difference in new and less stereotypical ways'. This means making efforts to go beyond the 'them' and 'us' and have local conversation in a globalised context. Examples of anti-oppressive youth work include tackling the issues around identity, ethnicity, lifestyle and societal circumstances. Batsleer also highlights the potential importance of youth work to 'transversal politics', through the youth worker being able to unsettle our perceptions of difference so that diversity is not expected to be normalised by the dominant, but discovered by the involvement of all forward-looking intercultural conversations (Gilroy, 1993). However, this may also mean that there will be times when the young person has to be challenged about, for example, racist or homophobic opinions. An example of the process involved in anti-racist work is detailed by the Bede detached youth work project (Dadzie, 1997).

Reflective Challenge – Questions

- What do you think is the need for, and potential of, a critical informal education approach to youth work?
- In what ways do you find the work of Paulo Freire a help to youth work practice?
- How important do you think the notion of community is to youth work?
- To what extent do you think youth work is about bringing about a fairer society through tackling injustices?

Comment

I think that critical informal learning provides both a logic and a practice for youth work which is community based and makes some suggestions about ways in which to start conversations about tackling injustice in society.

CONCLUSION

In summary, we have seen the ways in which both the law and youth make useful contributions to society. I have shown that there have been tensions between youth work and successive governments who each want different things from the practice. The government policies are based on a deficit understanding of the youth concept, and youth work strives to be free to develop a young person-based agenda instead of being driven into service areas, such as schools and employment initiatives, which potentially challenge and damage the traditional principle of voluntary association. The central problem is that politicians view young people as a short-term and non-voting category. The tension with policy arises as youth workers attempt to hold on to a special relationship with young people by working with them on their terms in spite of policy assertions. This fundamental principle of putting young people first is not concomitant with the state's agenda of prescribing outcomes as part of their centralist, managerialist approach to service delivery.

In democracies, such as the UK, it is vital that the judiciary act in a neutral capacity and that all citizens have the opportunity to play their full part in society, which includes acting as jurors in certain criminal cases to help bring about a just and reasonable adjudication. This active citizenship-based participation, not just in the legal systems but also through other mechanisms such as exercising political rights, including voting and volunteering, is a central part of democracy, and to that extent youth work could be viewed as a democracy practice which, among other things, aims to combat the democratic deficit that currently exists. Youth work encourages democratic participation to enable people to be full citizens, based on a set of values which holds that people are inherently good and aims to tackle injustice and discrimination as a contribution to securing continuous human development within a sustainable society. In this context, it could be argued that youth work is about protecting people's rights, seeking social justice, and working towards an increasingly equal society not just through law abidance but also through engendering solidarity in social practice and advocating for change that will improve young people's circumstances.

Descriptions and definitions of youth work practice are multifarious because the settings and purposes are multi-dimensional and this can be regarded as both a weakness and strength. However, for our purposes here we can draw out from this discussion that youth work provides social, group and individual functions to the extent that it encourages some participation in society and enables dialoguing a personal and collective critical understanding of social circumstances, develops a trustful relationship with young people, especially the excluded, and at its best seeks to create a more equal society by challenging discrimination at individual, group organisational and social structure levels to promote social justice.

As Taylor (2009) cogently posits the government in England has 'transformed youth work into an agency of behavioural modification [and] it wishes to confine to the scrapbook of history the idea that Youth Work is volatile and voluntary, creative and collective – an association and conversation without guarantees'.

Thus, we have to acknowledge that the whole notion and purpose of a youth policy are still disputed ideas with a considerable lack of ideological and operational consensus (Williamson, 2008: 66). In spite of this, directives and policies continue to be published which have increasingly influenced the intentions and approaches of youth work practice.

It is clear that youth work practice is often required to work around issues and within structures which it can neither influence nor control, based on a resource base which is wholly inadequate, which gives rise to the contention that it maintains the status quo (Jeffs and Smith, 1999) which 'masked an implicit, unconscious politicised practice "on the side of the powerful"' (Taylor, 2008: 253). There is a position in the youth work literature that youth work is at a crossroads and is in search of renewal, and it is now time to get political.

This discussion takes place at a time when trust in government is at an all time low as central ideas on work with young people, such as participation and citizenship, have been monopolised by untrustworthy politicians (Jeffs, 2005: 8) and used to 'oil the wheels of government by lessening irritating obstructions to what it wanted to achieve anyway' (Davies, 2008: 141).

There is a real need to continue to explore what is happening in practice, because the youth service is in a very fragile state and the vast majority of practice reports are aimed at justification for managers, funders and employers (Taylor, 2008: 255). What we require are honest reflexive accounts of practice which will articulate what happens in human development terms.

So youth work is not just confined to the individual, the group or the community: it also encompasses the contribution that it can make, as a social practice over time, to society and the development of human beings.

Case Study 10

Jon was annoyed with his boss because she had raised at a supervision session that a few young people had commented that he did not appear to care for them. This perplexed Jon, who was always on time, highly organised, and to his mind, showed great leadership skills by giving clear instructions about what should be done. He was highly efficient, very conversant with all the rules, knew all of (and complied with) all of the policies, and had his paperwork up to date.

The boss intimated that the skills he showed were relevant, appropriate and appreciated, but they were not enough: he had to develop stronger relationships with the young people.

Jon and his senior worker developed a plan to focus on getting to know young people which involved discussing with them what their lives were like and sharing what his experiences were. Over the months they discussed social, cultural, political and economic situations and understandings which gave rise to identifying a need for further learning where their knowledge was lacking. They tackled the hard issues of identity, ethnicity, lifestyle, and analysing societal circumstances. This led over time to developing a range of interests and expertise in particular subject areas. They grew in their understanding of themselves, their own and others' circumstances, and teased out ways of taking appropriate action to improve the local situation.

Eventually, with the help of the team, the young people were encouraged to identify and take on development opportunities which, with continuous support, resulted in an increase in their self confidence. They were encouraged to take on work in their local community where they had seen a need and to join a local political party. These young people felt empowered which grew into confidence in reading social circumstances and acting judiciously and collectively to meet local needs and improve people's circumstances.

As the years rolled by the young people took on their respective roles in society: a mechanic, a care worker, a politician, a police officer, a professional fundraiser, a business person, and a bus driver, and none of them forgot that youth work experience. Each one is now active in their local community and beyond, and they have strong networks, political allies and enhanced skills.

The police officer initiated one of the first community inter-cultural liaison committees. The bus driver started a credit union in his depot. The professional fundraiser started a charity to bring clean water to Africa. The business person runs a social enterprise cooperative. The politician is advocating having the laws around children and young people reviewed in light of the United Nations Convention on the Rights of the Child (UNCRC). The care worker has opened his first social enterprise.

Today that youth work practice has plenty of willing helpers who can use their expertise to develop the practice in that area, and the next generation are benefiting from a wide range of advice, action and advocacy.

Jon is now an excellent youth worker: highly organised and knowledgeable about policy and procedures, very caring and dialogically engaged with the young people, with an appreciation of the wider human development community role that this practice enables.

Summary of Key Points

- Compliance with the laws does not equate to good practice.
- Youth workers' political understandings are important to the way they view society and young people.
- Meaningful, active participation is an important democratic right for young people.
- Both youth work and the law provide key social functions.
- While the law has a defined public role, youth work has both a public and a latent role.
- Both youth work and the law are vibrant practices.
- The dominant social discourse about youth largely demonises young people.
- The youth category is dominated by ideas of young people being dependent and in need of control.
- Youth policy is inadequate and contradictory and seems to be based on political expediency.
- There are clear tensions between policy and youth work regarding their role and with different expectations from the government and young people.
- Youth work can develop with meaningful participation which needs to be politically motivated and sustained.
- Youth workers need to recognise the importance of power and aim for social justice.
- If we recognise young people's position then this provides the bedrock for developing actions through critical informal learning.
- What we need most at this point in time are honest accounts of youth work practice.
- Youth work is essentially about human development which is exercised by respecting the dignity of others.

REFERENCES

Albemarle Report (1960) *The Youth Service in England and Wales.* London: HMSO.

Baldrock, J., Manning, N., Miller S. and Vickerstaff, S. (1999) *Social Policy.* Oxford: Oxford University Press.

Banks, S. (2005) *Ethics, Accountability and the Social Professions.* Basingstoke: Palgrave Macmillan.

Banks, S. (ed.) (2010) *Ethical Issues in Youth Work* (2nd edn). Oxon: Routledge.

Barber, T. and Naulty, M. (2005) *Your Place or Mine? A Research Study Exploring Young People's Participation in Community Planning*. Dundee: University of Dundee, Department of Community Education.

Batsleer, J. (2008) *Informal Learning in Youth Work*. London: Sage.

Children Act 2004. Available at www.legislation.gov.uk/ukpga/2004/31/contents (last accessed 07.07.13).

Coles, B. (1995) *Youth and Social Policy*. London: UCL Press.

Considine, M. (2005) *Making Public Policy: Institutions, Actors and Strategies*. Cambridge: Polity Press.

Crooks, M. (1992) Social justice: Core value of youth work. In T. Corney (ed.), 'Value versus competencies: implications for the future of professional youth work education', *Journal of Youth Studies,* 7 (4): 513–527.

Dadzie, S. (1997) *Blood, Sweat and Tears: A Report of the Bede Anti-Racist Detached Youth Work Project*. Leicester: Youth Work Press.

Davies, B. (2008) *The New Labour Years, Vol.3, 1997–2007*. Leicester: Youth Work Press.

Denney, D. (2005) *Risk and Society*. London: Sage.

Department of Education and Science (1969) *Youth & Community Work in the 70's*. (The Fairbairn–Milson report). London: HMSO.

Department of Education and Science (1982) *Experience and Participation, Review Group on the Youth Service in England* (The Thompson Report). London: HSMO.

Dwyer, P. and Wyn, J. (2001) *Youth Education and Risk*. London: RoutledgeFalmer.

France, A. (2007) *Understanding Youth in Late Modernity*. England: Open University Press.

France, A. and Wiles, P. (1997) 'Dangerous futures: social exclusion and youth work in late modernity', *Social Policy & Administration,* 31 (5): 59–78.

Freire, P. (1972) *Pedagogy of the Oppressed*. London: Penguin.

Freire, P. (1992) *Pedagogy of Hope*. New York: Continuum.

Freire, P. (1998) *Teachers as Cultural Workers: Letters to Those Who Dare Teach*. Oxford: Westview.

Fulcher, J. and Scott, J. (1999) *Sociology*. Oxford: Oxford University Press.

Furlong, A. and Cartmel, F. (2007) *Young People and Social Change: New Perspectives* (2nd edn). Maidenhead: Open University Press.

Gilroy, P. (1993)*The Black Atlantic: Modernity and Double Consciousness*. Cambridge, MA: Harvard University Press.

Henderson, S. (2007) *Inventing Adulthood: A Biographical Approach to Youth Transitions*. London: Sage.

Holdsworth, C. and Morgan, D. (2005) *Transitions in Context*. Berkshire: Open University Press.

Ingram, G. and Harris, J. (2001) *Delivering Good Youth Work*. Dorset: Russell House.

Jeffs, T. (2005) 'Citizenship, youth work and democratic renewal', *Encyclopaedia of Informal Education*, available at www.infed.org.

Jeffs, T. and Smith, M. (1999) *Informal Education: Conversation, Democracy, Learning*. Tucknall: Education Now.

Lifelong Learning UK (2008) *National Occupational Standards for Youth Work*. Available at http://webarchive.nationalarchives.gov.uk/20110414152025/http.lluk.org/2010/11/national-occupational-standards-for-youth-work/ (last accessed 06.12.2013).

MacDonald, R. (2002) 'Crossing the Rubicon: youth transitions, poverty, drugs and social exclusion', *International Journal of Drug Policy*, 13 (1): 27.

Mauss, R.E. (1962*) Theories of Adolescence*. New York: Random House.

McCulloch. K. (2007) 'Democratic participation or surveillance? Structures and practices for young people's decision making', *Scottish Youth Issues Journal*, 9: 9–22.

Mizen, P. (2004) *The Changing State of Youth*. Basingstoke: Palgrave Macmillan.

Morrow, V. and Richards, M. (1996) *Transitions to Adulthood: A Family Matter?* York: York Publishing Services.

Ord, J. (2007) *Youth Work Process: Product and Practice*. Dorset: Russell House Press.

Packham, C. (2008) *Active Citizenship and Community Learning*. Exeter: Learning Matters.

Parry, G., Moyser, G. and Day, N. (1992) *Political Participation and Democracy in Britain*. Cambridge: Cambridge University Press.

Ratcliffe, R. and Taylor, T. (1981) 'Stuttering steps in political education', *Schooling and Culture* (9).

Roberts, R. (2009) *Youth Work Ethics*. Exeter: Learning Matters.

Silver, H. (1994) 'Social exclusion and social solidarity: three paradigms', *International Labour Review*, 133 (1994/5–6).

Smith, M. and Jeffs, T. (2007) *Fostering Democracy and Association*. Available at www.infed. org (last accessed 06.05.09).

Stuart, G. (2006) 'What does Gandhi have to say about youth work?', *Youth and Policy*, 93: 77–90.

Spence, J. (2004) 'Targeting, accountability and youth work practice', *Practice*, 16 (4): 261–272.

Spence, J. et al. (2006) *Youth Work: Voices of Practice*. Leicester: The National Youth Agency.

Taylor, T. (2008) 'Young people, politics and participation: a youth work perspective', *Youth & Policy,* 100 (summer/autumn).

Taylor, T. (2009) 'The open letter: in defence of youth work'. Available at http://indefenceofyouthwork.wordpress.com/2009/03/11/the-open-letter-in-defence-of-youth-work/ (last accessed 08.06.09).

Tett, L. (2010) *Community Education, Learning and Development*. Edinburgh: Dunedin.

Wenger, E. (1998) *Communities of Practice: Learning, Meaning and Identity*. Cambridge: Cambridge University Press.

Williamson, H. (2008) 'European youth policy', *Youth & Policy*, 100 (summer/autumn).

APPENDIX 1

Draft Example – Health & Safety Induction Checklist

Name of Employee   Start date _____

Employing Organisation

The following items should be included in your induction into the organisation, preferably on your first day. Please check off the items below when they occur. It may be that not all of the items below are applicable, for example, your work placement may not involve any manual handling. This list is not exhaustive and other topics may be covered, which you may note if you wish:

Table for Appendix 1

No	Health & Safety Issues	Date
1	Emergency procedures	
2	First Aid arrangements	
3	Fire procedures	
4	Accident reporting and location of accident book	
5	Safety policy received and location known	
6	COSHH Regulations/Risk Assessments	
7	Display Screen Equipment Regulations/Risk Assessments	
8	Manual Handling Regulations/Risk Assessments	
9	Other appropriate Risk Assessments	
10	Protective clothing arrangements	
11	Instruction on equipment you will be using	
12	Other issues (please specify in detail)	

Signed: _____
Dated: _____

APPENDIX 2

Record of Drug/Medication Administration Form

Name of Person: _____

Table for Appendix 2

Date	Confirm name of young person	Drug issued	Dosage	Signature of adult administering the drug	Witnessing signature of other adult

(Continued)

(Continued)

Date	Confirm name of young person	Drug issued	Dosage	Signature of adult administering the drug	Witnessing signature of other adult

APPENDIX 3

Accommodation Risk Assessment Checklist

Name of Accommodation _____

This form should be completed by the owner/manager of the accommodation under consideration. The following requirements are deemed to be necessary and if there are any negative answers on the following questions then the accommodation should be judged to be unsuitable for safe use.

1. Will there be 24-hour reception or concierge arrangements at the accommodation to be used by the group?

2. Will the premises be properly secured against possible intruders outside reception hours?

3. Will all bedrooms/sleeping accommodation have working locks on the doors, windows and shutters?

4. Will the group have adjoining rooms adjacent to the group leader's quarters?

5. Will the group leader's access to the young people's accommodation be available at all times?

6. Will a list of rooms and numbers of beds in each room be made available to the group leader at least two weeks prior to the visit?

7. Will a floor plan of the accommodation be made available to the group leader at least two weeks prior to the visit?

8. Are there appropriate emergency procedures, fire escape routes and fire doors?

9. Have all the company staff, including drivers, who will be in contact with the group during the stay, been vetted in keeping with child protection laws?

Signature: _____

Name: _____

Position: _____

Organisation: _____ Date: _____

Name of Group: _____

Name of Leader in Charge: _____

Contact Details: _____

_____

INDEX